DATE DUE

EXPLORING MANUFACTURING

by

R. Thomas Wright
Professor of Industry and Technology
Ball State University
Muncie, Indiana

Publisher
The Goodheart-Willcox Company, Inc.
Tinley Park, Illinois

About the Author

Dr. R. Thomas Wright is one of the leading figures in technology education curriculum development in the United States. He is the author or coauthor of many Goodheart-Willcox technology textbooks. Dr. Wright is the author of *Manufacturing Systems, Processes of Manufacturing,* and *Technology Systems.* He is the coauthor of *Exploring Production* with Richard M. Henak, and *Understanding Technology* with Howard "Bud" Smith.

Dr. Wright's educational background includes a bachelor's degree from Stout State University, a master of science degree from Ball State University, and a doctoral degree from the University of Maryland. His teaching experience consists of three years as a junior high instructor in California and 25 years as a university instructor at Ball State. In addition, he has also been a visiting professor at California State University, Oregon State University, and at Edith Cowan University in Perth, Australia. Dr. Wright is currently the George and Francis Ball Distinguished Professor of Industry and Technology at Ball State University.

Cover Credit: © 2000 Matsu Illustration

Copyright 2000

by

THE GOODHEART-WILLCOX COMPANY, INC.

Previous Editions Copyright 1993, 1985

Library of Congress Catalog Card Number 98-44627
International Standard Book Number 1-56637-530-4

2 3 4 5 6 7 8 9 10   00   03 02 01 00

Library of Congress Cataloging-in-Publication Data

Wright, R. Thomas.
    Exploring manufacturing/by R. Thomas Wright.

        p.   cm.
    Includes index.
    ISBN 1-56637-530-4
    1. Manufacturing processes. 2. Materials. 3. Production management. I. Title.
TS176.W74   2000
670--dc21   98-44627
                                                          CIP

INTRODUCTION

EXPLORING MANUFACTURING provides a complete picture of two important manufacturing activities: Material Processing Technology and Management Technology. You will learn about the types of materials from which manufactured products are made. Then you will learn about their properties (that is, what makes them what they are). Understanding the materials of manufacturing, you can better understand the story of the processing activities that change the materials into useful and attractive products.

You will learn about raw materials being extracted or harvested from nature. You will read how these materials are converted into standard stock which can be used in making useful products. EXPLORING MANUFACTURING explains secondary manufacturing processes. You will learn about casting and molding, forming, separating, conditioning, assembling, and finishing.

EXPLORING MANUFACTURING explains management activities and responsibilities. You will study the principles of good management and see how they are put to use. Then the book will show you step by step how a manufacturing company is organized and managed. You will see how engineers and other professionals change product ideas into actual products. You will also learn what is involved in marketing manufacturing products.

EXPLORING MANUFACTURING helps you understand five major areas of manufacturing:
1. Designing and engineering products.
2. Developing production systems.
3. Manufacturing products.
4. Marketing products.
5. Performing financial activities.

EXPLORING MANUFACTURING concludes with an overview of the history of manufacturing and a glimpse of what the future is likely to hold. You will be able to examine your own goals and aptitudes as they relate to the many career opportunities offered in this cluster of occupations. Using the information in EXPLORING MANUFACTURING you will be better able to assume the adult roles of consumer, citizen, and career person.

R. Thomas Wright

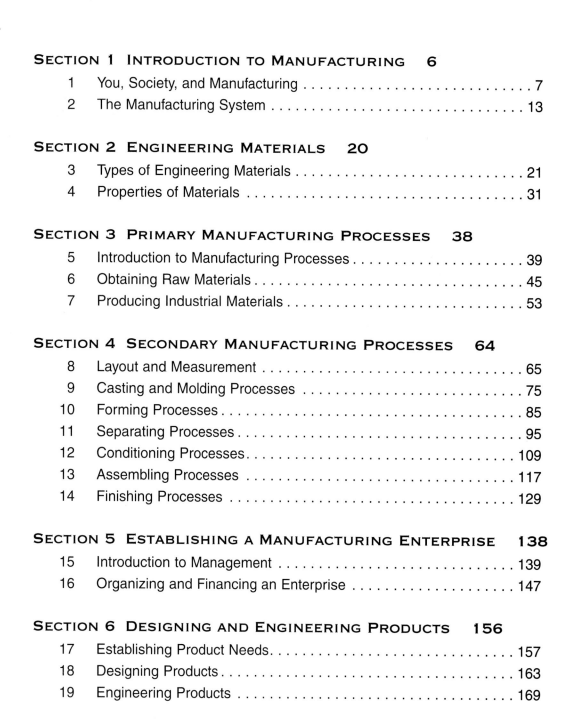

CONTENTS

INTRODUCTION TO MANUFACTURING

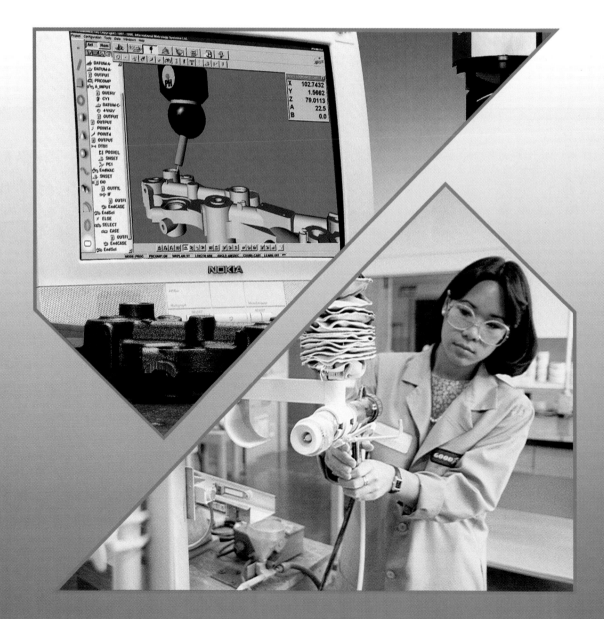

CHAPTER 1

YOU, SOCIETY, AND MANUFACTURING

After studying this chapter, you will be able to:
- ☐ Define manufacturing technology.
- ☐ List the important types of manufacturing activities.
- ☐ Explain the purposes for manufacturing.
- ☐ Define the term technology.
- ☐ List and describe technologies related to manufacturing.
- ☐ Explain the three different meanings of the term industry.
- ☐ Demonstrate an appreciation for manufacturing and give reasons for studying it.

You live in a manufactured (made by people) world. All around you there are manufactured goods. You may have been brought to school in a manufactured bus. You opened manufactured doors to enter the building. You sit on a manufactured chair at a manufactured desk. You write on manufactured paper with a manufactured pencil. You are reading a manufactured book. Whatever you do or wherever you go, you are in contact with and use manufactured products.

What exactly is manufacturing? Simply, it is changing materials to make them more useful.

Fig. 1-1. Manufacturing changes the form of a material to add to its value. A–Iron ore is changed into pig iron. B–Pig iron is converted into steel. C–Steel is rolled into strips. D–Steel strip is fabricated into a useful product. (U.S. Steel, American Iron and Steel Institute, White Consolidated Industries)

Manufacturing adds value to materials by making them more useful, Fig. 1-1. For example, trees are a common natural resource. They can be harvested and sliced into thin sheets called veneer. The veneer can be glued together to form plywood. The plywood can be used to make a bookcase. At each stage the material is *changed* and becomes more useful.

Manufacturing is done in a factory, as shown in Fig. 1-2. The products are made in one location then shipped to the customer, or user. Manufacturing adds to the value of materials by changing them.

HOW IMPORTANT IS MANUFACTURING?

Manufacturing is very important to all of us for several reasons. First, it provides us with products which make life easier and better. We live in more comfort because of manufacturing activities.

Manufactured products move us from one place to another in comfort. We ride in automobiles, buses, subway cars, railway cars, boats, and airplanes. These were all manufactured in a factory.

Manufacturing Provides Information

Each of us receives information daily by way of manufactured products. We watch television or listen to radios that were manufactured. The books, newspapers, and magazines we read are also manufactured in a factory called a printing plant.

Our food comes to us in manufactured containers such as boxes, bags, pouches, cans, jars, and bottles. Truly, manufactured goods are a key element in our way of life. Try to imagine what your

Fig. 1-3. Employment is important to people. (Goodyear)

life would be like for one day without manufactured products.

Manufacturing Provides Work

Secondly, manufacturing employs many workers to produce the products we buy. This employment is important to a large number of people, Fig. 1-3. It gives them:
• A source of income.

Fig. 1-2. Left. The manufacturing processes shown produce bottles. Right. The processes are done in a building or factory. The products are then shipped to customers. (Owens-Brockway)

- A chance to give something to society.
- A feeling of belonging to a group.

People need the opportunity to hold a job. They feel better if they earn their money through honest work. Manufacturing provides work for many people. Of course, some of them make the products. But many more are involved with other tasks. Some people manage (direct) the work of others. There are people busy selling manufactured products. Still others service (maintain and repair) the manufactured goods. Additional people transport the products from factories to warehouses and on to stores. Other people keep personnel and financial records. Manufacturing provides a variety of jobs requiring many skills and talents.

Manufacturing Gives A Sense Of Belonging

Each of us wants to belong to a group. We want to feel needed. Manufacturing gives people a chance to belong to a group. Individuals who are members of a company, may belong to a department within the company, or to an even smaller work group. A person might say, "I am part of the armature assembly group in the motor department of _____ Company." This is belonging.

Also, we all feel better if we can contribute to society. Manufacturing develops and produces products needed by people. Those working for a manufacturing company can take pride in helping people live better.

A third reason manufacturing is important is that it helps make a country strong. The strength of the United States is due, in part, to manufacturing. The U.S. has wealth, and people have jobs, partly because of manufacturing. We have goods to exchange with other countries. Technology (the knowledge of doing) developed by manufacturing companies is also sold to other nations. However,

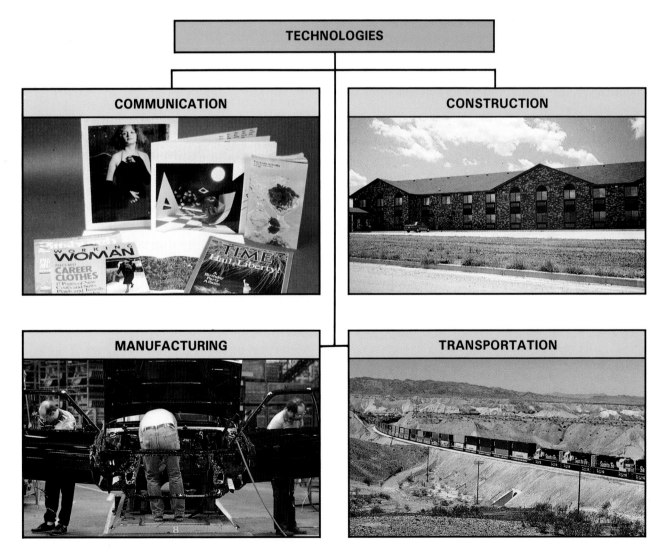

Fig. 1-4. There are four common industrial technologies.

this strength is being constantly tested. Other countries compete with the United States as they develop quality products at competitive prices.

MANUFACTURING AND OTHER TECHNOLOGIES

Manufacturing is a technology. It is a way of doing things efficiently. Manufacturing is an "action" activity. It requires knowing how to do the work well without wasting time or materials.

Manufacturing is one of four basic technologies, Fig. 1-4, that people use to produce goods and services. The other technologies are the industrial activities called communications, construction and transportation. The four technologies may be described as follows:

- *Manufacturing:* changing materials into usable products in a factory.
- *Communication:* changing information into messages. These can be transmitted (moved) from the source to a receiver.
- *Construction:* using manufactured goods and industrial materials to build structures on a site.
- *Transportation:* converting energy into power to move people and goods from one location to another.

Each of these activities is independent. Every system has its own way of doing things. However, the four are always working together, as seen in Fig. 1-5. They support each other.

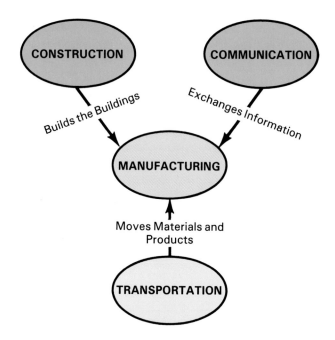

Fig. 1-5. The technological systems are related to one another.

Since you are studying manufacturing, let us look at how the other three work with this area. You know manufacturing is making products in a factory. The factory was built using construction activities, manufactured goods, and machines. The roads and rail lines leading to the plant, the parking lots, and the water, electrical, and sewer lines were also manufactured.

Manufacturing depends on transportation. The materials to build products arrive on transportation vehicles. The finished products leave the same way. Also, workers use buses, trains, automobiles, and even planes to get to work. In short, the resources and outputs of manufacturing are constantly being transported.

Communications is necessary in any complex (many plants or departments) organization. Information is shared between manufacturing plants. Drawings and other data are often sent over long distances using computer systems. The research and development center and company offices are sometimes miles away from the factory. Managers in these facilities must send and receive information. Also, companies send messages to customers through advertisements, announcements, and packages.

As you can see by these brief examples, no technological system can exist alone. Each depends on the others. All four systems form our economic system. They are the foundation of all efforts to produce and exchange goods and services.

TECHNOLOGY AND INDUSTRY

Technology and industry are two different things. *Technology* is the knowledge of efficient (timesaving) action. There are technologies (methods) involved in making products. There is an efficient way to cast metal, cut wood, form plastic, and so forth. These are technologies.

Industry, on the other hand, is a part of society. Industrial activity is undertaken to meet human needs. There are three meanings for the term industry, as shown in Fig. 1-6.

The first meaning is the broadest. It includes all economic activity. This means all businesses that do something for money. All activities that exchange goods and services for pay would be included, too. It would take in doctors and lawyers, entertainment activities, banking companies, farming, and manufacturing.

The second meaning limits industry to the four major human productive activities. The narrower definition would include all communication, construction, manufacturing, and transportation activities. Using this definition, major league baseball and retail selling would not be thought of as industries.

The third meaning is narrower still. It includes only companies that compete with each other. Examples of the use of this definition would be the steel industry, the telecommunications industry, and the aircraft industry.

All three uses of the term industry are correct. Many words have several meanings. However, it is very important to know how a word is being used as we hear or see it. *In this book, industry will mean those activities that are organized for communication, construction, manufacturing, and transportation purposes.*

INDUSTRY AND COMPANIES

Often people use the words, "industry" and "company" as if they had the same meaning. They do not. A *company* is a single business unit, often called an *enterprise*. Ford Motor Company, American Broadcasting Company, and Sears, Roebuck and Co. are companies. They are individual business enterprises.

However, as we said before, many companies make up an industry. The manufacturing industry includes all companies that produce goods in a factory. The steel industry includes all companies that convert iron ore into steel. Talking about the "automobile industry" is correct. Calling General Motors Corporation an "industry" is incorrect. It is a business enterprise.

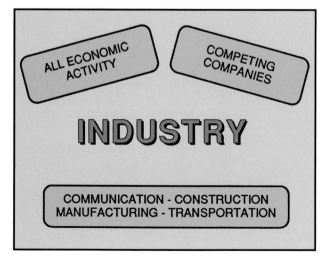

Fig. 1-6. There are three main definitions of the term industry.

Fig. 1-7. We all need answers to questions about manufacturing.

WHY STUDY MANUFACTURING?

You now know the meaning of the terms manufacturing, industry, and company. But why would anyone want to study manufacturing, Fig. 1-7? Stop and think about some possible answers. Are you planning to get a job after you finish your education? Do you know what jobs are available? Do you have any idea what the educational requirements are for these jobs? Do you know which jobs fit your interests and abilities?

Do you plan on voting for candidates for public office? Will you ever be asked to speak or vote on current issues? Will the candidates and issues affect your life and our industries?

Do you buy manufactured products? Can you decide if a product is really worth the selling price? Do you understand how products are made? Do you know how to maintain simple products? Do you know when a product needs servicing?

If you plan on being a worker, voter, consumer, and citizen, you need to understand the world around you. You are living in a complex industrial and technological world. A study of manufacturing will help you live in such a world.

KEY WORDS

All the following words have been used in this chapter. Do you know their meaning?

Communication
Company
Construction
Enterprise
Industry
Manufacturing
Technology
Transportation

TEST YOUR KNOWLEDGE

Please do not write in this text. Place your answers on a separate sheet of paper.

1. Manufacturing is _____ _____ to make them more useful.
2. Indicate which of the following are reasons for manufacturing's importance in our society:
   A. Provides products which make life easier and better.
   B. Provides many jobs for people.
   C. Is a source of income for people.
   D. Offers each worker a chance to contribute something to the community.
   E. All of the above.
   F. None of the above.
3. _____, _____, and _____ are other technologies related to manufacturing.
4. Industry and technology are the same thing. True or false?
5. In this text, _____ means those activities that are organized to communicate, construct, manufacture, or transport.
6. Is General Motors Corporation a company or an industry? Explain your answer.

ACTIVITIES

1. Read a national newspaper for one week or more, looking for articles covering products manufactured in other countries for sale to the United States or from the U.S. to other countries. Clip or photocopy the articles and set up a reference file. Create a bulletin board displaying a world map and the products bought or sold in each country reported on. Come up with a method for showing whether the product is an import or export to the U.S.
2. Working in pairs or small groups, obtain a state map and determine a 25-mile radius from your town or city. Using local telephone, business, industrial, and manufacturing directories in your library's reference section, identify as many companies in the geographic radius as you can that come under the headings of:
   A. Communication.
   B. Construction.
   C. Manufacturing.
   D. Transportation.
3. Working with a partner, build a model or create a pictorial representation of a factory being constructed to produce a manufactured product. Depict how production depends on communication between the factory and the research and development facility miles away. Show how transportation is utilized to move workers and products.

CHAPTER 2

THE MANUFACTURING SYSTEM

After studying this chapter, you will be able to:
- ☐ Define the term system.
- ☐ Describe the common parts of any type of system.
- ☐ List and define the seven inputs to a manufacturing system.
- ☐ Name the two manufacturing technologies.
- ☐ Explain what an output is and describe the outputs of manufacturing.
- ☐ Define the term goals and suggest common manufacturing goals.

A *system* is anything made up of parts or groups organized for a purpose. You are surrounded by systems. Your home has a heating system. The classroom has a lighting system. Your body has a digestive system. The products you use were produced by a manufacturing system. All of these systems, Fig. 2-1, have four common parts:
- *Inputs* (what goes into the system - such as energy or material).
- *Processes* (what is done to or by the input).
- *Outputs* (what comes out because of the inputs and processes).
- Goals (a *goal* is the purpose for the system).

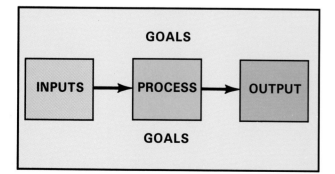

Fig. 2-1. This is a systems model. Every system has these four parts.

A heating system may use fuel and air as its inputs. These inputs are processed (changed) in a furnace. The fuel (energy) and air (material) enter into a reaction we call burning. The output is heat energy and exhaust gases. Of course, a warm building is the goal.

Like the heating system, the manufacturing system has inputs, processes, outputs, and goals.

MANUFACTURING INPUTS

Products are not built out of thin air. A number of inputs or resources are needed. These inputs may be grouped into seven main classes. As you can see in Fig. 2-2, these are:
- Natural resources (wood, iron ore, etc.).
- Human resources (workers).
- Capital (plant and equipment).
- Knowledge (skills and scientific information).
- Finances (money).
- Time.
- Energy.

Natural Resources

Natural resources are the raw materials that are changed into finished products. These resources, Fig. 2-3, are the product's "building blocks" found on earth: metal ores, trees, petroleum, water, natural gas, sand, and clay.

Human Resources

Human resources are people. People are a unique resource. People are individuals, each with special abilities and talents.

Manufacturing needs a wide variety of human talent. Some jobs require great physical skill.

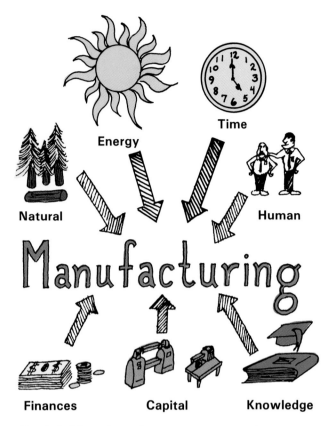

Fig. 2-2. Manufacturing resources come from these areas.

Others need a person who can organize tasks. Still others require the ability to manage people and work with them. Some jobs need workers who like to do the same thing over and over. Others need employees who like to do different things each day. There is a job for nearly every type of person.

Capital

Capital is the plant and equipment used to produce products, Fig. 2-4. Each enterprise must have capital. Buildings (factories, offices, and warehouses) are needed as a place to work. Equipment is needed to move material, change its form, and process data. *Capital* is the permanent (lasting) physical resources of a company.

Knowledge

Knowledge is a resource all companies have. It is called a hidden resource because it cannot be directly seen or measured. However, it is a vital (needed) resource. Often the difference between successful and failing companies is knowledge.

This knowledge may be of many kinds. It could be knowing how to process materials. It could be knowing how to manage the company's money. Understanding how to promote and sell a product is important. These, and many other types of knowledge, are needed by all successful companies.

Finances

An important resource is *finances*. You may have heard the saying, "It takes money to make money." This is very true. A company must have money to purchase the other resources. It costs money to develop and engineer new products. Also, a company must buy material, pay for labor, and purchase machines. Finances, or money, are the

Fig. 2-3. Timber is a common natural resource. (Freightliner Corp.)

Fig. 2-4. This rolling mill at a steel plant is a capital resource. (American Iron and Steel Institute)

very foundation of a company. Without it, nothing else can be done.

Time

Another technological resource is *time*. It includes the human time needed to produce and sell products and structures. Time also includes the machine time required to process materials.

Energy

The last type of resource is *energy*. This resource powers machines, lights work areas, heats and cools factories, moves materials, and performs many other tasks. The energy may be electrical, chemical, mechanical, thermal (heat), or nuclear.

MANUFACTURING PROCESSES

Having the proper resources is not enough for success. The company must use them properly. This activity is the "process" (doing) part of the manufacturing system. It uses two major technologies. These, as pictured in Fig. 2-5, are:
- Material processing technology.
- Management technology.

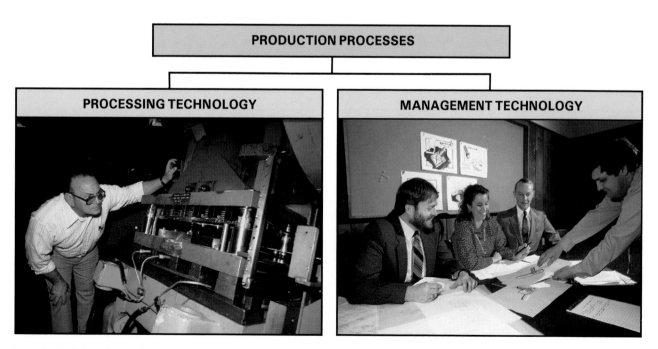

PRODUCTION PROCESSES

PROCESSING TECHNOLOGY

MANAGEMENT TECHNOLOGY

Fig. 2-5. Manufacturing processes include material processing technology and management technology. (Ohio Art Co.)

Material Processing Technology

Manufacturing changes the form of materials to make them more valuable. This form change is called material processing. It usually involves changing raw materials into industrial materials, such as lumber, sheet steel, and plastic pellets. The industrial materials are then changed into a finished product, such as a stool or garbage can.

Material processing is a "doing" activity. It involves action and is, therefore, a technology. To understand this technology, people must know:

- Materials and their properties (qualities).
- The ways (methods) of changing the form of materials.

Material processing technology, as shown in Fig. 2-6, has two parts: material properties and material

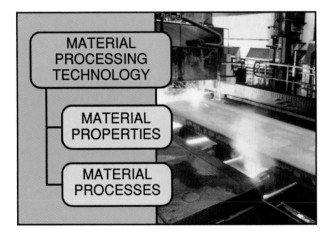

Fig. 2-6. Material processing technology has two parts or activities.

processes. These topics will be covered in Sections 2 through 4 of this book.

Management Technology

It is not enough to be able to process materials. To be successful, a company must do it efficiently (least amount of resources and highest quality). The enterprise must use as little material, labor, capital, and money as possible.

This is where management technology is used. *Managing* means "guiding and directing company activities to get efficient operation." Each company activity, from the time a product is just an idea until someone buys it, must be managed. Resources (material, machines, and people) must be wisely used. Material processing techniques must be efficient. Products must move from the factory to the customer easily. Basically, waste of resources must be kept as small as possible. The managed activities that are used to develop, manufacture, and market products will be presented in Sections 5 through 10 of this book.

MANUFACTURING OUTPUTS

It is easy to see that the output of a manufacturing system is a usable *product*. This is why people developed the system. There is almost no end to the number and kinds of products made. However, they can be grouped into three general types. These, shown in Fig. 2-7, are consumer products, industrial products, and military products.

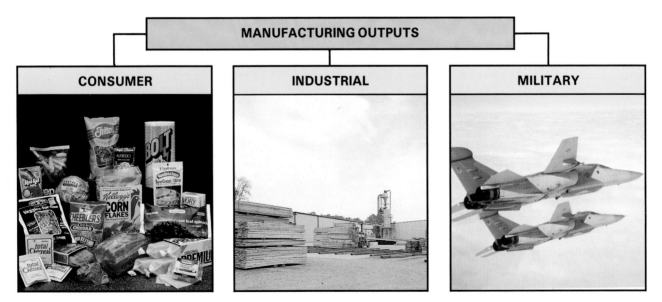

Fig. 2-7. There are basically three types of manufacturing outputs (products). Left. Consumer goods. (James River Corp.). Center. Industrial goods. (American Woodmark). Right. Military goods. (McDonnell Douglas)

Consumer Products

Consumer products are manufactured goods that are ready to use. Customers do not need to do further processing before they use the product. These products are bought from retail stores, dealers, or catalogs.

Consumer products, Fig. 2-8, are usually divided into two groups:
- Durable (hard) goods: things that are expected to last for a long time. Automobiles, kitchen appliances, and furniture are examples.
- Nondurable (soft) goods: things that are used up quickly, such as food, clothing, and beverages.

Industrial Products

Industrial products are materials and equipment used by industries. Industrial materials need further processing before becoming a useful product. A sheet of plywood is useful only after it is made into a doghouse, desk, or cabinet. The same is true for lumber, sheets of aluminum, or potter's clay. These and thousands of other items are industrial materials.

Capital *equipment* is also a form of industrial products. These are the machines that process materials. They are used to produce industrial, military, and consumer products.

Military Products

Military products are the materials and machines used for war. These goods are special products

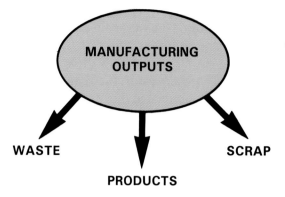

Fig. 2-9. Not all outputs of manufacturing are useful products.

made for the use of a country's military forces. Tanks, guns, and bombers are examples of military products.

Other Manufacturing Outputs

Not all outputs of manufacturing activities are products. There are other outputs. See Fig. 2-9.

Manufacturing processes often create *scrap*, such as chips, shavings, and cutoffs. Some of these can be recycled (used again). Metal scraps can be remelted. Wood chips may become paper, hardboard, or particleboard. Management should always work to reduce and recycle scrap.

Also, manufacturing processes will produce unusable *waste*. Many manufacturing processes have by-products which are not really wanted. Steelmaking produces slag (material that looks like rock) and chemical fumes. Papermaking produces strong

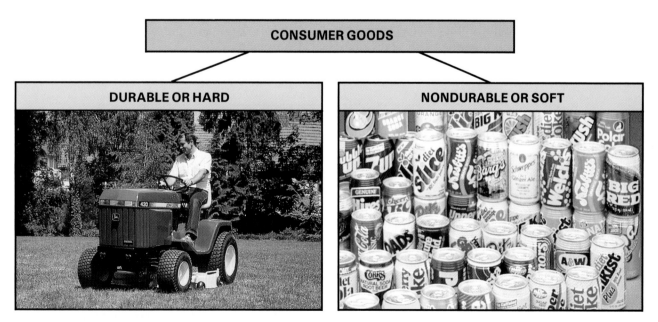

Fig. 2-8. Consumer goods are either durable or nondurable. (Deere and Co., Reynolds Metals)

smelling liquids. Many chemical plants produce hazardous wastes. This waste must be disposed of without causing pollution.

Management must deal with these undesirable outputs, too. In many cases, they cannot be easily or economically eliminated. For example, the automobile engine produces carbon monoxide gas as it burns fuel. This deadly poisonous gas is an undesirable by-product. The problem is to reduce it so that the air we breathe is safe. Likewise, manufacturers must carefully dispose of their waste.

MANUFACTURING GOALS

There are two types of goals for manufacturing. One is the goals of the company. The other is the goals that society has for manufacturing.

Company Goals

A company's a basic goal is to make money. The enterprise must have some of the money left over after all its costs are paid. The left over money is called *profit*. This profit allows the company to:
- Reward its owners for investing in the company (pay dividends).
- Become more productive.
- Develop new products and technology.
- Replace equipment.
- Invest in other businesses.

Without profits, companies soon disappear. They "go out of business." Workers lose their jobs. Without income they buy less from merchants in their towns. Families have to move away to find new jobs.

Managers have a responsibility (duty) to keep their companies making a profit. This does not mean they should be greedy. They should manage well so that the workers and the owners receive their fair share.

Society's Goals

Manufacturing firms must also consider the goals of society. As members of society we want companies to help their workers have a better life. Each of us wants a higher standard of living. Also, we expect companies to protect the environment (air, water, land). In addition, companies are asked to train and retrain workers, and to give money for community projects and similar activities. Companies are expected to be good "citizens."

SUMMARY

Manufacturing is a system that produces products for our use, Fig. 2-10. It uses inputs to create the desired outputs. The system is organized to change the form of materials, using material processing and management technologies. The activities within the system are controlled by company and society goals. If successful, manufacturing will provide goods at a fair price without harming the environment. The owners of the company will earn a profit.

KEY WORDS

All the following words have been used in this chapter. Do you know their meaning?
Capital
Consumer products
Energy
Equipment
Finances

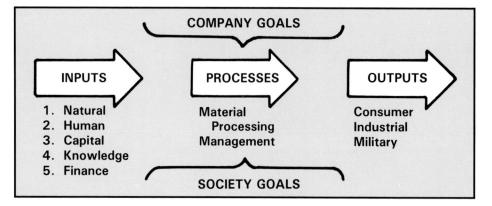

Fig. 2-10. This model of the manufacturing system sums up how a company performs in your community.

Goals
Industrial products
Inputs
Military products
Outputs
Processes
Product
Profit
Scrap
System
Time
Waste

TEST YOUR KNOWLEDGE

Please do not write in this text. Place your answers on a separate sheet of paper.

1. List and briefly describe the five major inputs to manufacturing.
2. Producing a change of form in materials is called _____.
3. _____ means guiding and directing company activities to get efficient operation.
4. Products can be grouped into three basic kinds. Indicate which of the following are included:
   A. Durable.
   B. Nondurable.
   C. Consumer.
   D. Industrial.
   E. Military.
5. Chips, shavings, and cutoffs are known as _____.
6. True or false? The basic goal of a company is to make money.

ACTIVITIES

1. Complete a simple line production product, then discuss it in terms of:
   A. Inputs.
   B. Processes used.
   C. Outputs.
   D. Goals.
2. The next time you spend the day shopping, keep track of the many products or materials you see. List them by category in this table format.

Industrial Materials	Industrial Equipment (Capital Goods)	Consumer Durable Goods	Consumer Nondurable Goods

3. With another class member, interview a production worker or a manager employed in a manufacturing enterprise. Find out all you can about the product manufactured, including:
   A. Kind of product manufactured (consumer, industrial, or military).
   B. The inputs, processes, outputs, and goals of the company.
   C. Problems in controlling waste.

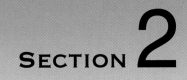

SECTION 2

ENGINEERING MATERIALS

CHAPTER **3**

TYPES OF ENGINEERING MATERIALS

After studying this chapter, you will be able to:

☐ List some properties of materials.
☐ Describe types of metals, plastics, and ceramics.
☐ List units of measurement for length, volume, and weight.
☐ Explain how to select and buy materials.

Scientists group all materials into three kinds: gases, liquids, and solids, Fig. 3-1. Each type has a use in industry. For example, burning gases produce heat for welding and heat-treating. Liquids lubricate surfaces. They also are solvents (liquid carriers) for finishes. Solids provide the mass and shape of many products.

In many ways, solid materials are the most important type. They are often called *engineering materials.* These materials have a rigid structure. They hold their size and shape under normal conditions.

There are more than 70,000 different kinds and grades of engineering materials. This number grows almost daily. Scientists and engineers develop new materials as our needs change. For instance, more than a thousand different materials are used to make an automobile. Products made from a single material are difficult to find. The simple lead pencil, for example, is made of four: wood, granite, rubber, and metal.

Even this vast number of materials can be classified into three basic families. These, as shown in Fig. 3-2, are:

• Metals.
• Polymers (plastics).
• Ceramics.

Combining two or more of these creates a fourth family of materials. For example, fiberglass is a combination of glass fibers and plastic resin. Concrete combines cement, sand, and gravel. Each material keeps its own properties. But combining them adds special properties to the new material. This fourth type of material is called a composite.

The materials in each of these families are solids. But they differ in their chemical makeup and in the ways their molecules are arranged. To understand these materials better, let us discuss these materials separately.

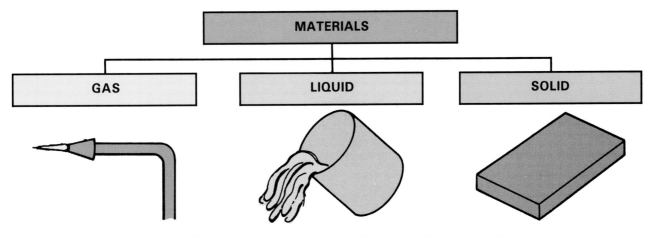

Fig. 3-1. These are the kinds of materials as classified by scientists.

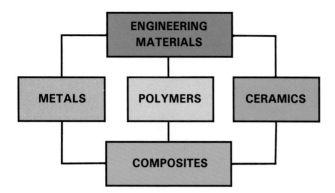

Fig. 3-2. Types of engineering materials. All are solids.

METALS

Look around you. How many things do you see that are made out of metal? Obviously, metals are a very important engineering material.

Metals are crystalline, inorganic (never were living matter) materials. The atoms are arranged in box-like shapes called crystals, Fig. 3-3. Crystals cluster together into grains. The grains form as molten metal cools. The grains stick together, forming a solid material. Fig. 3-4 shows magnified sections of two metals. Do you see the grain lines?

Combining Metals

In early history, metals were used in their pure state. Our ancient ancestors used pure copper and pure iron for many products. Today, however, pure metals are rarely used. Some pure gold is used in making small electronic parts. Pure copper is used in special electrical applications. Pure aluminum is used by the chemical and electrical industries.

Most metallic materials combine two or more pure metals. This combination is called an *alloy*. The mixture is carefully planned. First, the correct metals are chosen. Then they are combined using precise quantities of each metal.

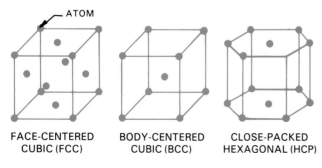

FACE-CENTERED CUBIC (FCC) BODY-CENTERED CUBIC (BCC) CLOSE-PACKED HEXAGONAL (HCP)

Fig. 3-3. Types of metal crystals. They combine to form grains.

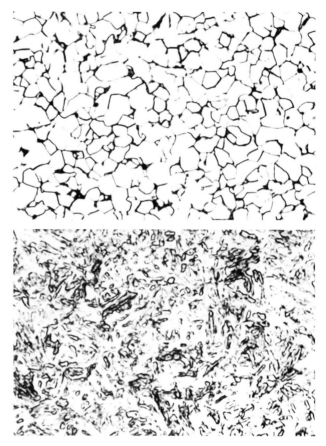

Fig. 3-4. Magnified sections of two metals. Top. Cold-rolled and annealed steel. Bottom. Hardened alloy steel. (Bethlehem Steel Co.)

Alloys are developed for many uses. They often have better properties than pure metals. They are usually stronger, harder, and resist corrosion (chemical attack) better.

You already know the names of some common alloys used in everyday life. Steel is a mixture of iron and carbon. Brass is an alloy of copper and zinc. Solder is a tin-lead alloy. Bronze is an alloy of copper and tin. Thousands of alloys are produced by the metals industry.

There are over 25,000 different steels. The Copper Development Association lists over 200 standard copper alloys. The Aluminum Association lists over 75 common wrought aluminum alloys. As you can see, there are thousands of metals to choose from. There is one for every job.

Common Metals

There are many common metals in use. The most widely used are:
• Iron-based alloys.
• Aluminum alloys.
• Copper alloys.

Iron-based alloys

The iron-based alloys are the most widely used of all metals. The Industrial Revolution was based on them. So is the Western technical culture. The settling of the American West depended on steel rails and railroad equipment. Steel barbed wire allowed us to farm the plains. Steel forms the skeleton of skyscrapers. Without iron and steel, progress would have been difficult.

Iron-based alloys are inexpensive, strong, and easily worked. They can be divided into two groups:
- Cast iron.
- Steel.

Cast iron

Cast iron is any iron-carbon alloy with more than two percent carbon. There are several types of cast iron. They are used to produce complex, heavy shapes. For example, engine blocks are often made of cast iron.

Steel

Steel is iron-carbon alloy with less than two percent carbon. Steel can be divided into carbon steels and specialty steels.

As the name suggests, carbon is the main alloying element in carbon steel. These steels are divided into three main groups:
- Mild Steel. This is a low-carbon, general purpose steel. The most common of all steels, it can be easily forged, bent, or welded.
- Medium-Carbon Steel. This steel is stronger than mild steel. It is easy to machine, forge, and cast.
- High-Carbon Steel. Heat treating will harden this steel. It is not easy to machine, weld, or forge.

Specialty steels

Specialty steels are developed for specific uses. The most common types are stainless steel and tool steel. Steel may also be coated to protect it from the environment. Two common coated steels are tinplate and galvanized steel. Tinplate is tin-coated steel and is used for food cans (tin cans) and other similar applications. Galvanized steel has a coating of zinc. It is used for siding, roofing, and automobile body parts.

PLASTICS

The scientific name for plastics is polymers. *Polymers* are made from molecules that contain

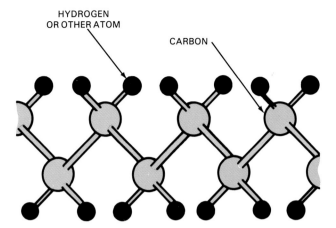

Fig. 3-5. This is a model of a polymer chain. If plastic molecules were large enough to see, they would look like this.

carbon. These molecules are called mers or monomers (meaning single mers).

Polymers are made by combining monomers as you would building blocks. The result is a chainlike structure of molecules. The structure is a group of repeating monomers, Fig. 3-5.

Polymers are both natural and synthetic (made by people). Animal and vegetable protein, starch, and cellulose are natural polymers. Almost all important industrial polymers are synthetic.

Making Synthetic Polymers

Polymers are formed by chemical action. Basic molecules are united to form the polymer chains. For example, vinyl chloride monomers are united to form polyvinyl chloride. As seen in Fig. 3-6, the result is a chain made up of many (poly means "many") vinyl chloride monomers.

Many different plastics are formed by this same action. The action is called polymerization (joining

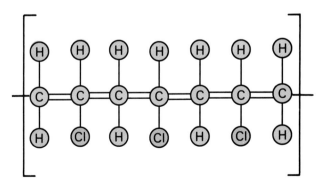

Fig. 3-6. A polyvinyl chloride polymer chain is a number of elements linked together by chemical action. The elements in the chain are carbon (C), hydrogen (H), and chlorine (Cl).

many molecules). Polymerization is used to make two classes of plastics:
- Thermoplastics.
- Thermosets.

Thermoplastics

A *thermoplastic* material contains many long polymer chains. These chains are independent. They are not directly connected to each other. They are held in place by weak electrical forces along the chains, Fig. 3-7.

The bonds will weaken if the material is heated. This action allows thermoplastics to be shaped over and over again. Any time heat is applied, the material becomes soft. If pressure is applied, the material will take a shape. When it cools the weak bonding forces return. The material is held in the new shape. At any time, the forming process may be repeated. The thermoplastic material may be made into a new shape as many times as desired.

Thermosets

Thermosetting polymers (also called *thermosets*) take on a permanent shape when heat and pressure are applied. These materials also have long polymer chains. However, heat causes the material to develop cross-links between the chains. These bonds form a rigid structure. The individual chains are now connected, Fig. 3-8. They cannot move past each other. Heat and pressure will no longer affect the plastic. It has cured into a permanent shape.

CERAMICS

The term ceramics covers a wide range of materials. This type of material may be used to make beautiful art works. Abrasives and cement are ceramics. So are window glass, and porcelain enamels used on bathroom fixtures. Ceramics are the broadest family of engineering materials.

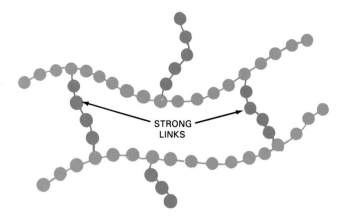

Fig. 3-8. Thermoset structure. Chains have strong links to one another.

Ceramic is a Greek word for potter's clay. Today, *ceramic* is used to describe a range of materials that:
- Have a crystalline structure.
- Are inorganic (were never living).
- Can be either metallic or nonmetallic.

Ceramic materials, generally, are very stable (not likely to change). They are not greatly affected by heat, weather, or chemicals. They have high melting points. Also, ceramics are stiff, brittle, and rigid. Ceramics are the hardest of all engineering materials.

Ceramic materials are grouped into four main classes, Fig. 3-9. There are:
- Clay-based ceramics.
- Refractories.
- Glass.
- Inorganic cements.

Clay-based Ceramics

Clay-based ceramics have two main parts. First, they have a crystalline body. This body is held in place by the second part, a glassy material. This material is the ceramic bonding agent. It holds the clay particles together. The most common types of clay products are:
- Earthenware–a useful but weak material used for dinner plates, flower pots, and drain tile.
- Stoneware–an improved earthenware used for ovenware and chemical ware.
- China–a translucent (passes light), strong product used for fine dinnerware.
- Porcelain–a hard, dense (heavy) product used for coatings on metal and ceramic materials.
- Structural clay–a material fired (cured by heat) at low temperatures and used for bricks, decorative tile, and drain tile.

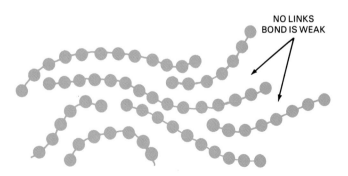

Fig. 3-7. Thermoplastic structure. Chains of polymers have a weak bond with each other.

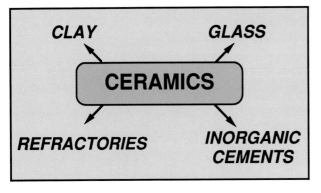

Fig. 3-9. Types of ceramics.

Refractories

Refractories are something like clay-based ceramics. They are made from crystalline materials. However, no glassy material is present to bond the grains together. Instead, the crystalline material is fused (bonded) by high temperatures.

After being fired the material is heat resistant. It is used for fire bricks that line furnaces and ovens. Refractory materials are also used in nuclear power plants, spacecraft, and jet engines.

Glass

Glass is an amorphous ceramic material. (Amorphous means it has no regular internal pattern.) Glass is mostly silica sand with other materials added. The mixture is melted at high temperatures. When it cools it forms a hard, brittle substance.

Glass actually is always a liquid. The internal structure is the same in its "liquid" state as it is when it is "solid." The material has a very high viscosity (resistance to flow) at normal temperatures. This feature makes it appear as a solid at room temperature. And in fact, it can be treated as a solid engineering material.

Inorganic Cements

Inorganic cements are hydrosetting materials. These materials are powders that harden when water is added. The three types of inorganic cements are:
- Plaster: a material made from rock gypsum that is used for wall board, molds, and decorative items.
- Lime: a calcium product used as stucco for wall covering and as mortar for bricks, blocks, and stone.
- Portland cement: a group of materials that are used to bond sand and gravel to form concrete.

COMPOSITES

Metals, ceramics, and plastics are single, uniform substances. Composites are not. **Composites** are made of two or more materials that are bonded together by adhesion (held together by physical force, or "stickiness").

A composite has two major parts, as shown in Fig. 3-10. These are:
- A filler.
- A matrix.

The *filler* usually provides the bulk (gives body) for the material. It is the fibers, flakes, sheets, or particles that are the base for the composite. The *matrix* (binding force) is the agent that holds the filler together. It is the bonding agent for the filler.

Composites can be either natural or synthetic. They can either appear in nature or be made by humans.

Natural Composites

Nature has produced the most widely used composite, *wood*. Wood is primarily hollow cellulose fibers (filler) held in place by lignin (matrix). It is like a group of soda straws glued together. Wood is divided into two major groups, Fig. 3-11.
- Hardwoods.
- Softwoods.

These categories have nothing to do with the hardness of the material. Hardwoods can be soft and softwoods can be hard. In fact, balsa is classified as a hardwood!

The difference between the two is the kind of tree the wood came from. Hardwood trees lose their leaves in the winter. They are called deciduous trees. Softwood trees are coniferous (meaning cone-bearing).

In general, hardwoods have shorter, open-ended fibers. Softwoods have longer fibers and a closed

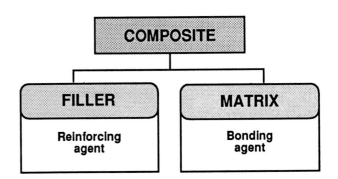

Fig. 3-10. This drawing shows the parts of a composite material.

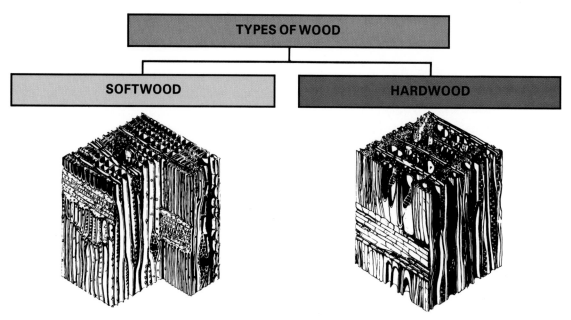

TYPES OF WOOD	
SOFTWOOD	HARDWOOD

Fig. 3-11. Types of wood. Cell structure varies between species.
(Forest Products Laboratory, U.S. Forest Service)

structure. Fig. 3-12 lists typical species (kinds) for each type of wood.

The length of the fibers and how closely they are packed together helps determine the property of a wood. Harder woods resist wear, but softer woods are easier to cut and nail. Therefore, most construction work uses softwoods. Furniture and flooring are usually made from hardwoods.

Manufactured Composites

Synthetic composites are not new. For centuries, people have mixed straw with mud to make adobe bricks. Adobe is still used in the southwestern U.S. In recent years, other composites have been devel-

IMPORTANT SPECIES OF WOOD	
Softwood	Hardwood
Cedar Cypress Fir Pine Redwood Spruce	White ash Basswood Beech Birch Cherry Gum Mahogany Maple Oak Pecan Poplar Walnut

Fig. 3-12. These species of wood are popular for many manufactured or constructed products.

oped. These can be grouped into three categories shown in Fig. 3-13:
- *Fibrous* composites use fibers to carry a load. A common example is glass fiber reinforcing plastic to make fiberglass.
- *Particulate* composites use particles held in a matrix. The load is shared by particles and matrix. Examples: flakeboard, particle board, concrete.
- Laminar composites are made up of layers glued together; the laminations carry the load. Examples: plywood, laminated beams, clad metals (coins, bi-metal thermometers).

Newer uses for composites are being found daily. In many new aircraft, the skin and some structural parts are now composites. These parts are lighter and stronger than parts made from other materials. The result is a more fuel efficient-airplane. Nose cones of rockets, fronts of trains and cars, sports car bodies, fishing poles, and many shower stalls are molded fiberglass. The newest tennis racquets use advanced composites. The uses for composite materials keep on growing.

SELECTING AND PURCHASING ENGINEERING MATERIALS

It is not enough to know about materials. You also need to be able to select and buy them. You will have to know how to determine the amount and type you need. This involves two major steps:
- Picking the type and grade of material needed.
- Determining the quantity needed.

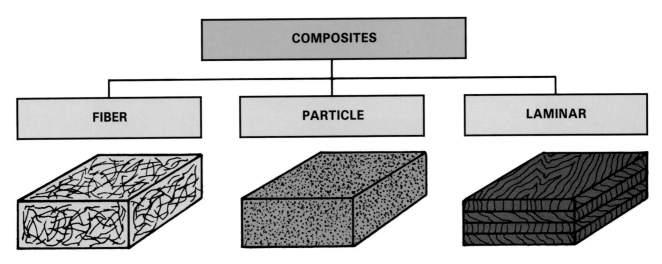

Fig. 3-13. Types of synthetic composites include fibers, particles, and sheets.

Material Grades

Materials come in different grades or compositions. Each material has a system for labeling these conditions. Metals generally use a number system to determine the composition of each alloy. For example, the Aluminum Association has developed a four-digit (number) system to identify aluminum. These four digits are then followed with a code to show the temper (hardness) of the aluminum. Fig. 3-14 is a typical aluminum code.

Steel, too, uses a number system for its alloys. The system developed by the American Iron and Steel Institute (AISI) and the Society of Automotive Engineers (SAE) is quite complex. The basis for it is a four digit number. The first two digits indicate the alloy. The last two show the carbon content.

Other metals have their own systems for identifying alloys. Each is different and somewhat complex.

Lumber Grades

As a natural material, wood is not very uniform.

Careful control can produce a uniform steel, aluminum, or polymer material. However, nature does not hold such tight controls. Therefore, wood must have a quality grade. The strength and percentage of knots and defects must be identified. There are separate systems for grading softwood lumber and hardwood lumber.

Softwood grading

There are a number of softwood lumber grades. Three important groups are: appearance-grade boards (selects), common boards, and framing lumber.

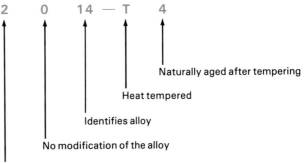

Fig. 3-14. The first four numbers in aluminum grading code stand for the type and percentage of different metals in the alloy.

Hardwood grading

Hardwood lumber is produced to a standard thickness, but it varies in width and length. It is said to be "random width and length." The hardwood grading system has three major grades. These are:
- First and seconds (FAS).
- Selects.
- Common.

Purchasing Materials

Engineering materials are purchased by many companies and individuals. These materials are sold in standard sizes or quantities. The typical measurements, as shown in Fig. 3-15, are:
- Unit.
- Weight.
- Surface measure.
- Volume.

Some materials are sold by counting **units.** Rolls of plastic are priced by the roll. Screws and bolts are sold by the hundred. Sheets of building materials

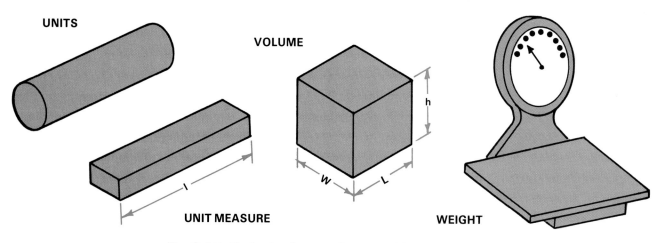

UNITS

VOLUME

UNIT MEASURE

WEIGHT

Fig. 3-15. Methods of measuring quantities of materials.

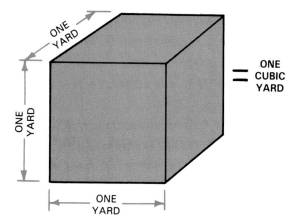

ONE CUBIC YARD

Fig. 3-16. A cubic yard measures a yard on all sides.

(plywood, particle board, hardboard, etc.) are sold individually.

Other materials are sold by their **weight**. Ceramic clay and Portland cement are sold by the pound, hundredweight, or ton. Plastic pellets are sold by their weight.

Surface measure is used in measuring many materials. The two typical measures are linear measure and area.

Linear measure is simply the length of the material in a unit. Small quantities of metal rod, strips, and angles are sold by length. Most indoor trim for houses is also sold by the foot. Most retail lumber yards sell wood by the foot or by the piece.

Area is a common way to measure building materials. Plastic laminate (Formica™) is sold by the square foot. Shingles are sold by the square (100 square feet). Area is determined by multiplying the length of the piece by its width.

The last way to measure materials is by **volume**. Two major methods used are cubic yards and board feet. (Lumber yards purchase lumber from mills by

the board foot.) Each of these measures requires you to calculate the volume of the material. You must multiply the thickness, width, and length together. Let us look at ways to determine each of these measures.

The *cubic yard* is the measure used for concrete. When you buy concrete you must decide the volume of material needed. A cubic yard can be thought of as a "container" that is one yard tall, one yard wide, and one yard long, Fig. 3-16.

The *board foot* is the measurement for lumber. A board foot is one inch thick and one foot square, Fig. 3-17. If the lumber is rough (not surfaced to size), you can use the material's actual size. However, for surfaced lumber, you cannot use the size of the part. Board feet must be figured using the nominal (normal or original) size of the material. For example, the nominal thickness of materials less than one inch thick *is* one inch. Typical nominal sizes for softwoods are shown in Fig. 3-18.

For softwood *finish* lumber you use the thickness and width nominal sizes. A 1 x 8 (nominal size) board is actually 3/4″ x 7 1/4″. However the "1" and the "8" are used in calculating the board measure.

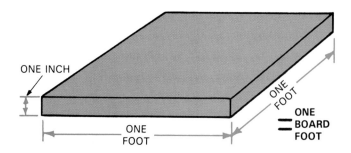

ONE INCH

ONE FOOT

ONE FOOT

ONE BOARD FOOT

Fig. 3-17. A board foot is determined by multiplying the width, length, and thickness and then dividing by a constant. A board foot is a measure of volume.

28   Exploring Manufacturing

SOFTWOOD LUMBER SIZES		
	NOMINAL SIZE	ACTUAL SIZE
BOARDS	1 × 4	3/4 × 3 1/2
	1 × 6	3/4 × 5 1/2
	1 × 8	3/4 × 7 1/4
	1 × 10	3/4 × 9 1/4
	1 × 12	3/4 × 11 1/4
DIMENSION LUMBERS	2 × 4	1 1/2 × 3 1/2
	2 × 6	1 1/2 × 5 1/2
	2 × 8	1 1/2 × 7 1/4
	2 × 10	1 1/2 × 9 1/4
	2 × 12	1 1/2 × 11 1/4

Fig. 3-18. Nominal sizes of lumber are not the same as actual sizes.

For thicker *construction* lumber, the same system is used. For example, a 2 x 4 is really 1 1/2″ x 3 1/2″.

Again, for rough lumber you use the actual sizes. Most hardwoods are sold this way.

SUMMARY

Materials are the foundation of our human-made world. Solid materials make up most of our permanent products. These materials are called engineering materials. They can be divided into metal, polymers, ceramics, and composites.

Material must be graded and sized for purchase. Commonly, materials are sold by the unit, weight, surface measure, or volume.

KEY WORDS

All the following words have been used in this chapter. Do you know their meaning?

Alloys
Area
Ceramics
Composites
Engineering materials
Filler
Linear measure
Matrix
Metals
Polymers
Surface measure
Thermoplastics
Thermosets
Weight
Units
Volume

TEST YOUR KNOWLEDGE

Please do not write in this text. Place your answers on a separate sheet of paper.

1. Name three common types of metal.
2. What is the difference between thermoplastic and thermoset materials?
3. Which of the following is or are NOT a ceramic material?
   A. Abrasives.
   B. Clay.
   C. Refractories.
   D. Glasses.
   E. Inorganic cements.
   F. Polymers.
4. Ceramics are the hardest of all engineering materials. True or False?
5. _____ is a name given material having grains made up of smaller boxlike structures or shapes. These small particles are called crystals.
6. The most common natural composite is:
   A. Ceramic.
   B. Glass.
   C. Steel.
   D. Wood.
7. What units are used in measuring materials for purchase?

ACTIVITIES

1. Interview a salesperson at a lumber yard or building supply store. Ask about the methods used to measure various materials for sale.
2. Gather pictures of various materials, then group them by type (metal, plastic, ceramic, composite). Use the pictures in a scrap book or bulletin board.
3. With your teacher's help, calculate the linear measure, surface measure, and volume (cubic feet and board feet) of several materials.

The properties of a material dictate how it will be used. Composites are light and strong, thus they are suited for uses such as this aircraft propeller. (Piaggio Aviation)

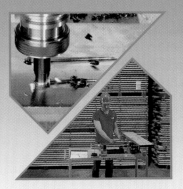

CHAPTER 4

PROPERTIES OF MATERIALS

After studying this chapter, you will be able to:
☐ Define terms like density, hardness, ductility, and opacity.
☐ Describe how some material properties are measured.
☐ Sketch how materials respond to stresses.
☐ List some requirements for selecting materials.

Product designers and engineers have a common problem. They must select a material to fit a need. The material must do a certain job.

The selection of the right material cannot be left to chance. It is a careful, thoughtful act. The designer must "know" materials. That is, she or he must know the properties of many different materials. *Properties* are qualities such as hardness, transparency, and so forth.

A material may need to satisfy several requirements to do the job. For example, it may have to be strong and look good (kitchen chair frame). It might have to be attractive, reflect light, and absorb sound (ceiling tile). Or the material may have to be strong and transparent (window glass). The examples are endless. All materials have a job to do.

Properties tell the designer how the material will perform or behave during use. Every material has many individual properties. These can all be grouped, as shown in Fig. 4-1, into the following categories:
• Mechanical.
• Physical.
• Thermal.
• Chemical.
• Electrical and magnetic.
• Optical.
• Acoustical.

MECHANICAL PROPERTIES

Mechanical properties are the ability of a material to withstand mechanical forces. Typically, these forces, as shown in Fig. 4-2, are:
• Compression.
• Tension.
• Shear.
• Torsion.

Basically, compression squeezes and crushes a material. Tension tries to pull it apart. Shear will

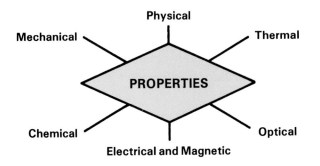

Fig. 4-1. This diagram shows the types of material properties.

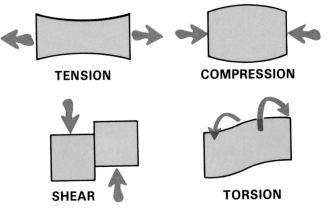

Fig. 4-2. Mechanical properties help a material stand up under these types of mechanical forces.

cause two parts of the material to separate and slide past each other. Torsion will twist the material. Torsion is actually a rotating shear force.

The ability to withstand these forces are measured in several ways. The common mechanical properties, as shown in Fig. 4-3 are:
- Strength.
- Elasticity, stiffness.
- Plasticity, ductility, malleability, brittleness.
- Hardness, wear resistance.
- Toughness.
- Fatigue.

Strength

Strength is the material's ability to bear a mechanical load. There are four strengths: tensile, compression, shear, and torsion.

Tensile strength is the amount of force needed to pull a material apart. *Compression strength* is the force that will cause a material to rupture (bulge out). *Shear strength* is the force that is required to cause parts of a material to slide past each other and

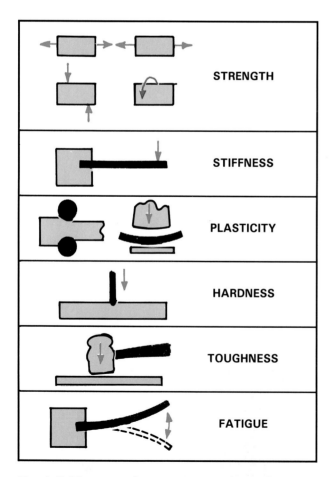

Fig. 4-3. These are the common mechanical properties that designers and engineers look for in a material.

separate. *Torsional strength* is the twisting force needed to cause the material to shear and separate.

Besides strength, other mechanical properties are important. There are six properties in this list: elasticity, plasticity, brittleness, hardness, toughness and fatigue.

Elasticity and stiffness

The ability to be flexed or stretched, then return to the original size, is called *elasticity*. The resistance to elastic forces is called stiffness. *Stiffness* is the ability to hold a load without flexing. A rubber band is elastic. A piece of glass has high stiffness.

Plasticity

The ability of a solid material to flow into a new shape under pressure is *plasticity*. Two measures of plasticity are:
- *Ductility*–plasticity under tension forces. This is a material's ability to be drawn (pulled) out. Chewing gum is highly ductile.
- *Malleability*–plasticity under compression force. This is a material's ability to be pounded into shape. Modeling clay has high malleability.

Brittleness

Brittleness is the tendency of a material to fracture before material flow (deformation) happens. Brittleness is the opposite of plasticity. Glass has high brittleness. It breaks easily.

Hardness

Hardness is an ability of a material to resist denting. It is directly related to abrasion and wear resistance. Harder materials will wear less under use. A diamond is very hard.

Toughness

The ability of a material to absorb energy without breaking is known as *toughness*. A hammer head must have high toughness so that it does not shatter when used to strike other materials.

Fatigue

Fatigue is the ability of a material to absorb repeated stress. A material with high fatigue strength can withstand constant flexing or bending. A spring must have high fatigue strength.

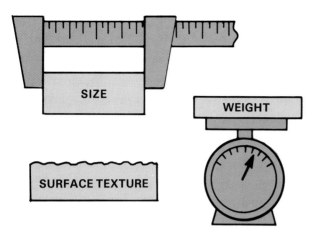

Fig. 4-4. Physical properties refer to size, surface appearance, and weight.

PHYSICAL PROPERTIES

Physical properties describe the size, density, and surface texture of a product, Fig. 4-4. *Size* describes a material by its thickness, width, and length. This overall size is a physical property.

Density is a measure of the weight of a certain volume of material. The volume of the sample objects must be constant. Typically, density is given as pounds per cubic inch (lb/in^3), pounds per cubic foot (lb/ft^3), or grams per liter (g/L).

Fig. 4-5. Density of a new rubber shoe sole is demonstrated in tank of water. (Goodyear Tire and Rubber Co.)

Different materials can be compared using their densities. For example, red oak has a density of 43.8 pounds per cubic foot (lb./cu. ft.) Ponderosa pine's density is 28.6 lb./cu. ft. We can see that red oak is almost 1 1/2 times as dense as pine. That is to say, an oak board will weigh 50 percent more than the same size pine board.

Closely related to density is *porosity*. This is the relationship of open space to solid space in a material. A more porous material will generally be lighter (less dense) than a nonporous material, Fig. 4-5. Also, a porous material will contain air within it. It will be a better heat insulator.

Wood is more porous than aluminum. Therefore, wood window frames will insulate a home better than aluminum frames. If you live in a colder area you know this is true. You have probably seen aluminum window frames frost up on the inside.

The final physical property is *surface texture,* Fig. 4-6. We have all used the terms smooth and rough. These describe surface texture. Some surfaces must be smooth, while others need to be rough. A rough surface on a pair of skis would not work well, nor would a smooth surface on sandpaper.

THERMAL PROPERTIES

Thermal properties relate to a material's response to changes in temperature. Three important properties relate to heat:
- Melting and freezing point.
- Thermal conductivity.
- Thermal expansion.

Fig. 4-6. This technician is measuring the surface texture of a part. (Rohm & Haas)

Everyone knows about melting and freezing points. Both involve thermal (heat) energy. Thermal energy is measured in BTUs (British thermal units) or calories. A BTU is the heat energy needed to raise the temperature of one pound of water one degree Fahrenheit. Another measure of heat is the calorie. It is the energy needed to raise the temperature of one gram of water one degree Celsius.

It takes thermal energy to melt a solid material. Likewise, a material gives up thermal energy as it freezes. This is important in all processes that heat and cool materials, Fig. 4-7.

Thermal conductivity is a material's ability to allow heat to flow within it. Heat energy tends to flow from a hotter area to a colder area. The speed at which this happens in a set period of time is called the coefficient (measure) of thermal conductivity. An insulation material should have a low coefficient of thermal conductivity. It should not allow heat to move from one area to another. However, the liquid in a cooling system must have a high coefficient of thermal conductivity. It should move heat away rapidly.

Thermal expansion is the degree to which a material changes size with a change in temperature. Solid materials usually expand when heated and shrink when they cool. The increase in length per degree rise in temperature is called the coefficient of thermal expansion.

CHEMICAL PROPERTIES

All environments are full of chemicals. The world, in fact, is totally made up of chemicals. The air is a chemical mixture. It has nitrogen, oxygen, sulfur dioxide (a component of acid rain), and many other compounds. Water has many minerals mixed in it. It is said to be "hard" when it contains chemicals that prevent soap from working properly.

The *chemical properties* of a material are the measurement of its ability to resist chemicals. Many chemicals cause engineering materials to corrode. Corrosion is a very complex action. In fact, its process is not totally understood by scientists. However, we all see the results of it. Steel rusts. Glass becomes pitted. Plastics become etched or simply fracture. These are the results of corrosion, Fig. 4-8.

ELECTRICAL AND MAGNETIC PROPERTIES

Electrical and magnetic properties measure a material's reaction to:
• Electrical current.
• External electromagnetic forces.

Fig. 4-7. It is important to know the thermal properties of the steel slab and its shear strength during this operation. (U.S. Steel)

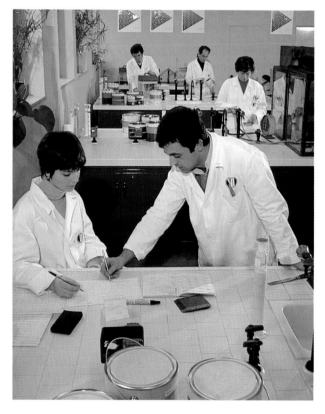

Fig. 4-8. Materials are subjected to numerous chemicals in this laboratory to determine their chemical properties.

One principal measure of these properties is electrical conductivity. This is the ability of a material to conduct electric current. Materials that can carry current are called conductors. Those that do not are called insulators, and resist current flow.

Electric conductors (wires, bus bars, etc.) must have high electrical conductivity. They should *not* have high electrical resistance. In short, little electrical energy should be converted to heat energy because of resistance.

The opposite of electrical conductivity is electrical resistivity. It is a measure of the resistance to the flow of electric current. Insulators have very high resistivity. They should not conduct electric current. Also, heating coils have high resistivity. They convert electrical energy to heat energy.

Magnetic properties relate to a material's ability to be magnetized by an outside electromagnetic force. This measure is called permeability. The higher the permeability, the easier it is to magnetize a material.

OPTICAL PROPERTIES

Optical properties relate to a material's reaction to light waves, Fig. 4-9. Two main optical properties of general importance are:
- Opacity–The ability to stop light waves. Opaque materials will block light. The opposite is transmittance. Windows should have high transmittance. Window shades should have high opacity.

Fig. 4-9. The reaction of materials to a laser is checked in a laboratory. (Air Products)

- Color–The ability of a material to absorb certain light waves and reflect others. This property determines which light waves are reflected to the human eye for us to see.

ACOUSTICAL PROPERTIES

Acoustical properties relate to a material's reaction to sound waves, Fig. 4-10. Materials will vary in their ability to:
- Absorb sound.
- Transmit sound.
- Reflect sound.

Fig. 4-10. The materials in this "quiet room" have high sound absorption. (Goodyear Tire and Rubber Co.)

SUMMARY

Each material has a unique set of properties. These properties are what make materials different from one another. A material's properties must be carefully considered as it is chosen for a specific use. Properties are commonly grouped into seven categories: mechanical, physical, thermal, chemical, electrical and magnetic, optical, and acoustical.

KEY WORDS

All the following words have been used in this chapter. Do you know their meaning?

Acoustical properties
Brittleness
Chemical properties
Compression strength
Density
Elasticity
Electrical and magnetic properties
Fatigue
Hardness
Mechanical properties
Optical properties
Plasticity
Porosity
Properties
Shear Strength
Size
Stiffness
Strength
Tensile strength
Thermal properties
Torsional strength
Toughness

TEST YOUR KNOWLEDGE

Please do not write in this text. Place your answers on a separate sheet of paper.

1. _____ is a force that squeezes and crushes a material; _____ attempts to pull it apart.
2. Describe the difference between ductility and malleability.
3. Select the property most important when forming material under pressure:
   A. Ductility.
   B. Plasticity or malleability.
   C. Elasticity.
   D. Fatigue.
   E. Toughness.
4. A spring should have the property of brittleness. True or False?
5. Wood floats in water because of the property of (surface texture, porosity).
6. What property explains why heating one end of a copper rod will also cause the other end to become warm?
7. Chemical properties measure a material's ability to resist:
   A. Rust.
   B. Corrosion.
   C. Water.
   D. Sunlight.
8. _____ is the ability of a material to absorb certain light waves and reflect others.

ACTIVITIES

1. Collect a variety of materials that are used to make drinking cups. They are often made from steel, aluminum, paper, plastic, and clay (china).
   A. Arrange these materials according to their hardness, density (weight), thermal conductivity, and strength.
   B. Which material would you use to make a cup for the following uses? Explain the reasons for your selections:
      Camping trip.
      Picnic.
      Formal dining.
      Vending machines.
2. You are asked to select a material for a diving board. Which properties would you consider in your selection? Why?
3. Working with a partner, design a test to determine a major material property such as hardness, thermal conductivity, or electrical resistance.

The properties of a material will determine how it will be processed. The properties of this aluminum sheet make it easy to process using a separating machine such as the one shown. (Ira Wexler, Reynolds Metals)

PRIMARY MANUFACTURING PROCESSES

CHAPTER 5

INTRODUCTION TO MANUFACTURING PROCESSES

After studying this chapter, you will be able to:
☐ Identify manufacturing processes as primary or secondary.
☐ List and discuss major steps in the manufacturing processes.
☐ Define primary and secondary processes.
☐ Describe six types of secondary processes.
☐ Name outputs of manufacturing activities.
☐ Discuss the impact of manufacturing processes on the environment.

Throughout history, people have changed the size, shape, and looks of materials. They have tried to make materials better fit their needs. In so doing, people have manufactured products.

The actual changing of the form of material is one part of manufacturing. This activity is called *material processing*. Management, you remember, is the other part of successful manufacturing.

Changing the form of materials takes three major steps. These stages, as shown in Fig. 5-1, are:

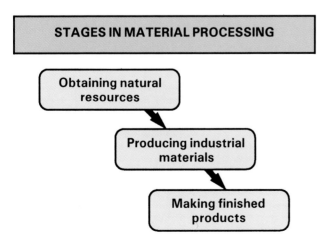

Fig. 5-1. There are three stages of material processing.

• Obtaining natural resources.
• Producing industrial materials by changing raw materials into them.
• Making finished products from industrial materials.

Keep in mind that we are going to talk mostly about materials. However, this is only one resource in manufacturing. People, energy, time, knowledge, capital, and finances are also important. However, converting materials into products is the task of manufacturing. The other resources (inputs) support this activity.

OBTAINING RESOURCES

We cannot build a product without materials. The materials must be located and gathered. The typical processes for collecting materials are listed in Fig. 5-2. These are:
• Mining–Digging the material from the earth by means of a hole or tunnel.
• Drilling–Pumping material from below the earth's surface through a narrow, round shaft.
• Harvesting–Cutting a mature, renewable resource from the land.

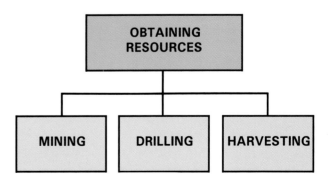

Fig. 5-2. Resources are gathered in three ways.

PRIMARY PROCESSING

Once raw materials are obtained, they are moved to a mill. Here the resource is changed into an industrial material. Trees are made into lumber, plywood, fiberboard, and particleboard. Iron ore, limestone, and coke are used to produce steel. Natural gas is a feedstock (source) for many plastics. These outputs are called standard stock. They are the products of primary processing.

Primary processing is the first major step in changing the form of materials. Three major processes are used to convert raw materials into industrial materials. These, as shown in Fig. 5-3, are:
- Thermal (heat) processes.
- Chemical processes.
- Mechanical processes.

These processes are not entirely separate. For example, thermal processes heat crushed (mechanically processed) ores. *Thermal processes* use heat to change the properties of materials. The hot ores enter into a chemical reaction. This reaction separates the metal from impurities. Crushing the ore makes it easier to extract the metal using heat. The two processes worked together.

Mechanical processes cut or crush resources. Trees are cut into lumber, veneer, and chips. Rocks are crushed into gravel. Wool is sheared from sheep. All are mechanical processes. They use mechanical force to change the resource.

Chemical processes use chemical reactions to refine raw materials. Plastics are formed by chemical reactions. Simple compounds are combined to form the complex polymer chains we call plastics. Fig. 5-4 lists some resources that are processed by each type of primary processing.

SECONDARY PROCESSING

Industrial materials (standard stock) can now be changed into finished products. Lumber is made into furniture and houses. Leather is made into shoes and belts. Steel is used to make cars, appliances, and reinforcing bars for concrete. Thousands of products are made from the outputs of primary processing.

Finished products are produced by *secondary processes*. These activities, as shown in Fig. 5-5, are:
- Casting and molding–Pouring or forcing liquid material into a prepared mold. The material is allowed to become solid. Then it is removed from the mold.
- Forming–Using force to cause a material to permanently take a shape. A die, mold, or roll is used to shape the material.
- Separating–Changing a material's size and shape by removing excess material. The material is cut or sheared by these processes.
- Conditioning–Using heat, mechanical force, or chemical action to change the internal properties of a material.
- Assembling–Temporarily or permanently holding two or more parts together.

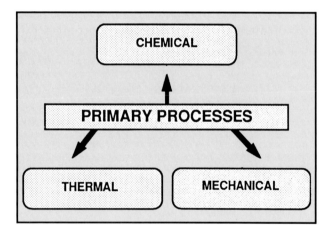

Fig. 5-3. Types of primary processing. Sometimes more than one type is used to produce a primary material.

PRIMARY PROCESSES		
THERMAL	CHEMICAL	MECHANICAL
Steelmaking	Aluminum refining	Lumber manufacture
Copper smelting	Polymer formation	Plywood manufacture
Zinc smelting	Gold refining	Particleboard making
Lead smelting	Papermaking	Rock crushing
	Leather tanning	

Fig. 5-4. Resources processed by each type of primary processing.

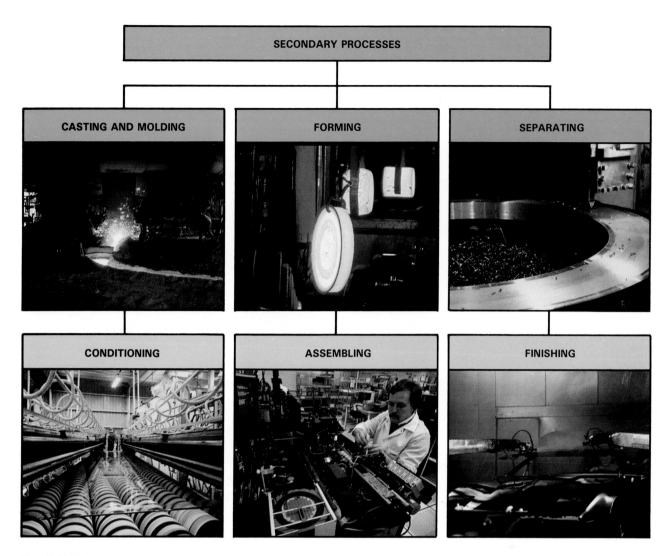

Fig. 5-5. Secondary processes are casting and molding, forming, separating, conditioning, assembling, and finishing.(Rohm & Haas; Bethlehem Steel; Inland Steel Co.; PPG Industrial; AT&T; DeVilbiss)

• Finishing–Protecting or improving the appearance of the surface of a material.

PRODUCTS, WASTE, AND SCRAP

Almost all manufacturing activities create unwanted by-products. Mining creates holes and shafts in the ground. Harvesting timber requires roads through peaceful woods and camps for workers. Steel plants and foundries give off fumes, dust, noise, and wastes. Machining activities create chips, scraps, and shavings. There is no such thing as a scrapless, pollution-free manufacturing activity. People must carefully plan to reduce and control undesirable outputs. By doing this we can make sure that the environment is not harmed.

The protection of the environment is the responsibility of all citizens. We need clean air, water, and soil. Each of us must do our part to save our precious natural resources. Also, we should expect—*and demand*–that industry help. Companies must consider:

■ Their practices in obtaining raw materials:
  • Are they efficient?
  • Is the land returned fully to productive use, Fig. 5-6?
■ Pollution caused by manufacturing processes:
  • Can it be avoided and minimized?
  • If not, can it be controlled and cleaned up?
  • Scrap and waste:
■ Does the manufacturing process produce unnecessary scrap and waste?
  • Is every effort being made to recycle scrap? See Fig. 5-7.
  • Is unusable waste material disposed of properly?

Our future will be more secure with industrial and personal resource conservation. You and tomorrow's children can have the "good life" if we use our resources wisely.

Fig. 5-6. This is land that was once an open pit mine. (American Electric Power)

Fig. 5-7. Scrap metal can be recycled and used in the steelmaking process.

SUMMARY

Manufacturing materials are converted from raw materials to finished products in three stages, Fig. 5-8. Raw materials are first located. They are then obtained from the earth by harvesting, drilling, or mining. Secondly, the raw materials are converted into standard stock. Thermal, chemical, and mechanical processes are used. Finally, the industrial goods are changed into finished products. The form change is done through casting and molding, separating, forming, conditioning, assembling, and finishing processes.

Throughout the processing, the environment must be protected. Resources must be used wisely. Scrap and waste must be kept to a minimum. Pollution needs to be reduced and controlled.

With environmental concern and efficient manufacturing, we can all live better. We will have useful products and a healthy world.

KEY WORDS

All of the following words have been used in this chapter. Do you know their meaning?

Chemical processes
Material processing
Mechanical processes
Primary processes
Secondary processes
Thermal processes

TEST YOUR KNOWLEDGE

Please do not write in this text. Place your answers on a separate sheet of paper.

1. Changing the form of materials takes (three, four, five) major steps.
2. List and describe three ways of obtaining natural resources.
3. Which of the listed processes are called primary processes?
   A. Chemical processes.
   B. Heating processes.
   C. Mechanical processes.
   D. Electrical processes.
   E. Extracting processes.
4. Crushing is a primary process called _____ processing.
5. List and describe the six types of secondary processes.
6. Name the three outputs of manufacturing activity.
7. Protection of the environment is _____ responsibility.

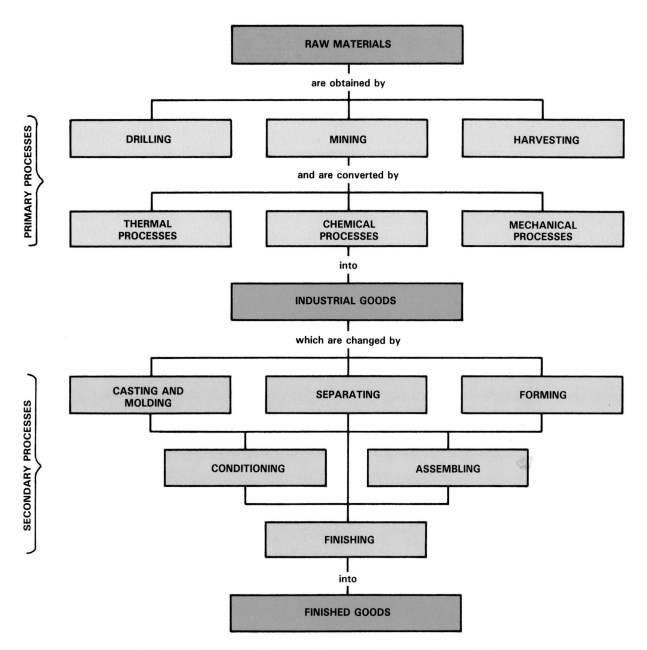

Fig. 5-8. A summary diagram of the material processing activities.

ACTIVITIES

1. Invite a person from a manufacturing company to discuss the inputs, processes, and outputs of manufacturing.
2. Find out about the Pollution Prevention Act of 1990. Learn how manufacturers or users of a toxic chemical must be responsible to the environment. Begin by writing to the U.S. Environmental Protection Agency, Public Information Center (3404), 401 M Street, SW, Washington, DC 20460 or on-line at http://www.epa.gov. Request a copy of *Guide to Environmental Issues.*
3. Go on a field trip to a manufacturing company. Observe and list the resources, sequence of operations, and outputs.

Materials are gathered by mining, drilling, and harvesting. Trees are harvested by skilled workers called fellers. (Weyerhaeuser)

CHAPTER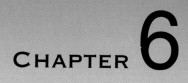

OBTAINING RAW MATERIALS

After studying this chapter, you will be able to:
☐ Define renewable and exhaustible resources and give examples of each.
☐ Describe three different methods for mining raw materials.
☐ Define and describe two methods of drilling for oil or gas.
☐ Describe three methods of harvesting forests.
☐ Explain methods by which raw materials are moved to mills and refineries.

Most products are made from many different materials. All of these materials were once in a "raw" condition. **Raw materials** are natural resources found on or in the earth or seas.

All manufacturing starts with raw materials. These materials are of two basic types, Fig. 6-1. They are renewable or exhaustible.

RENEWABLE RESOURCES

Renewable resources are biological materials (growing things). Each growing unit (plant or animal) has a life cycle. First, it is planted or born. It

RESOURCES	
RENEWABLE	**EXHAUSTIBLE**
Trees	Metal ores
Cotton	Petroleum
Wool	Natural gas
Flax	Coal
Animal hides	Clays

Fig. 6-1. There is no limit to the supply of renewable resources. Exhaustible resources will be gone one day and cannot be replaced.

then grows through stages to maturity (full size). Finally, it becomes old and dies.

A tree is a good example of a renewable resource. It is planted by nature or people. It grows and, after a number of years, reaches its full size. Then, growth slows and finally stops. Limbs die and fall off. Insects, wind, and decay attack the tree. In time, it dies and falls to the forest floor. There it rots, providing nutrients (food) for other plants.

Managing Resources

Managing a resource means making sure that there is always a supply to use. It means seeing that future generations will also have it to use.

Even though some resources are renewable, managing them is still important. People must plan and work at growing new resources and knowing when and how to harvest them. For instance, a forester should not cut down all the trees in a forest without planting new ones.

We depend on many renewable resources for manufactured products. They provide us with wood products (such as furniture), leather, and natural fibers (wool, cotton, silk, and linen) for making cloth.

Exhaustible resources, discussed next, also must be managed. Unlike renewable resources, we cannot replace them. Management means collecting and using resources carefully so they are not wasted.

EXHAUSTIBLE RESOURCES

Not all natural resources are renewable. Some have a limited supply. There is a fixed amount of them on earth. Once used up, there will be no more. These resources are called *exhaustible*. They can be used up. Like the dinosaurs, a material can become extinct.

For example, there is only so much petroleum, gold ore, natural gas, or iron ore on the earth. If we use them all up, that's it. Thus, all resources MUST be used wisely.

LOCATING RAW MATERIALS

Obtaining raw materials for manufacturing is a three-step process. This includes:
- Locating resources.
- Gathering resources.
- Transporting (moving) resources.

A large part of getting raw materials is finding them. Aerial mapping (using an airplane to take pictures) can help locate trees. Geological (under the ground) searches will find minerals and petroleum. See Fig. 6-2.

Other resources are easier to find. They are grown commercially (for money). Trees in the south are often grown like a crop. Livestock provides us with leather.

The search for raw materials can be costly and disappointing. For example, our future supplies of petroleum cause us concern. Oil companies spend millions of dollars searching for new pools of oil. Often they come up dry. Several multimillion dollar "dry holes" have been drilled off the east coast of the United States. No oil was found.

On a smaller scale, some persons spend a lifetime looking for minerals. The prospectors (gold hunters) of old still live. Today they use better equipment, but are still unlikely to "strike it rich."

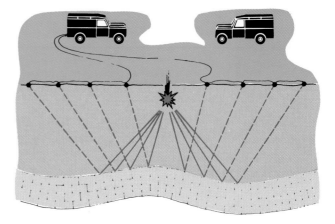

Fig. 6-2. Seismic studies send shock waves into the earth to detect promising locations for raw materials. (Shell Oil Co.)

Working with them are trained geologists (people who study the structure of the earth) from mining companies. Such teams constantly look for gold, silver, uranium, and other metal ores.

Even with all the scientific knowledge and equipment available, finding underground resources is hard, but it is necessary. Our lifestyle is built on materials. Our society must have a continuing flow of raw materials.

GATHERING RAW MATERIALS

Once found, raw materials must be gathered. This is done using three major methods. These methods were introduced in Chapter 5, and are shown in Fig. 6-3.

Fig. 6-3. Materials are collected by mining, drilling, and harvesting. (AMAX Corp.; OMI; Boise-Cascade Corp.)

Mining

Mining involves digging resources out of the earth. If the raw material is close to the surface, it can be mined from the surface. The topsoil is removed and often stored. The mineral is then scooped up by giant power shovels and put in huge trucks. They haul the material to a conveyor or to the surface, Fig. 6-4. This is called *open-pit mining* or surface mining.

Often the mineral is in a narrow vein (strip) like many coal deposits. In this case, the topsoil is replaced after mining. The land is returned to productive use. Lakes, pastureland, and farms are developed over the mine pit.

In other cases, the mineral is in a very deep (thick) deposit. As it is removed, a huge pit is produced. The Bingham Canyon copper mine in Utah is over 1/2 mile deep and 2 miles wide. Over 2,000,000,000 (two billion) tons of material have been removed since the mine opened in 1904.

Other ore deposits require digging tunnels to reach the material. This is called *underground mining*. There are three major underground mining methods. As seen in Fig. 6-5, these are:

- *Shaft mining*. This method is used for deeply buried mineral deposits. A shaft is dug down to the level of the deposit. These shafts can extend several thousand feet into the earth. The main vertical (up-and-down) shaft is used to move people and equipment in and out of the mine.

The mineral is also lifted out through the vertical shafts. Other vertical shafts are dug to bring in fresh air and remove stale air and gases. The material is mined by digging horizontal (level) tunnels from the vertical shaft.

- *Drift mining*. This method is used when the mineral vein comes to the surface at one point. A tunnel is dug at that point. The tunnel follows the ore vein into the earth. People and materials are moved by railcars that travel along the drift shaft.

- *Slope mining*. This method is used for a shallow mineral deposit. A sloping tunnel is dug down to the deposit. Workers can walk or ride motorized cars down to the deposit. There they dig the mineral out of the vein. The materials are often carried to the surface on a moving platform called a conveyor.

Drilling

Drilling involves cutting a round hole deep into the earth, Fig. 6-6. A drilling rig or derrick is brought to the site. A drilling bit is attached to a drill pipe. The pipe is clamped in a rotary table in the middle of the drilling floor. The table turns and the hole is drilled. More drill pipe is added as the hole deepens.

Throughout the drilling, "mud" is pumped down the drill pipe. It comes out through the drill bit. The mud is forced to the surface, carrying with it the

Fig. 6-4. An open pit mine in operation. This type of mining is suitable when ores are near the surface.

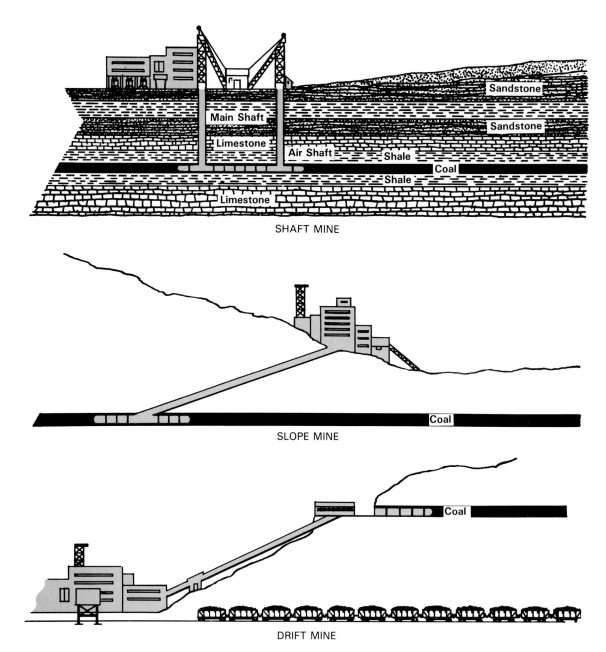

Fig. 6-5. Types of underground mines. (National Coal Assoc.)

cuttings from the bit. Casing (pipe the diameter of the hole) is forced into the hole to keep it from caving in.

Drilling stops when the hole reaches the underground reservoir (pool). The drilling rig is removed. Valves to control the flow and a pump are attached. Drilling is used to reach petroleum, water, natural gas, and other liquids normally found underground.

Drilling may be done either on land or in the water, Fig. 6-7. Generally, the drill produces a straight hole. This type of drilling is called *vertical drilling*. Newer techniques allow the drilling of a curved well. This method is called *directional drilling*. It allows us to reach a reservoir that would be

hard to get to with vertical drilling. Also, several wells can be drilled from a single platform.

Harvesting

Harvesting is a method used to collect a growing resource. Trees are the major "growing" resource that produce engineering materials. Trees are harvested using one of three methods. These, shown in Fig. 6-8, are:

- *Selective cutting.* Mature trees are selected and cut. This method is used for trees that can grow in the shade of others. The stands will have all ages of trees present. Selective cutting is used in western pine areas and in hardwood forests.

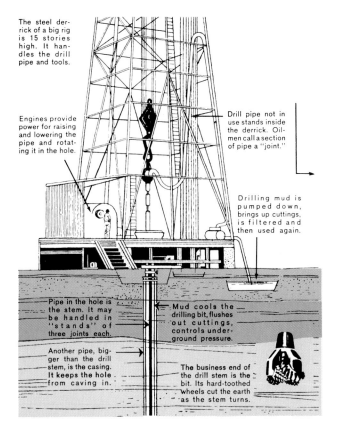

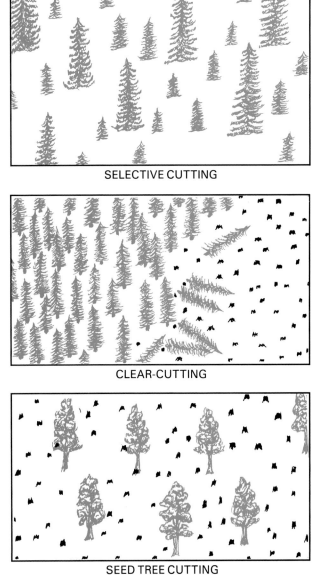

Fig. 6-6. A typical oil drilling rig. The derrick supports a block and tackle for raising and lowering drill pipe. (Shell Oil Co.)

- **Clear-cutting** (Block cutting). All trees in a block of about 100 acres are cut. Trees in areas around the block are left alone. They will provide the seed to reforest the area. This technique is used for trees that will not grow in the shade, such as Douglas fir. Clear-cutting is widely used in the western coastal forests.

SELECTIVE CUTTING

CLEAR-CUTTING

SEED TREE CUTTING

Fig. 6-8. Types of tree harvesting.

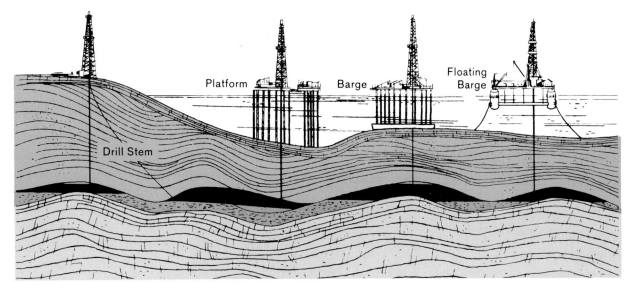

Fig. 6-7. Some common drilling locations and methods.

- *Seed tree cutting*. All trees in an area, except for four or five large ones, are cut. The large trees reseed the area. This technique is used in the southern pine forests.

Harvesting requires several steps. First, either trees or the area to be harvested must be selected. Fallers then fell (cut down) the trees, Fig. 6-9. A bucker removes the limbs and top. The tree is cut to standard lengths for the mill.

The lengths, called logs, are moved to a central location for loading on trucks or railcars. This task is called *yarding*. From the yard, the trees are hauled to the mill. They are placed in a pond to help retain their moisture and reduce insect damage.

Newer practices are now using more of the tree. Chippers are placed in the woods. Limbs and tops are chipped up for boiler fuel, hardboard, and paper.

TRANSPORTING RESOURCES

Nearly every type of land and water transportation is used to move raw materials. Pipelines move petroleum and natural gas. Coal can be ground up and mixed with water, forming a *slurry*, for pipeline transport. Trucks of all kinds and sizes move mineral and forest products. Barges and ships are used on inland waterways and oceans. In short, the most economical method is used to move raw materials from mine, well, or forest.

Fig. 6-9. A tree is cut or felled by a skilled worker. (Weyerhaeuser Co.)

SUMMARY

Raw materials are the foundation for all manufactured goods. These materials are either a renewable or an exhaustible resource. They are located, gathered, and transported to primary processing mills or refineries.

Commonly, raw materials are gathered through mining, drilling, and harvesting. The gathered resources move over land and on water. There they are transformed (changed) into industrial materials.

KEY WORDS

All the following words have been used in this chapter. Do you know their meaning?

Clear-cutting
Directional drilling
Drift mining
Drilling
Exhaustible resource
Harvesting
Mining
Open-pit mining
Raw materials
Renewable resource
Seed tree cutting
Selective cutting
Shaft mining
Slope mining
Slurry
Underground mining
Vertical drilling
Yarding

TEST YOUR KNOWLEDGE

Please do not write in this text. Place your answers on a separate sheet of paper.

1. A material that is still in its natural form is called a _____ material.
2. Explain the difference between a renewable and an exhaustible resource.

Matching questions: Match the definitions on the left with the correct term on the right.

3. _____ Sloping tunnel   A. Shaft mine.
   is dug to get   B. Surface.
   at shallow deposit.   C. Drift mine.
4. _____ Tunnel follows   D. Slope mine.
   surface ore vein
   into earth.

5. _____ Deep shaft is dug straight down to deposit.
6. _____ Deposit is dug from open-pit.
7. List 10 renewable resources.
8. List 10 exhaustible resources.
9. _____ searches are used to find underground resources such as petroleum, coal, copper, and other mineral resources.
10. If you want to drill for oil on a certain spot but cannot because a lake is in the way, which of the following methods would you use?
    A. Vertical drilling.
    B. Directional drilling.
11. Describe the difference between the following methods of harvesting trees: selective cutting, clear-cutting, and seed tree cutting.

ACTIVITIES

1. Visit a drilling, mining, or harvesting operation to see how natural resources are obtained. Then, visit a recycling center to see how manufactured products are recycled for reuse.
2. Working in a team, design a process to separate gravel from a sand-soil-gravel mix.
3. Plant or adopt a tree. Observe its growth throughout the year and the variety of mammals, birds, and insects that utilize it as a resource. Discuss the possible effects on creatures, soil, and air if this tree were removed and not replaced.
4. Start a recycling program at your school or expand an existing program. Recycle all types of waste including paper, cardboard, plastic, glass, and aluminum.

Industrial materials are produced so that manufacturing companies can make finished products. (Inland Steel Co.)

CHAPTER 7

PRODUCING INDUSTRIAL MATERIALS

After studying this chapter, you will be able to:
- ☐ Explain primary processing.
- ☐ Define and identify various kinds of standard stock.
- ☐ Describe four major types of synthetic wood composites.
- ☐ List forms of plastic standard stock.
- ☐ Describe steps in making iron and steel stock.
- ☐ Explain how forest products are converted to standard stock.

When raw materials arrive at the mill, they are ready for a change in form. They will be refined or converted into standard stock. Trees will become lumber or plywood. Natural gas will be changed into plastic. Bauxite will become aluminum sheets. Lime, silica sand, alumina, iron, and gypsum are processed into Portland cement. The first step in manufacturing is called *primary processing*, Fig. 7-1. Raw materials are processed into industrial materials. Another name for them is standard stock.

STANDARD STOCK

What is standard stock? *Standard stock* is a material that has been changed so it has certain characteristics (qualities). It has a particular grade, size, and shape.

Each type of material has its own standards. Let's look at some major types of standard stock.

Standard Forest Products

Forest products include all things made from wood. Even in its natural state, wood is a composite. It is made up of fibers held together by lignin, a natural adhesive. The common natural wood composite is *lumber*.

Fiberboard, particleboard, and laminated boards are synthetic wood composites. Paper is also a synthetic wood composite, but is not an engineering (structural) material.

Hardwood lumber standards

Hardwood is cut to standard thickness–4/4 (four quarters of an inch), 5/4, 6/4, 8/4, and so on. The boards are random (varying) widths and lengths. The diameter and length of the log determine the width and length of the lumber. Other manufacturing steps may produce standard hardwood products. Examples of these are flooring and interior trim for houses.

Softwood lumber standards

Softwood lumber is generally produced to standard sizes for all of its dimensions. Boards are cut to set thicknesses, widths, and lengths. For example, you can buy a 2 x 4 x 8 (1 1/2 in. thick by 3 1/2 in. wide by 8 ft. long) or a 1 x 8 x 16 (3/4 in. thick by 7 1/4 in. wide by 16 ft. long). Do you remember that softwood lumber is sold by its nominal (in name only) size?

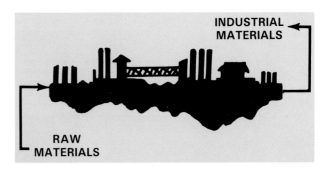

Fig. 7-1. The primary processing system changes materials from a natural state to one more suitable for a useful product.

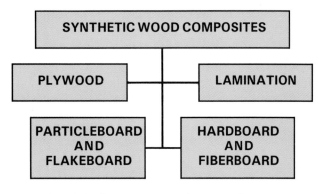

Fig. 7-2. Synthetic wood composites can be classified.

Synthetic wood composites

The typical synthetic wood composites, as shown in Fig. 7-2, are:

- *Plywood*–A panel composed of a core, (middle layer), face layers of veneer (thin sheets of wood), and crossbands. The grain of the core and the face veneers run in the same direction. Except in thin plywood, the crossbands are at right angles to the face veneers, Fig. 7-3. Three-

ply material has a core that is at right angles to the face veneers. Most plywood is made entirely from a series of layers of veneer. Other plywood has cores made of particleboard or solid lumber (lumber-core), Fig. 7-4.

- *Particleboard*–A panel made from chips, shavings, or flakes of wood. The actual name of the material comes from the type of particles used. The most common types are called standard particleboard, waferboard, flakeboard, and oriented strand (placed in a certain direction) board. The particles are held together with a synthetic glue.

- *Fiberboard*–A panel made from wood fibers. The most common fiberboard is hardboard, commonly referred to as Masonite™. This material is very dense. Fibers are held in place by natural glue (lignin).

- *Laminations*–Heavy timbers produced from a series of layers of veneer or lumber. The grain of all layers run in the same direction. The timber is held together by synthetic adhesives. Many wood beams in churches, schools, and other buildings are laminations.

Except for laminations, synthetic wood composites are produced in sheets. The most common sheet

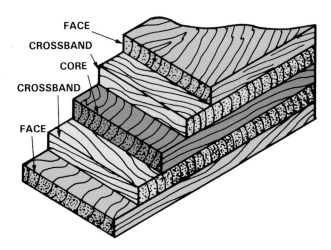

Fig. 7-3. A diagram of plywood construction. Note the crossbanding that gives it strength.

SIZE	PLYWOOD	PARTICLEBOARD	HARDBOARD
1/8			*
1/4	*	*	*
3/8	*	*	
1/2	*	*	
5/8	*	*	
3/4	*	*	
1	*	*	

Fig. 7-5. Standard sheet sizes for wood composites.

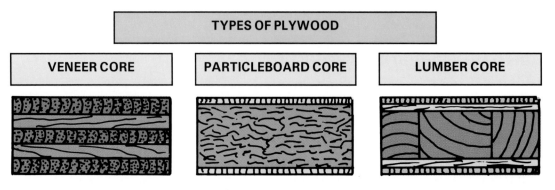

Fig. 7-4. Types of plywood are named for their core.

size is 4 ft. by 8 ft. Materials are made in a number of standard thicknesses. Fig. 7-5 lists the most common ones.

STANDARD METAL STOCK

Like wood, metals also come in several standard sizes and shapes. Basically, the standard determines the cross section and the length of the material. Typical shapes are shown in Fig. 7-6.

STANDARD PLASTIC STOCK

Plastic materials are typically produced in pellets and powders, or as sheets and film. Pellets and powders are sold by the pound. They are the inputs for many molding processes.

Sheets and films are used for thermoforming processes and in packaging. These materials are sized by thickness and width. The thickness is given in mils. A *mil* is 0.001 in. thick. Width for these materials is given in inches.

Films are sold in single thickness sheets, tubing, and folded forms, Fig. 7-7. Folded film is used for shrink packaging, such as is seen on games, puzzles, and compact disc packages. Tubing can be made into bags.

Single-thickness film has many uses. These include vapor barriers (between gypsum board and insulation in homes), heat-sealing wraps (meats and vegetables in grocery stores), and temporary storm windows.

PRODUCING STANDARD STOCK

Each material has its own primary processing method. Aluminum is refined differently than is copper. Lumber is produced by techniques not used for manufacturing plywood. Each plastic is produced by a special chemical process.

It would be impossible to cover all primary processing systems. That would take many books. Instead, two common primary processing activities–steelmaking and forest product manufacturing–will be presented. This will give you an idea of the steps a raw material goes through to become standard stock.

Steelmaking

Steelmaking started in North America over 300 years ago. It is now a large industry. The process is a complex one. Complicated chemical actions

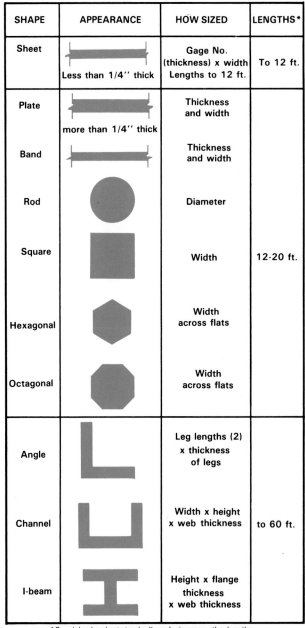

SHAPE	APPEARANCE	HOW SIZED	LENGTHS*
Sheet	Less than 1/4" thick	Gage No. (thickness) x width Lengths to 12 ft.	To 12 ft.
Plate	more than 1/4" thick	Thickness and width	
Band		Thickness and width	
Rod		Diameter	
Square		Width	12-20 ft.
Hexagonal		Width across flats	
Octagonal		Width across flats	
Angle		Leg lengths (2) x thickness of legs	
Channel		Width x height x web thickness	to 60 ft.
I-beam		Height x flange thickness x web thickness	

*Special orders (not standard) can be in many other lengths.

Fig. 7-6. Standard metal shapes and their names.

occur at high temperatures. We say that the processes are *thermally activated.*

Steelmaking requires three basic raw materials. These are iron ore, coke, and limestone. Other materials are added as alloys (mixtures of metals) are manufactured. Steelmaking is a four-step process:
- Preparing raw materials.
- Making iron.
- Making steel.
- Producing standard stock.

Preparing raw materials

Steelmaking is a process of removing impurities from iron ore. The early processes used high-grade

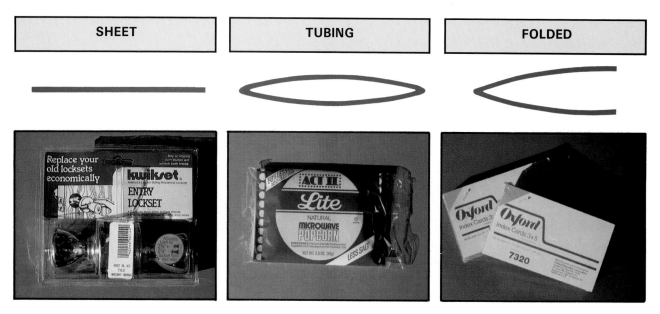

SHEET	TUBING	FOLDED

Fig. 7-7. Plastic film shapes.

iron ores. These ores then contained large amounts of iron. Now, such deposits are hard to find. Instead, low-grade ores called *taconite,* are often used. They must be preprocessed at the mines. The iron content is increased by removing many unwanted minerals. The remaining material is *sintered* (heated to high temperatures) and made into pellets. The pellets contain about 65 percent iron combined with oxygen.

Coke also must be produced. It is a clean-burning carbon product made from coal. The coal is loaded into chambers in a coke oven. The ovens, seen in Fig. 7-8, look like a series of drawers set on edge. Each chamber is about 18 in. wide, 20 ft. high, and 40 ft. deep. The coal is heated by gases burning between each chamber.

As the coal is heated to 2400°F (1316°C), gases, oils, and tar are driven off. These materials are caught and used for many products, such as lipstick and plastics.

After being heated for about 18 hours, the door of the chamber is opened. The coke is pushed into a quench (rapid cooling) car. The cooled coke is a high-carbon fuel.

The final ingredient of steel–limestone–must be mined and purified. It is crushed and screened. At the same time, impurities are removed by magnets and the screens.

Environmental protection (reducing pollution) is considered during the preprocessing of the iron ore, coke, and limestone. Land and water are reclaimed at the mine sites. Dust is controlled at the taconite mines and limestone crushers. Coal gases are carefully collected at the coke ovens. Workers are careful to collect as many pollutants as possible. Some are useful by-products.

Making iron

Iron is the first product of the steelmaking process. Most iron is made in a blast furnace like the one shown in Fig. 7-9. Layers of coke, limestone, and iron ore are loaded in the top. They move slowly down to the furnace. The coke is ignited by super hot gases moving upward.

The burning coke removes oxygen from the iron ore. (Iron ore is really iron oxide, a combined form of iron and oxygen.) The limestone combines with

Fig. 7-8. This 80-slot coke oven battery can produce 850,000 tons of coke a year. (Bethlehem Steel)

Fig. 7-9. This blast furnace produces iron. It towers 270 ft. into the sky.
(American Iron and Steel Institute)

Fig. 7-10. This 330 ton capacity car carries molten iron away from the blast furnace.
(Bethlehem Steel)

impurities in the molten iron. It produces a substance called slag that is drawn off.

The iron ore, by this time, is a mixture of iron and carbon (from the coke). This material collects at the bottom of the blast furnace. Now and then it is drawn off into railcars. These cars, shown in Fig. 7-10, move the iron-carbon mixture (called pig iron) to steelmaking furnaces.

Making steel

Steel is made from pig iron and steel scrap. It can be produced in one of two kinds of furnaces:
- Basic oxygen furnace.
- Electric furnace.

The older open hearth furnace is being rapidly replaced by these newer furnaces.

Most steel is produced by the *basic oxygen process,* Fig. 7-11. The furnace is charged with steel scrap and hot iron from the blast furnace, Fig. 7-12. A water-cooled lance is lowered into the furnace. Pure oxygen is blown through the lance into the metal. The oxygen burns (combines with) the extra carbon and any impurities in the iron. They form gases that are collected and cleaned. Also, lime and other materials are added to absorb more impurities. They form slag that is drawn off. Alloying elements (other metals) are added to the molten steel. The resulting steel is drawn off into a ladle.

Fig. 7-13 is a flowchart for the steelmaking process. You can study it to see the steps in producing steel as standard stock. Note the environmental control systems used at each step.

The electric furnace, seen in Fig. 7-14, is used to recycle steel scrap. These furnaces are generally smaller than basic oxygen furnaces. Many high-

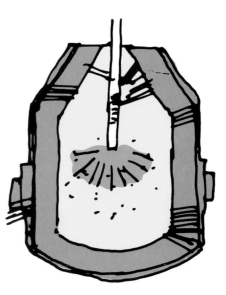

Fig. 7-11. The basic oxygen furnace in cross section.

Fig. 7-12. Molten iron from a blast furnace is charged into a basic oxygen furnace.
(Bethlehem Steel)

Producing Industrial Materials 57

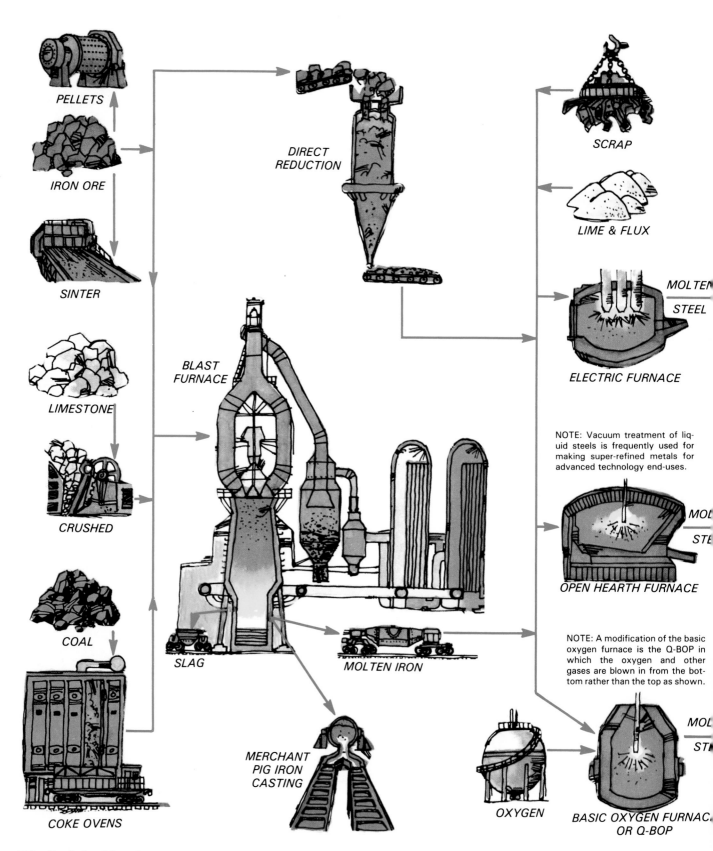

Fig. 7-13. A flowchart summarizing steps for steelmaking. (American Iron and Steel Institute)

PELLETS

IRON ORE

SINTER

LIMESTONE

CRUSHED

COAL

COKE OVENS

DIRECT REDUCTION

BLAST FURNACE

SLAG

MERCHANT PIG IRON CASTING

MOLTEN IRON

OXYGEN

SCRAP

LIME & FLUX

ELECTRIC FURNACE

MOLTEN STEEL

NOTE: Vacuum treatment of liquid steels is frequently used for making super-refined metals for advanced technology end-uses.

OPEN HEARTH FURNACE

MOLTEN STEEL

NOTE: A modification of the basic oxygen furnace is the Q-BOP in which the oxygen and other gases are blown in from the bottom rather than the top as shown.

MOLTEN STEEL

BASIC OXYGEN FURNACE OR Q-BOP

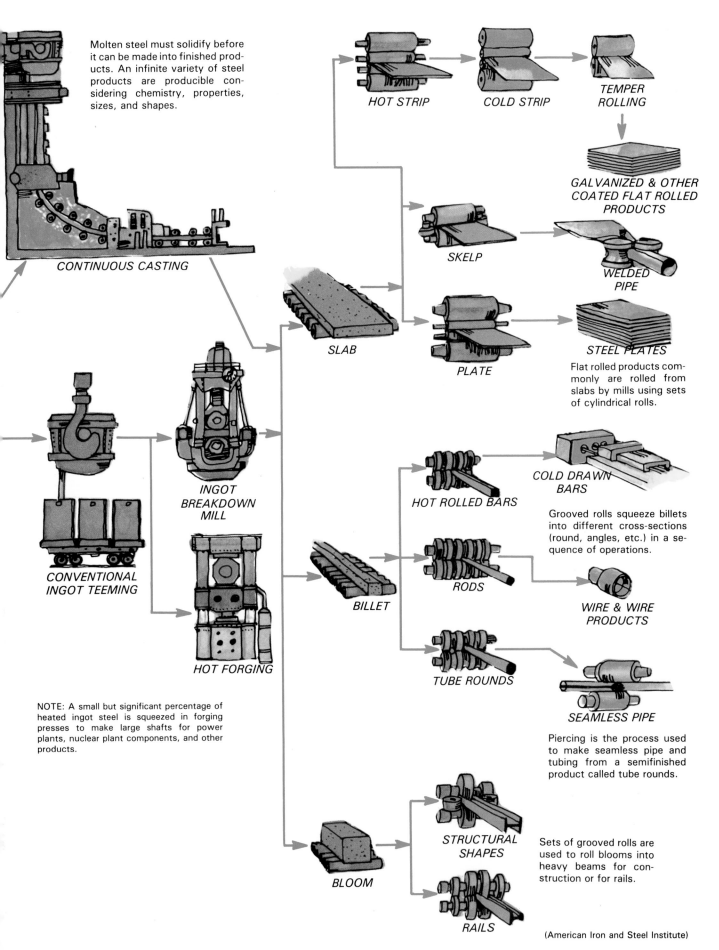

Molten steel must solidify before it can be made into finished products. An infinite variety of steel products are producible considering chemistry, properties, sizes, and shapes.

CONTINUOUS CASTING

HOT STRIP

COLD STRIP

TEMPER ROLLING

GALVANIZED & OTHER COATED FLAT ROLLED PRODUCTS

SKELP

WELDED PIPE

SLAB

PLATE

STEEL PLATES

Flat rolled products commonly are rolled from slabs by mills using sets of cylindrical rolls.

CONVENTIONAL INGOT TEEMING

INGOT BREAKDOWN MILL

HOT FORGING

HOT ROLLED BARS

COLD DRAWN BARS

Grooved rolls squeeze billets into different cross-sections (round, angles, etc.) in a sequence of operations.

BILLET

RODS

WIRE & WIRE PRODUCTS

TUBE ROUNDS

SEAMLESS PIPE

Piercing is the process used to make seamless pipe and tubing from a semifinished product called tube rounds.

NOTE: A small but significant percentage of heated ingot steel is squeezed in forging presses to make large shafts for power plants, nuclear plant components, and other products.

BLOOM

STRUCTURAL SHAPES

RAILS

Sets of grooved rolls are used to roll blooms into heavy beams for construction or for rails.

(American Iron and Steel Institute)

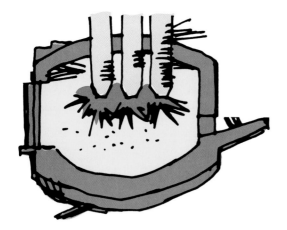

Fig. 7-14. The electric furnace uses heat from an electric arc to melt the charge.

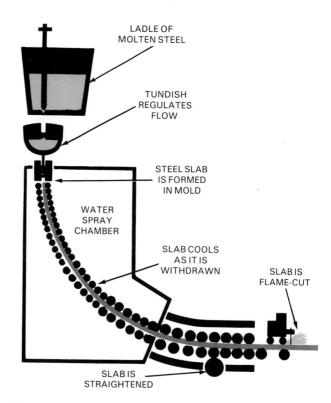

Fig. 7-16. The continuous casting process. Molten steel moves from ladle to mold to rollers in an unbroken flow.

alloy steels are produced in them. The output is typically stainless, tool, and specialty steels. Recently, larger electric furnaces have been developed to produce carbon steels.

Producing standard steel stock

The molten steel from the steelmaking furnaces must be processed further. It is usually cast into a workable shape first. Then, the steel is rolled into a final shape (standard stock).

Older mills first cast an ingot, Fig. 7-15. This is a solid casting that will be shaped in later processes. The ingots are first cooled in soaking pits to solidify the steel. Then, they are reheated to a rolling temperature.

More modern mills use a continuous casting process, as shown in Fig. 7-16. The metal is cast and cut

into slabs, Fig. 7-17. The hot slabs move directly to the rolling mills. Continuous casting saves large amounts of time and conserves energy.

Workers in control centers, Fig. 7-18, oversee many rolling processes. These processes change slabs into many shapes, Fig. 7-19.

Forest Products Manufacturing

All forest products start with logs. The logs are debarked (bark removed) as they enter the mill, Fig.

Fig. 7-15. Molten iron is poured into ingot molds. (Bethlehem Steel)

Fig. 7-17. A steel strand from a continuous caster is flame cut to length. (Bethlehem Steel)

Fig. 7-18. Modern electronics help these technicians in an elevated pulpit to control the steel rolling process. (American Iron and Steel Institute)

Fig. 7-20. Logs enter a mill after debarking.

7-20. In the mill, they move through one of four distinct paths. The logs can be used to make lumber or sheet materials.

Lumber manufacturing

The lumber manufacturing process varies slightly according to the size of the log. Basically, the logs go through seven steps, as seen in Fig. 7-21:
- Larger logs are squared at a head rig. The outer slabs produce wider boards that are fairly knot-free.
- The square center, called a *cant,* and smaller logs are cut into boards at a gang saw.
- The edges of the boards are sawed parallel by the edger. This process removes wane (sloping

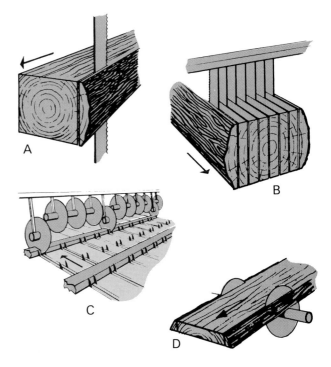

Fig. 7-21. Major steps in the lumber manufacturing process. A–Squaring up large logs. B–Sawing a cant into boards. C–Trim saws cut out defects. D–Board moves through the edger.

edges). Wider boards may also be cut into two or more narrower boards at this step.
- Trim saws cut out defects and square the ends of the boards. They also produce standard length.
- The lumber is graded as it moves down a conveyor called a green chain. Different grades are piled in separate stacks.
- The lumber is air and/or kiln (oven) dried.
- The dry lumber is often planed and edged (smoothed) to a standard thickness and width, Fig. 7-22.

Fig. 7-19. A steel plate is being rolled in a 160 inch wide plate mill.
(American Iron and Steel Institute)

Fig. 7-22. Dry lumber is planed and edged to a standard size. It is then sorted and graded. (Weyerhauser Co.)

Plywood manufacturing

Most plywood is made from softwood. Douglas fir and southern pine are the main species (types) used. Logs are steamed so they can be cut more easily. They are then placed in a veneer lathe, Fig. 7-23. The lathe turns the log against a sharp knife, as shown in Fig. 7-24. A thin sheet of wood, called *veneer*, is cut from the log. The log is simply "unwound" much like paper from a roll.

The veneer is dried and graded. The better pieces will have knots and defects cut out. Patches are placed in the holes.

The veneer is then laid up into plywood. The inner layers, as shown in Fig. 7-25, are coated with glue. Veneer strips for outer layers are edge glued to produce a single sheet. They are placed on top of the inner layers. The "veneer sandwich" is placed in a heated press. Heat and pressure squeeze the sheet together and cure the glue.

After a predetermined curing time, the panel is removed from the press. After the sheet has cooled, saws trim it to a standard size and sanders smooth and reduce it to a standard thickness. Finished sheets are inspected, grade marked, and shipped to customers.

Particleboard manufacturing

Particleboard is a sheet material made from logs and mill waste. Chips and flakes are mixed with glue. The mixture is formed into a mat, Fig. 7-26. The mat is pressed while heat is applied. The heat cures the glue, producing a rigid sheet. The cured sheet is sanded to thickness and cut to a standard size.

Fig. 7-23. A veneer lathe "unpeels" a log section to make veneer. (American Plywood Association)

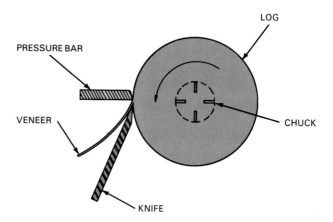

Fig. 7-24. A diagram of a veneer lathe. (American Plywood Association)

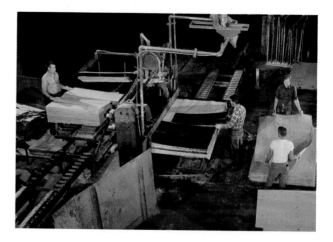

Fig. 7-25. Veneer is coated with an adhesive. The curtain glue spreader is in the center of the picture. (American Plywood Association)

Fig. 7-26. A particleboard mat is formed by a machine. (American Forest Products Industries)

Fig. 7-27. Defibered wood is the basic ingredient of hardboard. (American Forest Products Industries)

Hardboard manufacturing

Hardboard also uses mill waste and chips. These materials are broken down into single fibers. This process is shown in Fig. 7-27. The fibers are then formed into mats. The mat is placed in a heated press. Pressure is applied. The natural lignin on the fibers bonds them tightly together. The result is a very hard, dense sheet. The sheet is then cut to a standard width and length. The sheet is so smooth after it leaves the press that it does not need to be sanded.

SUMMARY

Raw materials are converted into standard stock. Each material has its own standard sizes, shapes, and compositions. These standards determine the materials that are available to small manufacturers and individuals.

All standard stock is produced by primary processing practices. Each material has its own processing methods. The basic processing activities for steel and forest products were presented. You may want to check books out of a library to read about other materials.

KEY WORDS

All of the following words have been used in this chapter. Do you know their meaning?

Basic oxygen process
Cant
Coke
Fiberboard
Forest products
Laminations
Lumber
Particleboard
Plywood
Primary processing
Sintered
Standard stock
Taconite
Veneer

TEST YOUR KNOWLEDGE

Please do not write in this text. Place your answers on a separate sheet of paper.
1. List and describe the three major types of structural synthetic wood composites.
2. Describe the major steps in making iron and in making steel.
3. List the steps in manufacturing lumber from logs.
4. How is plywood made?

ACTIVITIES

1. Write to a producer of forest products or steel. Request information describing their manufacturing processes. Share these materials with your class.
2. Make plywood from several sheets of veneer. Test it for strength and compare it with a piece of solid wood of the same thickness and species.

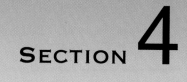

SECTION 4

SECONDARY MANUFACTURING PROCESSES

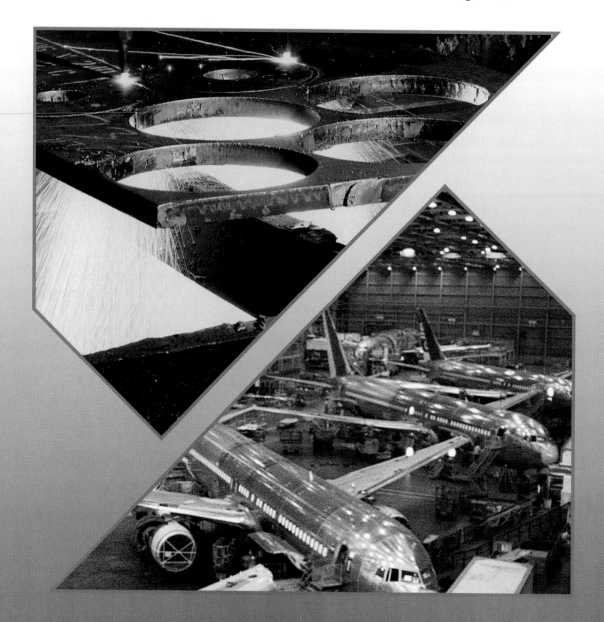

CHAPTER 8

LAYOUT AND MEASUREMENT

After studying this chapter, you will be able to:
□ State the meaning of the terms "measurement" and "layout."
□ Identify surfaces of a part.
□ Identify special features on a part.
□ Identify measuring and layout tools.
□ List principles of measurement for round and flat stock.
□ Describe how to lay out a part.

Before any part or product can be made it has to be measured and laid out. You need to measure to find the distance between two points. *Measurement* tells you how thick, wide, and long a part is. It tells you the diameter and depth of any holes. You also find the width and depth of grooves and dados by measurement.

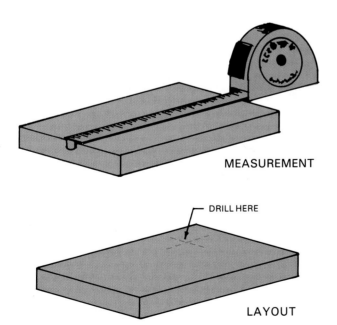

MEASUREMENT

DRILL HERE

LAYOUT

Fig. 8-1. These drawings show the difference between measurement and layout.

The word *layout* means to measure and mark a part so that it can be made. The markings tell you where every feature (hole, notch, etc.) should be on the part. It also shows where a part is to be cut from a larger piece of material. The difference in these terms is shown in Fig. 8-1.

Before you can lay out or measure parts and features you must know:
• Names of the surfaces on a part.
• Special features or cuts.
• Basic measuring and layout tools.
• Layout practices.

SURFACES OF A PART

There are some basic terms that describe a part. Everyone must know these terms so they can communicate with other workers. These terms, as shown in Fig. 8-2, are:
• *Length*–Largest dimension of a part.
• *Width*–The second largest dimension.
• *Thickness*–The smallest dimension of the part.
• *Diameter*–The distance across the end of a round part.
• *Face (or side)*–The largest surface.
• *Edge*–The second largest surface.
• *End*–The smallest surface.

Dimensions are all the size measurements of a part. They are always given in a certain order. For rectangular pieces, the order is "thickness × width × length." A round part's diameter is given first followed by its length.

Wood Measurement

These basic measurement terms are used differently for wood. Length is always measured along

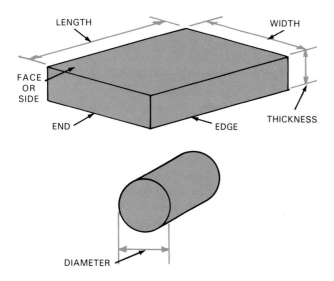

Fig. 8-2. Common terms used in most layout and measurement.

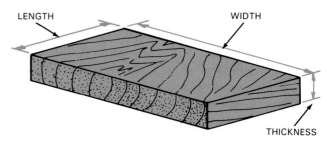

Fig. 8-3. Measurement of wood. Length is always with the grain of the wood.

the grain of the piece. Width is measured across the grain.

It is possible, as shown in Fig. 8-3, to have a board wider than it is long. Whenever you see a dimension listed, you can tell grain direction. A piece of wood, 3/4 × 6 × 24, has the grain parallel with the longest dimension. However, a part 1/2 × 12 × 6 is a board with the grain parallel to the 6 inch measurement.

SPECIAL FEATURES

Special features are the cuts that change a part from a square or rectangle. They are holes, cuts for joints, and specially shaped cuts. There are many special features. The most common are pictured in Fig. 8-4.

MEASURING TECHNIQUES

Measuring determines sizes of parts and features. Typically, we measure the external (outside) sizes and angles or the internal (inside) sizes and angles.

External measurement basically determines the thickness, width, and length of a part. It also mea-

GENERAL SAFETY

1. Always think "**SAFETY FIRST**" before performing any operation.
2. Dress properly. Avoid wearing loose clothing and open-toed shoes. Remove jewelry and watches.
3. Control your hair. Secure hair that may come into contact with machine parts.
4. Wear safety glasses, goggles, or a face shield in danger zones or other areas where they are required.
5. Wear ear protection around machines or equipment that produce a loud or high-pitched sound.
6. Do not use tools, machines, or equipment unless the instructor has demonstrated their use to you.
7. Stay alert! Always keep your mind on what you are doing.
8. Before using any tools, machines, or equipment, notify your instructor of any unsafe conditions.
9. Keep the floor clear of scrap materials.
10. Report even the slightest injury to your instructor. Small cuts or other minor injuries may become serious if left untreated.
11. Respect the rights of other people and their property.
12. Avoid horseplay. Do not distract the person performing an operation.
13. Concentrate on your work. Daydreaming and watching other people can cause accidents.
14. Know your own strength. Do not try to lift or move heavy materials or machines.
15. Follow all specific safety rules for tools and machines.
16. Do not use compressed air to blow chips or dust from machines, workbenches, or other surfaces. Use a brush.
17. If you have any questions about an operation, always ask them first before beginning.

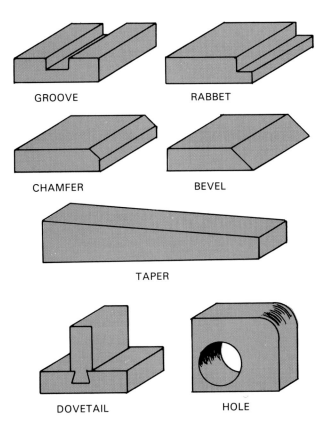

Fig. 8-4. Common features on parts change them from a basic square or rectangular shape.

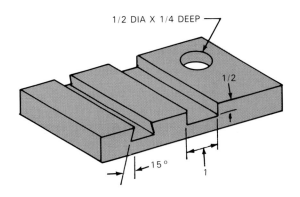

Fig. 8-6. Examples of internal measurements. They are on the inside surfaces.

sures the outside diameter of round parts. Special features that change external features, such as angled or shaped edges, must also be measured, Fig. 8-5.

Internal measurements determine the sizes of holes, grooves, slots, and other "inside" features. Typical internal measurements are width, inside diameter, angle, and depth. Fig. 8-6 shows some common internal dimensions.

These measurements are generally either standard or precision (very accurate). In *standard measurement*, you would measure to the nearest fraction of an inch. *Precision measurement* is generally given in thousandths of an inch (0.001″).

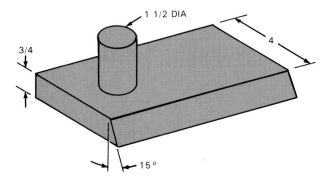

Fig. 8-5. Samples of external measurements. They are on the outside surfaces of parts.

Standard measurement is used for most woodworking, carpentry, and sheet metal work. Precision measurement is commonly used in metal machining, plastic molding, and material-forming practices. The type of measurement to be used depends on the accuracy needed and the stability of the material.

SI Metric Measurement

SI metric measurement is used by some U.S. industries and by most countries of the world. In this system, standard measure is taken to the nearest millimeter, which is much smaller than the inch (1 mm = 0.0394 in.). Precision measurement is accurate to the nearest tenth or hundredth of a millimeter (0.1 mm = 0.004 in.; 0.001 mm = 0.0004 in.).

The more accurate a part must be, the more precise the system of measurement is needed. Engine cylinders or transmission gears must be very accurately manufactured. Therefore, these are held to thousandths (0.001) or ten-thousandths (0.0001) of an inch.

However, some materials do not lend themselves to that type of precision. Wood, for example, is not very stable. It expands and contracts as the humidity of the air changes. It is useless to measure wood in thousandths. It will vary in size from day to day as the weather changes.

MEASURING AND LAYOUT TECHNIQUES

Layout and measuring is always done with the aid of tools and gages. The basic measuring tools may be grouped by what they measure:
- Linear (length) distances.
- Diameters.
- Angles.

Linear Distance Measuring Tools

Certain tools measure distances between two points in a straight line. They will determine the basic size measurements: thickness, width, and length. The most common measuring tool is the *tape rule.* It provides an easy way to measure long parts. Shorter parts may be measured with *machinist's rules* and *bench rules,* Fig. 8-7. Machinist's rules usually have scales (markings) that will measure down to 1/64 in.

A *micrometer,* Fig. 8-8, makes precision measurements. The most common type is an outside

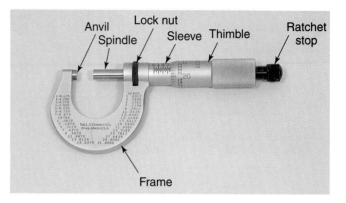

Fig. 8-8. Basic parts of a micrometer caliper.

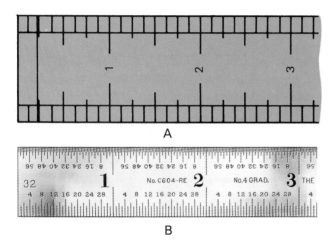

Fig. 8-7. Rules such as these measure distance along a straight line. A. Bench rule. B. Machinist's rule. (The L.S. Starrett Co.)

micrometer. They come in various sizes. The 0-1 inch micrometer, which measures in thousandths of an inch, is typical. Others measure larger sizes, but within a one inch range. For example, a 1-2 inch micrometer is available. So is a 3-4 inch.

Calipers and *dividers,* can also be used to measure linear distance, The caliper, Fig. 8-9, is set against the two parallel surfaces. It is then removed from the part. The distance between the caliper legs is measured with a rule. Dividers are similar, but they measure between two individual points.

Depth is also a linear measurement. It may be the depth of a hole, groove, or other feature. Measurements can be made with a rule if it will fit into the

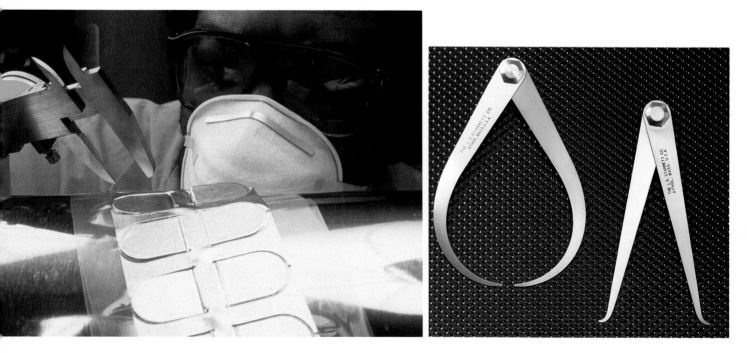

Fig. 8-9. Calipers and dividers can be used for measuring. (Goodyear Tire and Rubber Co., The L.S. Starrett Co.)

feature. Also, special **depth gages,** as shown in Fig. 8-10, are available.

Diameter Measuring Tools

Rules can be used to measure diameter. However, accurate measurements are hard to make. Typically, outside diameters are measured with a micrometer, Fig. 8-11, or calipers. Micrometers provide precision measurements while calipers are accurate up to 1/64 in.

Inside diameters can be measured with inside micrometers or inside calipers. Again, micrometers are more accurate than calipers, Fig. 8-12.

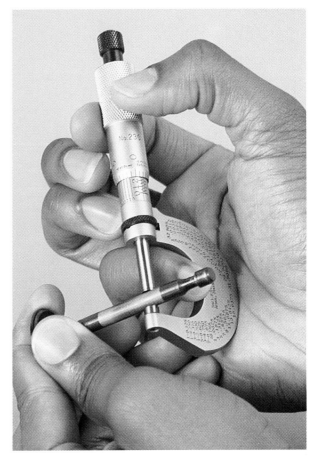

Fig. 8-11. Measuring a piece using a micrometer.

Fig. 8-10. A direct reading depth gage is used to check depth of a tire mold.
(Goodyear Tire and Rubber Co.)

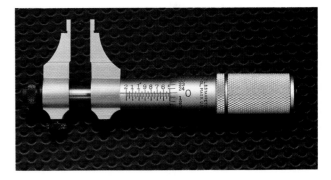

Fig. 8-12. Inside micrometers allow quick and accurate measurements of internal features.
(The L.S. Starrett Co.)

Angle Measuring Tools

Angles can be any value either greater or smaller than 90 degrees. The common 90 degree or right angle is checked with a **square.** There are many kinds of squares, as shown in Fig. 8-13. These include rafter squares, try squares, and combination squares. Combination squares will check both 90 degree and 45 degree angles.

Angles other than 90 degrees or 45 degrees can be checked with a **protractor,** Fig. 8-14. This may be a separate tool or part of a combination set. The **combination set** has a 45 & 90 degree head, a protractor head, and a center-finding head. All the heads will fit on a single rule, but are used separately, Fig. 8-15.

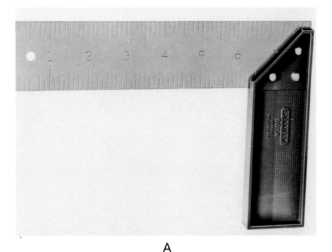

A

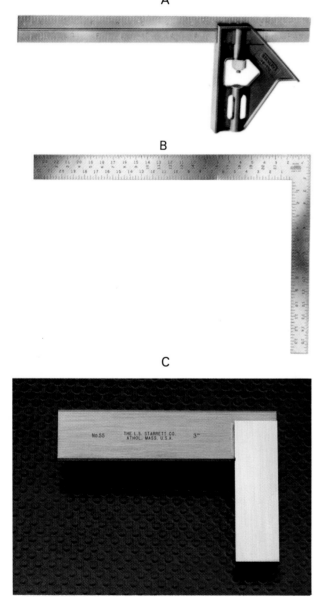

B

C

D

Fig. 8-13. Types of common squares. A–Try square.
B–Combination square. C–Steel square.
D–Machinist's square.
(Stanley Tools; The L.S. Starrett Co.)

Fig. 8-14. A protractor can check many angles.
(The L.S. Starrett Co.)

LAYOUT PRACTICES

One principal use of measuring tools, as shown in Fig. 8-16, is layout. The shape of the part itself must be laid out (drawn) on the standard stock. Proper layout is essential to making good parts. Layout should follow some basic steps.

First, the part size is measured off on the stock. Lines for length and width are scribed or drawn on the piece of material. Look at Fig. 8-17. It shows a way to use the square to do this. The part blank is then cut out of the standard stock.

Second, the features of the part should be located on the blank. The centerlines for holes and arcs are drawn first. Rules and squares are used to make these lines square and parallel.

Holes and arcs are then located. Dividers or a compass are used to lay out the circumference of (distance around) circles.

Centers of holes should be marked. A prick punch or center punch is used for this task. Tangent lines (lines that connect circles) are then drawn. Finally, straight cuts are laid out. Fig. 8-18 shows a typical layout process.

SUMMARY

Layout and measurement are important in all manufacturing processes. Measurement determines sizes of a manufactured part. Layout determines the location of features and the size of parts to be produced. We lay out something to be made. We measure the part after manufacturing operations are completed.

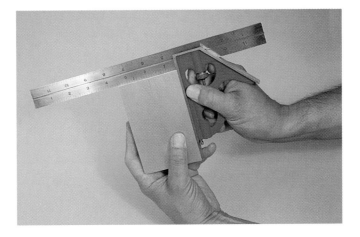

Fig. 8-15. The combination set can be used to check squareness and measure depth.

Fig. 8-16. A worker uses a square to lay out a piece of wood.

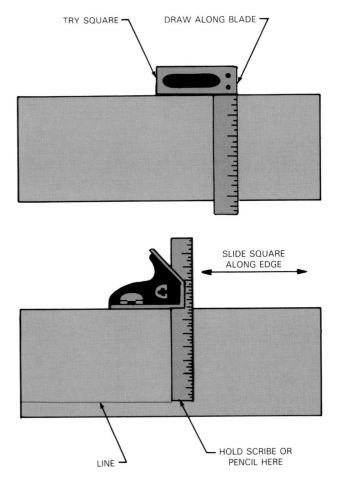

Fig. 8-17. Laying out the length and width of a part. Top. Marking the length. Bottom. Using a combination square to scribe a parallel line for width.

The principal surfaces of a part are its face, edge, and end. They are measured as a width and thickness (or a diameter) and a length.

Measurement may be very accurate (precision) or simply in fractions of an inch. These measurements may be for internal or external surfaces and features. All measurements are done with tools that measure linear distances, diameters, and/or angles.

KEY WORDS

All of the following words have been used in this chapter. Do you know their meaning?

Bench rule
Calipers

Combination set
Depth gage
Diameter
Dimensions

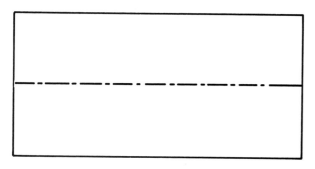

1. LOCATE CENTERLINE FOR PART

2. LOCATE CENTERLINES FOR ARCS AND CIRCLES

3. DRAW ARCS AND CIRCLES

4. CONNECT ARCS

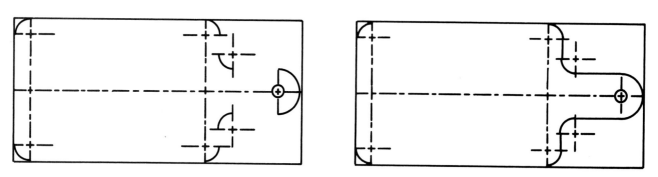

Fig. 8-18. Procedure for laying out product features.

Dividers
Edge
End
Face
Layout
Length
Machinist's rule
Measurement
Micrometer
Precision measurement
Protractor
Square
Standard measurement
Tape rule
Thickness
Width

TEST YOUR KNOWLEDGE

Please do not write in this text. Place your answers on a separate sheet of paper.

1. What is meant by precision measurement?

2. Which measuring tool would you use to measure the following features?
   A. Diameter of a hole in thousandths.
   B. Length of a board.
   C. Diameter of a wood dowel.
   D. Diameter of a steel shaft in thousandths.
   E. Length of a metal part in 1/64ths.
3. The proper order for listing the dimensions of a part is: _____.
   A. For rectangular parts: thickness x width x length; for round parts: diameter x length.
   B. Always length x width x thickness.
   C. Always list in descending order of size.
4. _____ _____ are the cuts that change a part from a square or a rectangle.
5. In laying out and measuring a part, which would you do first?
   A. Locate features on the piece of stock.
   B. Saw off the piece of stock to right length.
   C. Lay out the length and width of the part on the stock.
6. _____ of holes should be marked before they are drilled. A _____ _____ is used for this task.

ACTIVITIES

1. Working with a partner, design a device to measure the angle of cuts made on a saw. The device should be able to measure 0° to 45° in 1° increments.

2. Measure the lengths, diameters, and angles of various objects in the room using linear distance, diameter, and angle measuring tools.

3. Lay out the features of a door. Use tools that measure linear distances, diameter, and/or angles.

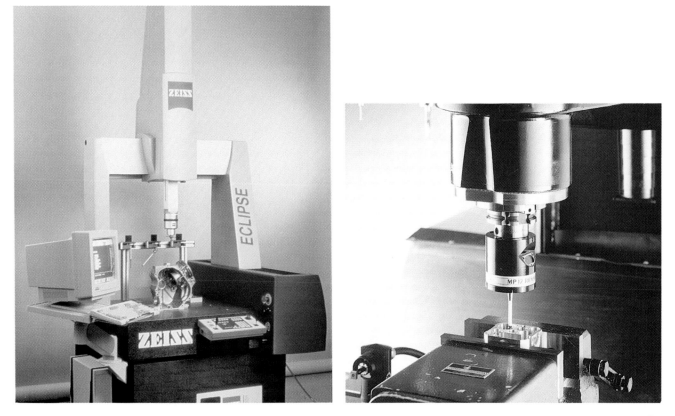

The coordinate measuring machine (CMM) makes measurements electronically. A CMM can achieve accuracy far higher than any manual measuring method. The probe shown in the right figure is being used to verify the accuracy of the holes machined into a complex part. (Renishaw. Inc.)

A liquid material is the starting place for all casting processes. (Inland Steel)

CHAPTER 9

CASTING AND MOLDING PROCESSES

After studying this chapter, you will be able to:
- [ ] Identify the parts of a mold.
- [ ] Describe how patterns and cores are used.
- [ ] List ways to make materials liquid.
- [ ] State requirements for removing parts from a mold.

The first step in secondary processing is giving a material size and shape. The dimensions (size) of the part must be worked out. Then, the part can be produced in the desired shape, Fig. 9-1.

WHAT IS CASTING AND MOLDING?

What is casting? Have you ever eaten an ice cube? Have you washed your hands in a sink or seen an automotive engine? If you have experienced any of these things, you have come into contact with or used a cast product, Fig. 9-2.

Casting and *molding* are a family of processes in which an industrial material is first made into a liquid. The liquid material is poured or forced into a prepared mold. Then, the material is allowed or caused to solidify (become hard). The solid material is then removed from the mold.

Casting and molding are really terms that describe the same general process. *Casting* is the word generally used when working in metal and ceramic materials. The term *molding* is often used when working with plastics.

STEPS IN CASTING

All casting processes have five basic steps. They are used no matter what material (clay, metal, plastic, wax, or glass) is being cast. These steps are:
- A mold of proper shape is made.

- The material is prepared for casting.
- The material is poured or forced into the mold.
- The material is allowed or caused to solidify.
- The finished item is extracted (removed) from the mold.

Some products come from the mold almost complete. They need little extra processing. Other products need cleaning, machining, heat treating, assembling, and/or finishing.

In all cases, their basic size and shape has to be set in the first step. Other processing simply adds features, trues surfaces, or completes other similar shaping activities.

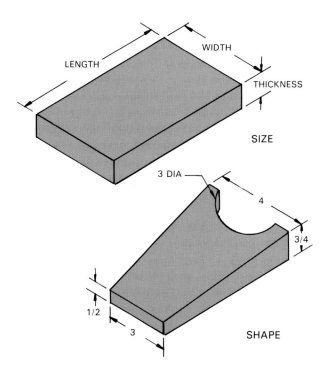

Fig. 9-1. Establishing size and shape. Casting and molding, forming, and separating, produce size and shape characteristics.

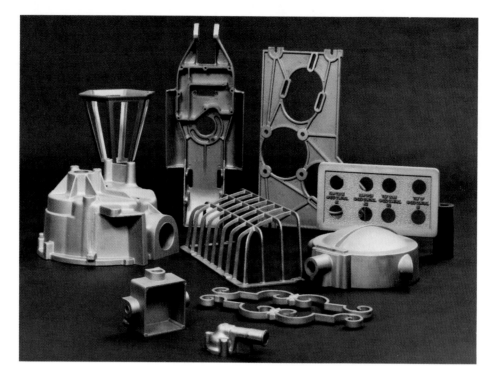

Fig. 9-2. This photo shows typical cast products.

Molds

A casting process needs a container for the liquid material. The material must be held in the right shape as it solidifies.

The container for casting processes is called a **mold.** The mold is a carefully prepared **cavity** (hole). The cavity, as seen in Fig. 9-3, must be of proper size and shape. Molds for castings are of two basic types: expendable molds and permanent molds.

Expendable molds

Expendable molds are so-called because they are used only once. They must be broken to remove the casting. Inexpensive materials like sand or plaster are used to make expendable molds.

Expendable molding requires two items. First, a pattern is needed. A **pattern** is a device that is the exact shape of the finished casting. Most molded materials shrink as they cool. Therefore, patterns are usually slightly larger than the finished product.

The second item you need is a molding material. It is something to place around the pattern to form a mold.

Casting process

It is easier to understand the use of patterns and molding materials by studying an actual casting process. Let's look at green sand casting, Fig. 9-4.

Green sand casting uses moist sand packed around a pattern.

The first step is to make a pattern. Patterns are usually made from wood, Fig. 9-5. If they are to be used many times, they may be made from metal or epoxy.

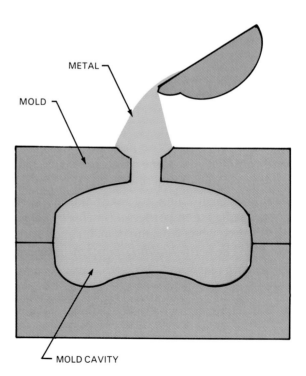

Fig. 9-3. The mold cavity must be the proper size and shape.

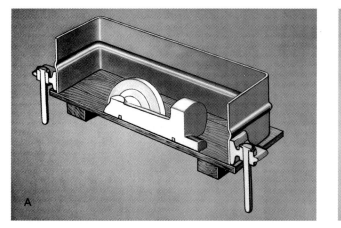

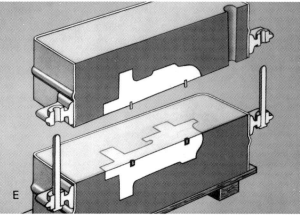

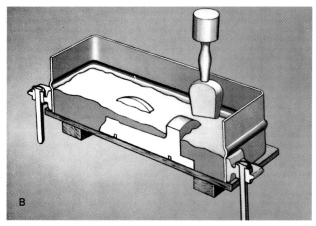

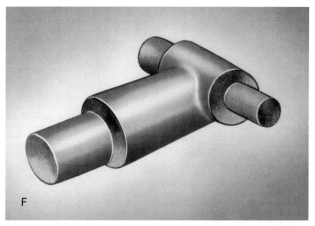

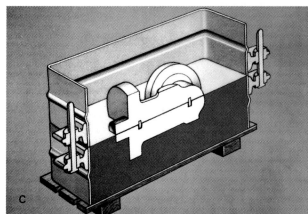

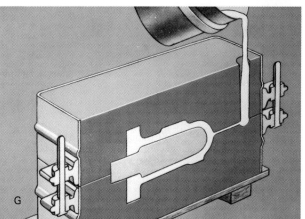

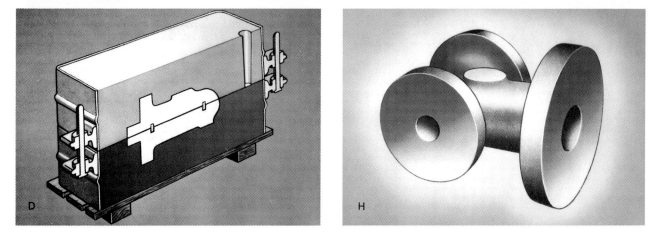

Fig. 9-4. These cutaway drawings show how a green sand mold is prepared. A—Pattern is placed in the drag and dusted with parting compound. B—Sand is riddled and packed around the pattern. C—Drag is filled and then turned over. The cope and second half of the pattern are put in place. D—Parting compound is sifted over pattern. Cope is rammed full of sand. E—The flask is separated and the pattern is removed. F—A core of baked sand is placed in the cavity. G—The mold is assembled and molten metal is poured into the cavity. H—The finished casting is removed from the mold. (Gray and Ductile Founders' Society)

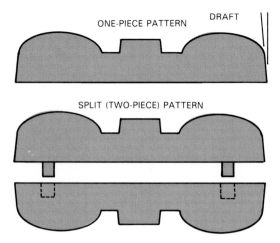

ONE-PIECE PATTERN   DRAFT

SPLIT (TWO-PIECE) PATTERN

Fig. 9-5. There are two types of patterns.

The pattern must have **draft** (sloped sides). Otherwise, the pattern cannot be removed from the sand without causing damage to the mold.

The green sand mold is produced in a two-part flask. Each part of the **flask** is a four-sided con-

tainer without a top or bottom. The bottom half is called the **drag.** The **cope** is the top half.

The molding process starts by placing the drag on a board. Half of the pattern is placed in the drag. The pattern is coated with a thin layer of powder called **parting compound.** It makes removing the pattern easier.

Next, molding sand is **riddled** (sifted) into the drag. The sand is rammed (packed) against the pattern with a special tool. The drag is filled and receives a final ramming.

The drag is then turned over and the cope is put on top. The other half of the pattern is placed exactly over the first half. Again parting compound is applied. Sand is riddled into the cope and rammed as with the drag. The top is then **struck** (leveled off).

The cope and drag are now separated. Pattern parts are carefully removed. The **gating** (a path into the cavity for the molten metal) is then cut. Finally, the mold is put back together. Metal can now be poured in. When the metal is solid, the sand mold is shaken apart.

Other one-shot molds are:
- Plaster investment molds, Fig. 9-6.
- Glass molds.
- Shell (baked sand and resin) molds, Fig. 9-7.

Fig. 9-6. Wax patterns are dipped in plaster as the first step in producing an investment (lost wax) casting. (Arwood Co.)

Fig. 9-7. Sand-resin core (inserts) and a shell mold drag is in place. (Brush Wellman Co.)

Permanent molds

Permanent molds can be used over and over again. They will produce many castings before they wear out. Most permanent molds have cavities that are machined into them. This makes permanent molds more expensive.

Permanent molds are either gravity or pressure molds. *Gravity molds* are filled by pouring the material into the mold from the top.

Pressure molds must be built to allow the material to be forced into the cavities. The molds must be much stronger than gravity molds. They must withstand the force of a strong clamping system that holds the mold together. Also, pressure is produced from inside by the material being forced into the molds.

Preparing the Material

Casting requires a liquid or semiliquid material. Several methods are used to prepare the materials for casting, Fig. 9-8.

Most plastics and metals are heated to the molten or flowable state. Metals are heated in a furnace. The metal, as shown in Fig. 9-9, is then moved to the mold in a ladle.

Some casting processes use a machine that first melts the material. Then the machine causes the material to flow directly into the mold. Most pres-

Fig. 9-9. Precious metals are poured from a ladle into a mold. (FMC Corp.)

HEAT

DISSOLVE

COMPOUND

Fig. 9-8. Methods of preparing materials for casting and molding.

Fig. 9-10. Injection molding machines use pressure to fill molds with plastic. (Stokes)

sure molding processes, such as die casting, use this type of system, Fig. 9-10.

Other materials are not melted. Instead, the material is suspended in a liquid. The mixture, called a *suspension,* is poured into molds where it hardens. Clays and certain plastics are cast as a suspension.

Finally, some materials are already a liquid. Water is a good example. Another widely used liquid material is liquid acrylic (casting plastics).

Many liquid materials must have a hardening agent compounded (mixed) into them. They then harden by chemical reaction.

Introducing Materials to the Mold

Once the mold is produced and the material is prepared, they need to be brought together. The material must be put into the mold. Two basic techniques are used to do this. The material may be

poured into the mold as was shown in Fig. 9-9. Gravity causes the mold to be filled. Most sand molds, slip casting molds, and nonpressure permanent molds are gravity filled.

Materials may also be forced into a mold. Several casting techniques use pressure to fill molds, including die casting and injection molding.

In *die casting,* nonferrous (not iron or steel) metals are melted in a "pot." A ram then forces some of the molten metal into the mold. The mold is water-cooled and, therefore, cools the metal. The dies (molds) open and the solidified part is *ejected* (pushed out). A typical die casting process is shown in Fig. 9-11.

Injection molding is another very important process. In principle it works exactly like die casting. The difference is in the material being molded. Die casting uses metals while injection molding works with plastic. Fig. 9-10 shows an injection molding

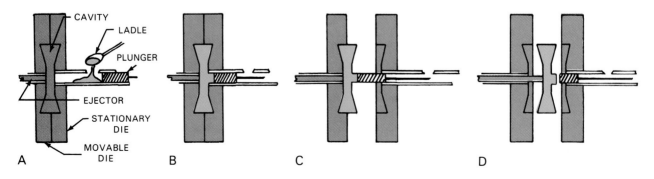

Fig. 9-11. Steps in cold chamber die casting. A—Metal is placed into the chamber. B—Metal is forced into the die. C—Die is opened. D—Casting ejected from die.

machine. Cold plastic pellets enter a heating chamber. The heat in the chamber softens the plastic. Then a ram forces the plastic into the mold. There the plastic solidifies. The mold opens and automatically ejects the molded part, Fig. 9-12.

Solidifying the Material

The liquid or soft material in a mold must become hard. One way to cause this is to remove heat. If the material was melted, cooling will solidify it. Liquids harden as heat is removed.

The heat can also be allowed to radiate (escape) into the air. This is natural cooling. It is the method used by most expendable molding techniques.

High-speed permanent molding processes require rapid cooling. Water or other liquids are

Fig. 9-12. This computer-controlled injection molding machine produces one plastic dishwasher tub every 68 seconds. The tubs are removed from the press by a robot. (Whirlpool Corp.)

STEPS IN SLIP CASTING

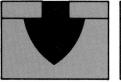 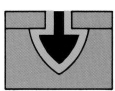 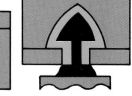 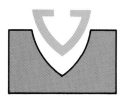 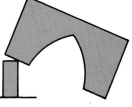

A. Mold filled with slip.   Wall thickness builds.   B. Excess slip poured out.   C. Casting removed. Mold opened.   D. Mold is dried.

BRACING MOLD

FILLING MOLD

PULLING BODY CORE

REMOVING FULL MOLD

Fig. 9-13. Top. Major steps in slip casting. Bottom. Photos showing slip casting of a toilet base.

common coolants. Channels in the molds allow cooling liquids to circulate and remove excess heat. Suspended materials must dry. The liquid must evaporate or be drawn off.

Slip casting of clay, shown in Fig. 9-13, uses this method. The slip (water/clay suspension) is poured into plaster molds. The molds absorb water. As a result, clay against the mold walls starts to become a solid. As additional water is absorbed, the outside wall of clay thickens. The center material is still liquid. When the wall reaches the correct thickness, the slip left in the center is poured out. This results in a hollow clay product.

The clay is allowed more time to dry. Then, the mold is opened and the casting is removed. It continues to dry under controlled conditions. The clay is then fired (heated to harden) in a kiln. The plaster mold must also be dried before it can be used again. Many clay products, such as figurines, teapots, lavatories (sinks), and toilets are produced using slip casting.

The last method of hardening a material is through chemical action. This process is really a conditioning technique (discussed in detail in Chapter 12). A chemical reaction is caused by an agent called a hardener. This process is generally used with plastics. It causes simple organic molecules to form rigid, complex molecules.

Removing the Casting

After a cast material is solidified it must be removed from the mold. The method to remove

Fig. 9-14. Expendable molds are destroyed to remove the casting. (Crouse-Hinds Co.)

castings is directly related to the type of mold used. Expendable molds are broken up to remove the casting, Fig. 9-14.

Permanent molds are opened. The parts (castings or molded items) are removed. Often, ejection pins built into the mold automatically push the parts out.

SUMMARY

Casting is the only process that directly converts an industrial material into a finished part in one major step. It moves from a liquid to a sized and shaped part in a single process. Casting and molding involves producing an expendable or a permanent mold. The material to be cast is then prepared. It is melted, dissolved, or compounded with hardeners. The prepared material is then poured or forced into the mold.

The material is caused to solidify by cooling, drying, or chemical action. The solid part is then removed by destroying an expendable mold or opening a permanent mold.

KEY WORDS

All of the following words have been used in this chapter. Do you know their meaning?

Casting
Cavity
Cope
Die casting
Draft
Drag
Eject
Expendable mold
Flask
Gating
Gravity mold
Green sand casting
Injection molding
Mold
Molding
Parting compound
Pattern
Permanent mold
Pressure mold
Riddle
Slip casting
Struck
Suspension

TEST YOUR KNOWLEDGE

Please do not write in this text. Place your answers on a separate sheet of paper.

1. What is the difference between "size" and "shape?"
2. List the five major steps in casting.
3. _____ and _____ are the two major types of molds.
4. List and describe the three main ways of preparing materials for casting or molding.
5. Molten materials are forced into the mold by _____ casting and _____ molding.

6. Indicate which of the following are methods of solidifying material cast into a mold:
   A. Freezing of the material.
   B. Natural cooling by radiation.
   C. Drying and/or evaporation.
   D. Chemical action.
   E. Pressure.

ACTIVITIES

1. Cast a candle in a permanent (metal or plastic) mold and another in a sand mold. Compare the results of these processes.
2. Prepare a meal in which the food is made in molds. Serve the meal to your family or deliver it to a shut-in or elderly person.
3. Learn how the dental profession makes use of castings. Collect information from dental journals, your dentist, a local dental supply laboratory. Give a short report to your class.

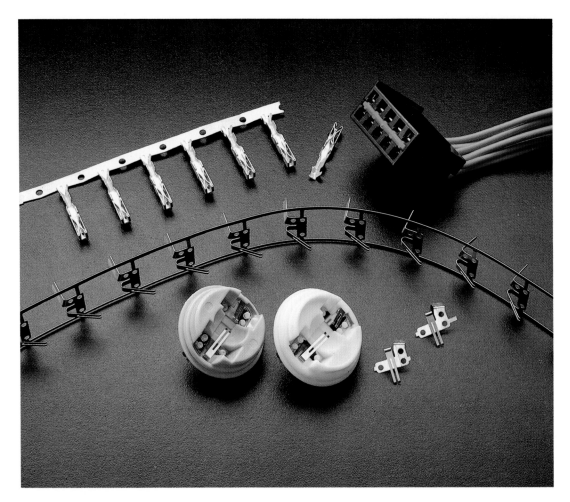

Forming process bend and cut metal to make many manufactured products.
(Brush-Wellman)

CHAPTER 10

FORMING PROCESSES

After studying this chapter, you will be able to:
☐ Define the term "forming."
☐ Identify the major stages of forming and describe what happens in each stage.
☐ List various shaping devices and explain the process to which each is related.
☐ Discuss the relationship of a material's temperature to forming.
☐ List the types of force used in forming.

Forming is a second method of giving a part size and shape. *Forming* processes changes the size and shape, but not the volume of the material. The material will weigh the same before and after a forming process.

STAGES OF FORMING

Forming uses pressure. All engineering materials being formed go through two major stages as stress (pressure or force) is applied. These stages, as shown in Fig. 10-1, are:
• Elastic stage. Stress will stretch the material in the *elastic stage*. However, when the stress is removed, the material will return to its original size and shape. At the end of the elastic range is the *yield point.* Beyond this point, additional stress will permanently deform (change shape of) the material.
• Plastic stage. This stage starts at the yield point. During the *plastic stage* the material starts to give in (yield) to the stress. It will be permanently stretched into a new shape. Added stress will cause more change in the shape. The plastic stage continues up to the *fracture point.* At this point the material breaks into two or more parts.

Forming is always done between the yield point and the fracture point. Pressure is applied to cause

permanent reshaping (deformation) without breaking the material.

All forming practices have three major things in common:
• A shaping device is used.
• A material forming temperature is established.
• There is a method for applying force.

SHAPING DEVICES

The shaping tool is to forming as the mold is to casting. The tool gives size and shape to the material. Two basic types of shaping devices are used in forming processes: dies and rolls.

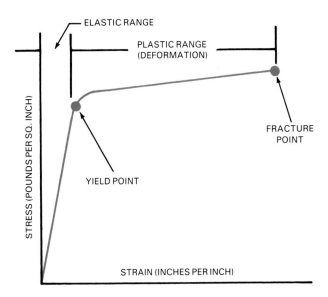

Fig. 10-1. This is a simple stress-strain curve showing material forming stages. The part of the curve that is nearly vertical is the elastic range. Up to the yield point, the material will return to its original shape if the stress is removed. Past the yield point, permanent changes in shape occur.

Fig. 10-2. An example of a two-piece die with cavities machined in them.

Dies

Dies are flat pieces of hard materials. They must be harder than the material they are forming. Tool steel is used for metal and many plastic-forming dies. Plaster can be used for ceramic dies. Certain plastic forming processes can use wood, ceramic, or epoxy dies.

The dies generally have a shape cut into them. This may be a cavity or raised portion, Fig. 10-2. Three major types of dies can be used:
• Open dies.
• Die sets.
• Shaped dies or molds.

Open dies

This is the simplest type of die. An *open die* is basically two flat, hard plates. One half of the die does not move. The other half moves to hit (hammer) or put pressure (squeeze) on the material between the dies.

The blacksmith's hammer and anvil work like open dies. The anvil is the stationary half of the die. The hammer is the striking force. Today, open dies

are used in smith forging to form special material, Fig. 10-3. These materials cannot be shaped easily by other processes.

Die sets

Die sets have shapes machined or engraved on their faces. Usually the shape on one half of the die fits the shape on the other half. Fig. 10-4 shows the two types: closed and mated. These dies either fit together or mate with each other.

Some important processes use die sets to shape material. Forging squeezes material into a shape. First, a heated metal workpiece is placed between shaped die halves. The upper die is pressed or dropped on the work. The material is forced to take the shape of the dies, Fig. 10-5. The dropping die process is called *drop forging*. Many wrenches, sockets, and pliers are drop forged.

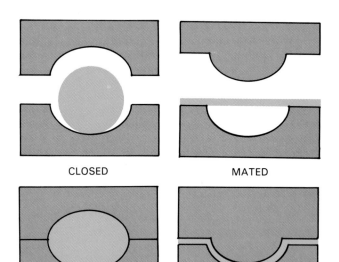

CLOSED   MATED

Fig. 10-4. These drawings show examples of two-piece closed and mated dies. Top. Dies are open. Materials are ready to be shaped. Bottom. Dies are pressed shut to shape the part.

Fig. 10-3. A steel ingot is forged with an open die forging press. (Bethlehem Steel)

Fig. 10-5. This forged steel truck axle was produced with closed dies. (Forging Industry Assn.)

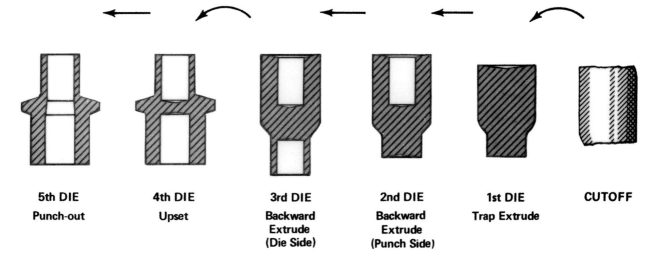

5th DIE	4th DIE	3rd DIE	2nd DIE	1st DIE	CUTOFF
Punch-out	Upset	Backward Extrude (Die Side)	Backward Extrude (Punch Side)	Trap Extrude	

Fig. 10-6. Steps in cold forming a part. The part was formed on a single die with five stations. (National Machinery Co.)

Press forging also uses squeezing action. It is used to shape many automotive and aircraft parts. Included are camshafts, piston rods, and crankshafts.

In many cases, a single die will have several cavities called *stations*. The material is moved from one station to the next. At each station, Fig. 10-6, a single forming act is completed. When the part leaves the die it is completely formed.

Drawing is another shaped die process. One die pulls sheet metal into the other die. This makes pan-shaped products such as automotive body parts, dry cell battery cases, and baking pans. See Fig. 10-7.

Drawing is often called *stamping.* Many stamping processes combine shearing (cutting) with drawing (bending). Fig. 10-8 shows a complex progressive (several stations) stamping die. The part on the lower die is partly shaped. A die like this one can cost over $100,000.

Shaped dies or molds

Shaped, or *one-piece dies* and molds are used when air or liquid pressure forms the part. Pressure or vacuum forces the material against the die. This type of die is called a *mold.*

This process is called *thermoforming,* Fig. 10-9, when it is used to make plastic parts or products. The material is held in a frame and heated. The hot material is lowered over the die. The air in the mold cavity is drawn out. Atmospheric pressure forces the plastic into the cavity. After the part is cool, it is

Fig. 10-7. Stamped pieces coming off a production line. These pieces will be used in automobile production. (Ford Motor Co.)

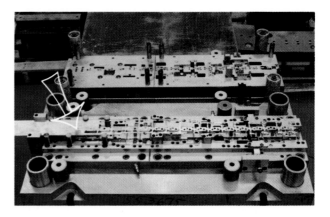

Fig. 10-8. A progressive carbide stamping die. The workpiece (indicated with the arrow) is partly formed. (Minister Machine Co.)

removed from the mold. Fig. 10-10 shows some thermoformed products.

Metal spinning

Another process that uses one-piece molds is *metal spinning.* A thin spinning disc of metal is forced over a spinning mold called a *chuck,* Fig. 10-11. Large lighting reflectors, satellite antennae, and tank ends are formed using the metal spinning process.

Blow molding

A third one-piece die process is called *blow molding.* This process actually uses a multipiece (several parts) die. The die, Fig. 10-12, forms the outside

Fig. 10-10. Typical thermoformed products. (Packaging Industries, Inc.)

shape of the product. A *parison* (heated glob) of plastic or glass material is placed in the mold. Air is blown into the parison. The material expands and takes the shape of the mold. Blow molding is very versatile. It produces light globes, children's toys, and bottles and jars of all shapes, Fig. 10-13.

Extrusion

Extrusion also uses a one-piece die. In the *extrusion process,* the material is forced through a shaped hole in the die, Fig. 10-14. As the material

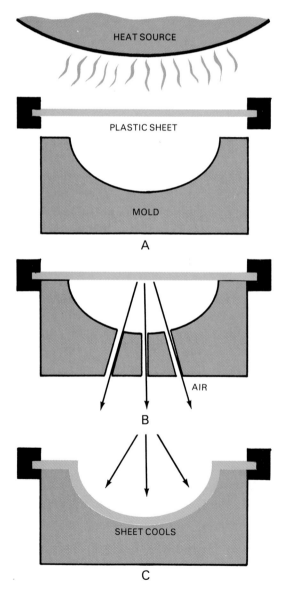

HEAT SOURCE

PLASTIC SHEET

MOLD

A

AIR

B

SHEET COOLS

C

Fig. 10-9. Steps in thermoforming. A–Sheet is heated. B–Heat source removed and air drawn out of mold. C–Atmospheric pressure forces sheet into mold.

Fig. 10-11. Metal spinning workpiece is rotated as tool forces it over a chuck (pattern). (Alcan Aluminum Co.)

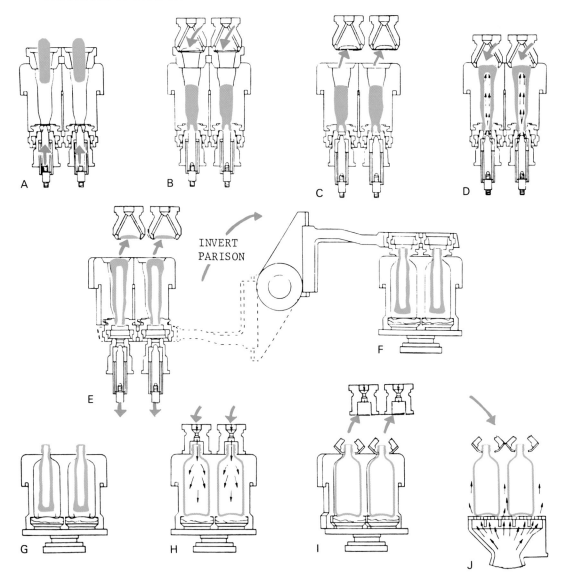

Fig. 10-12. Diagram of a two-step blow molding process for producing glass bottles. A–Gob of heated glass is delivered into closed blank molds. B–Subtle blows, pushing glass downward onto plunger. C–Gob reheats. D–Air from plungers shapes parison (gob). E–Blanks open; parison allowed to reheat. F–Parison released into blow molds. G–Parison reheats and gets longer. H–Bottles formed to blow mold shape. I–Molds open. Bottles taken out. J–Bottles released and swept off onto conveyor. (Owens Illinois)

flows through the die, it takes on the shape of the opening. As shown in Fig. 10-15, extrusion can produce different shapes in metals, plastics, and ceramics.

Roll Forming

Rolls are a second type of shaping device. They can be either smoothed or formed. *Roll forming* uses smooth rolls to give a curve to a straight piece without changing its cross section. For example, roll forming will produce a curved I-beam. However, the "I" shape of the beam will not change, Fig.

10-16. Curved members for storage tanks, rocket bodies, and large-diameter pipe are roll formed.

A set of matched rolls can also be used to produce formed sheets. The "quilting" on some aluminum foil is produced by matched roll forming. Metal barn siding and roofing is also produced using matched roll forming. Fig. 10-17 shows corrugated sheet material being formed.

MATERIAL TEMPERATURE

Material temperature is an important factor in all forming processes. Forming can occur at room

Fig. 10-13. Glass blowing process. A–Product being moved. B–Gob being placed in mold. C–Closed mold.

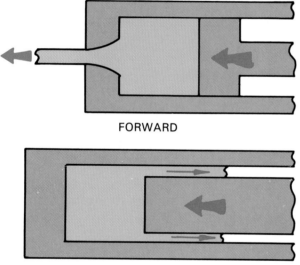

FORWARD

BACKWARD

Fig. 10-14. Diagrams of two major types of extrusion. Top. Hydraulic extrusion. Material is heated to soft, but not molten state, and is forced through opening under pressure. Bottom. Impact extrusion. This process is used to make cans and tubes.

Fig. 10-15. A bundle of aluminum shapes produced using an extrusion process. (Reynolds Metal Co.)

temperature with some materials. Other materials must be heated for forming. The material must flow, under pressure, into a new shape.

Forming is usually described by its temperature. Thus we have:

• Hot forming.
• Cold forming.

Hot forming is the name given all processes done above the point of recrystallization. The *point of recrystallization* is the lowest temperature that a material can be formed without causing internal stress. At this point, the material will form easily. Upon cooling, the material returns to its original stress-free state.

Forming below the point of recrystallization is called *cold forming*. The material may be at room temperature or it may be heated. Sometimes the term *warm forming* is used. This describes forming

Fig. 10-16. A heavy-duty roll former bending an I-beam. Note that the other features of the beam are not changed. (Buffalo Forge Co.)

heated materials that are not above the point of recrystallization.

Both hot and cold forming have advantages and disadvantages. These must be considered in choosing material temperature. The advantages of each are shown in Fig. 10-18.

KINDS OF FORCE

Forming processes use three kinds of force: *compression* (squeezing), *drawing* (stretching), or *bending.* These forces are developed in a number of ways. Most common techniques use one of four types of machine tools. These, as shown in Fig. 10-19, are:

- Hammers.
- Presses.
- Roll formers.
- Draw benches.

Fig. 10-17. A series of matched, shaped rolls form corrugated aluminum roofing. Note the position of the rolls at each stage. (Reynolds Metal Co.)

COLD FORMING	HOT FORMING
No heat required.	Hardness not charged.
Close dimensional control.	Porosity eliminated.
Smooth oxide free surface.	Less force required.
Increased hardness.	Smaller machines needed.
Improved strength.	Large shape changes possible.
	Clean surfaces not required.

Fig. 10-18. Both hot and cold forming have advantages that may lead to choosing one over the other.

SAFETY WITH FORMING PROCESSES

1. Do not attempt a process that has not been demonstrated to you by the instructor.
2. Always wear safety glasses, goggles, or a face shield.
3. Always hold hot materials with a pair of pliers or tongs.
4. Place hot parts in a safe place to cool, keeping them away people and from materials.
5. Follow correct procedures when lighting torches and furnaces.
6. Never place your hands or foreign objects between mated dies or rolls.
7. Always use a spark lighter to light a propane torch or gas furnace.

Hammers

Hammers and presses are alike in some ways. This fact can be seen in Fig. 10-19. The hammer pounds the material into shape. It produces a sharp blow.

Many forging operations require this type of force. A hard blow is delivered. A movable ram and die hit a stationary die, Fig. 10-20. Some hammers use gravity to move the upper die. The die is raised and drops onto the lower die. These hammers are called *drop hammers.* Steam or air hammers use force to produce the quick impact needed.

Presses

Presses have movable upper dies and stationary lower dies similar to hammers. The upper die is moved in a uniform, powered stroke to produce a squeezing action. Typical processes using presses are drawing, bending, shearing, crimping, and press forging, Fig. 10-21.

Sheet metal and band metal can be bent on machines that act like presses. They have two dies (bending leaves, radius posts, etc.). The machine applies uniform pressure to cause the material to bend, Fig. 10-22.

Roll Former

A roll former (sometimes called a rolling machine) has two or more rolls. The rolls may be smooth or shaped. The material bends as the rolls apply pres-

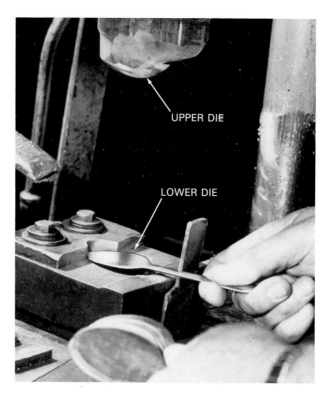

Fig. 10-20. The bowl of this spoon is cold forged by a set of mated dies. (INCO)

sure. As they turn, the rolls draw material between them. This squeezes and bends the material.

Draw Bench

A *draw bench* is a forming machine with a shaped one-piece die and a drive mechanism. It can:
• Stretch a bar or sheet over a die. This process, shown in Fig. 10-23, is called *stretch forming.* The draw bench pulls the material beyond its elastic limit. Then, a convex (curved outward) die is pushed into the material. The aircraft

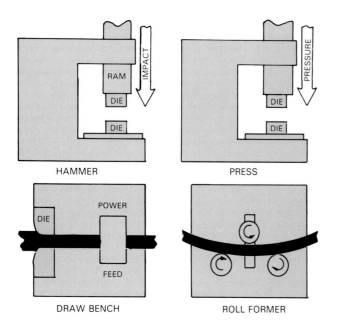

Fig. 10-19. Diagrams of typical forming machine tools.

Fig. 10-21. This giant press is being used to press forge a part. (Bethlehem Steel)

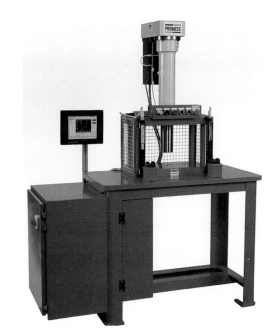

Fig. 10-22. Common press-like machines. A–Electromechanical press for use in crimping automotive fittings. (Promess Inc.) B–A computer numerical controlled (CNC) bending machine. (Di-Acro)

industry uses stretch forming to make airplane skin and structural parts.

• Pull a wire or bar through a hole in a die. Metal rod is pulled through smaller and smaller die openings. The material is finally drawn into the proper diameter. Reducing the diameter causes the length of a material to increase, Fig. 10-24.

Other Forming Systems

Other forces are used to form certain materials. As mentioned earlier, air pressure can mold plastics

Fig. 10-23. This powerful stretch forming press is being used to form this large beam.

and glass (blow molding). Vacuum is used to form thermoplastics (thermoforming).

High energy sources are also used. These include:
• Explosive materials.
• Rapidly changing electromagnetic fields.

These and other *high-energy rate (HER) processes* are used in special applications.

SUMMARY

Forming is changing the size and shape, but not the volume, of a material. The change is caused by applying a force above the yield point and below the fracture point. The force causes the material to take the shape of a die or forming roll.

Material temperature is important in all forming processes. Some use heated materials while others operate at room temperature.

Fig. 10-24. A draw bench (wire drawing machine) produces wire by drawing rod through a series of forming dies. (The Wire Assn.)

Forming processes must have a source of pressure. The most common source is a machine tool. Four machine tools are used: hammers, presses, roll formers, and draw benches. Other sources of pressure, such as air, vacuum, and high energy rate systems are used to produce forming pressure.

KEY WORDS

All of the following words have been used in this chapter. Do you know their meaning?

Bending
Blow molding
Chuck
Cold forming
Compression
Dies
Die sets
Draw bench
Drawing
Drop forging
Drop hammers
Elastic stage
Extrusion process
Forming
Fracture point
High-energy rate (HER) process
Hot forming
Metal spinning
Mold
One-piece die
Open die
Parison
Plastic stage
Point of recrystallization
Press forging
Roll forming
Rolls
Shaped dies
Stamping
Stations
Stretch forming
Thermoforming
Warm forming
Yield point

TEST YOUR KNOWLEDGE

Please do not write in this text. Place your answers on a separate sheet of paper.

1. When a material has been stretched so that any additional load will cause it to permanently deform, the material has reached its:
   A. elastic stage
   B. plastic stage
   C. change of shape stage
   D. yield point

2. The shaping tool or device is to forming what the _____ is to casting.

Matching questions: Match the definitions on the left with the correct term on the right.

3. _____ Two hard, flat plates; one is stationary, the other is movable.
4. _____ Usually, shape on one die half fits the shape on other die half.
5. _____ The several cavities found in die sets.
6. _____ Used when air or liquid pressure forms the part.
7. _____ The shape or pattern used when forming a part by metal spinning.
8. _____ One-piece die process used for forming bottles, glass, and ornaments.

A. Open die.
B. Stations.
C. Shaped die or mold.
D. Die sets.
E. Chuck.
F. Blow molding.

9. In _____, rolls are used to shape metal sheets, beams, or pipe.
10. What are the four major types of machines used to produce forming forces?
11. Two high energy forming sources are _____ materials and rapidly changing _____ fields.
12. List five parts or products that were manufactured using forming processes.

ACTIVITIES

1. Working with a design team, develop a method for producing a large number of single cupcake "pans" from aluminum foil.
2. Make a poster or chart with an automobile theme. Label the various auto parts made by forging.
3. Prepare a presentation on the various types of forming and show actual products made by each type of process.

CHAPTER 11

SEPARATING PROCESSES

After studying this chapter, you will be able to:
☐ List and describe the three elements common to all separating processes.
☐ Define and give examples of cutting motion, feed motion, and depth of cut.
☐ List six types of separating machines and describe how they work.

Separating processes remove excess (extra) material to change the size, shape, or surface of a part. There are two major groups of separating processes, Fig. 11-1.

• *Machining.* Changing size and shape by removing excess material such as chips or particles.
• *Shearing.* Using opposed edges to fracture (break) the excess material away from the workpiece.

Manufacturing would not be possible without separating processes. They shape and size parts so they are interchangeable. This means that all like parts will fit any assembly.

Separating processes are also used to build jigs, fixtures, patterns, and templates. These devices, called *tooling,* are used in manufacturing many products. Separating machines are used to build other machines and tools. They are the machines that build machines. We often call them *machine tools.*

ESSENTIALS OF SEPARATING

Every separating process has three elements. These are:
• A tool or cutting element.
• Movement between the workpiece and the cutting element.
• Clamping or holding of the tool and the workpiece to maintain their positions.

Tool or Cutting Element

Separating processes use several types of cutting elements or tools. See Fig. 11-2. Shearing and chip-removing machines generally use hard steel or ceramic tools. New machining (nontraditional) methods use other cutting elements such as light, sound, chemicals, and electric sparks. Flame cutting uses burning gases to separate the scrap material from the workpiece.

Chip removing tools

Many manufacturing processes depend on the basic property of all materials: hardness. A harder material will form, shear, or cut a softer material. This works better if the hard material has the proper shape. In separating, the hard, properly shaped material is called a *tool.*

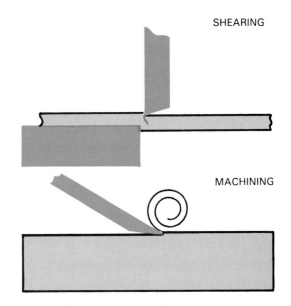

Fig. 11-1. The two types of separating processes—machining and shearing.

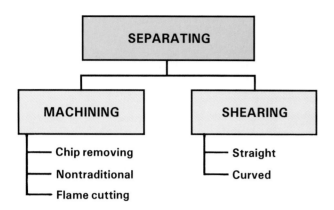

Fig. 11-2. These are the types of machining and shearing processes.

Fig. 11-4. The jack plane is a typical single-point hand tool.

When the tool moves against a softer material it will form a chip. A particle of material will be cut from the workpiece. If the cutting action continues, additional chips will form. The excess material will be cut away. This leaves a properly shaped and correctly sized part.

There are two major groups of cutting tools: single-point tools and multiple-point tools.

Single-point tools. Single-point tools are the simplest. They have *one* cutting edge, Fig. 11-3. A number of machines and hand tools, Fig. 11-4, use single-point tools. The most common of these are:

• Hand tools–Chisel, plane, gouge, and scraper.
• Machines–Lathe, metal shaper, and metal planer.

Multiple-point tools. Multiple-point tools are two or more single-point tools that form one unit,

Fig. 11-5. A tool with more than one cutting surface speeds up the cutting action.

Multiple-point tools have either uniformly spaced or random (no pattern) cutting edges, as seen in Fig. 11-6. Most cutting tools have teeth spaced uniformly around or along the tool. Abrasive cutting tools, such as sandpaper and grinding wheels, have randomly spaced cutting elements.

Multiple-point cutting is used for both hand tools, Fig. 11-7, and machine cutters. Typical examples of each are:

Uniformly spaced teeth

• Hand tools–Saw, file, tap and die, and hand drill.
• Machines–Milling machine, drill press, wood shaper, router, jointer, and surfacer.

Randomly spaced teeth

• Hand tools–Abrasive paper.
• Machines–Abrasive machines and grinders.

Cutting tool designs. Cutting tools come in many sizes and shapes. However, they are basically either

Fig. 11-3. A single-point tool is the simplest type. It has one cutting edge. (Inland Steel Co.)

Fig. 11-5. A multiple-tooth tool, such as this table saw blade, increases cutting speed.

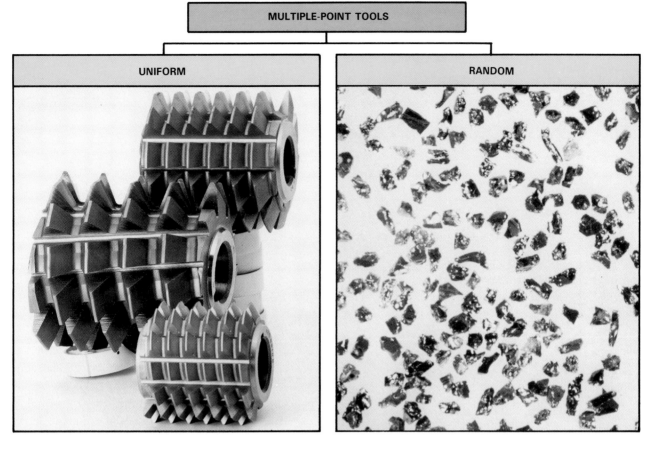

MULTIPLE-POINT TOOLS

UNIFORM

RANDOM

Fig. 11-6. Multiple-point tools may have uniformly spaced or randomly spaced teeth. The gear hobs on the left have uniform teeth. The magnified abrasive grains on the right are random cutting elements.

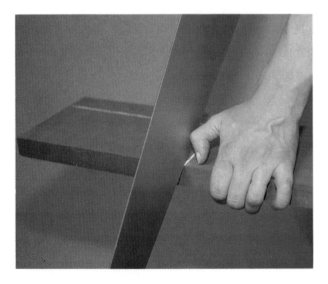

Fig. 11-7. A crosscut saw is a typical multiple-point hand tool. (John Walker)

straight or round. On straight tools, the teeth may be set along the edge or at the end of a straight piece of material. Band saw blades and handsaws are arranged along a strip of metal. Chisels and lathe tools have a point at the end of a flat strip.

In some tools, the teeth are located around or on the end of a cylindrical (round) tool. Drills have cutting lips at the end of a "rod." Milling cutters and circular saw blades have teeth spaced on the circumference (edge) of a disc or drum.

Each tooth on a tool must be designed to cut properly. These designs follow certain rules:
- Tooth or cutting surface shape must be correct. Each surface to be machined needs a certain shape, Fig. 11-8. A rounded edge on a board would require one shape of cutter. A straight edge would need another shape.
- Sharp corners must be avoided whenever possible. They wear or break easily. Sharp points give a rougher cut than a rounded edge. Does a knife cut more smoothly on its point or its edge?
- The cutting edge must be able to enter the workpiece. This requires *relief angles* for clearance behind all cutting parts of the tool, Fig. 11-9. Relief angles also keep most of the tool from rubbing on the workpiece. This keeps the tool cool and stops it from burning the workpiece.

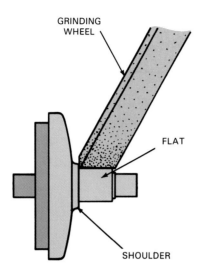

Fig. 11-8. This grinding wheel machines the flat and the shoulder of this product at one time. (Landis Tool Co.)

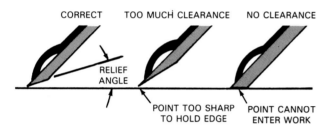

Fig. 11-9. Cutting edges must have the correct relief angle.

- *Rake* must be shaped into the tool. This is a slope of the tool face away from the workpiece, Fig. 11-10. Rake causes the chip to curl away from the cut. It also reduces the power necessary to make the cut.

Other cutting elements. *Nontraditional machining* and *flame cutting* do not use a "tool" as we use the word. They use heat, light, chemical action, or electrical sparks to produce a cut.

The oldest of these "nontool" separating practices is flame cutting. This process uses an oxyacetylene gas system with a special tip. (This system will be discussed in Chapter 13.) The material is first heated. Then, a blast of oxygen burns the material away, Fig. 11-11.

Heat is also used for cutting plastic materials. Instead of a flame, a hot wire or strip can be used to melt the plastic apart.

A number of processes use an electric arc to cut material. *Electrical discharge machining (EDM)* was the first process of this type.

EDM, as shown in Fig. 11-12, uses a carbon electrode or "tool." It is attached to a movable head.

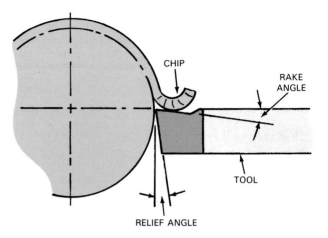

Fig. 11-10. Rake and relief angle are shown on a common metalworking lathe tool.

The workpiece is placed in a tank of dielectric (nonconductor) material. The workpiece is attached to one terminal (side) of an electric circuit. The tool is attached to the other side. When the tool is lowered, a spark will jump from it to the workpiece. The spark will dislodge (break away) particles of the workpiece. As the tool continues to be lowered, a cavity is machined. EDM is used to cut holes in metal. Also, it is widely used to produce cavities (holes and recesses) in various forming molds and dies made from steel.

Newer machines, Fig. 11-13, produce electric sparks between moving wires, bands, and wheels. These processes are called electric discharge wire cutting, electric discharge sawing, and electric discharge grinding.

Fig. 11-11. Flame cutting separates metal parts from a workpiece.

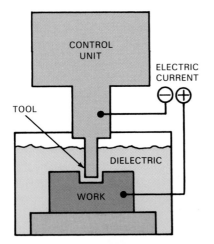

Fig. 11-12. Diagram and photo of electrical discharge machining (EDM) equipment. (Agie Losome)

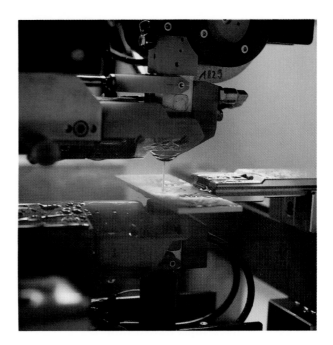

Fig. 11-13. An electro-discharge wire cutting machine. (Agie Losome)

Fig. 11-14. A general-purpose laser cutting system. (Strippit, Inc.)

Intense light is also used for cutting. The process uses a *laser* (**L**ight **A**mplification by **S**timulated **E**mission of **R**adiation). A laser changes electromagnetic radiation (energy waves) into light of a single color. It then amplifies (makes stronger) the light. This strong light produces heat when it strikes a surface. The heat will cut a workpiece, as shown in Fig. 11-14.

Other processes use chemicals and a combination of chemicals and electrical current. These processes accurately cut parts from various materials.

MOVEMENT

In all separating processes there is movement between the workpiece and tool. This movement, shown in Fig. 11-15, consists of two types: cutting motion and feed motion.

Cutting Motion

Cutting motion is the movement between the workpiece and the tool that creates a chip. The motion is created by three basic patterns that are shown in Fig. 11-16. These are:

• Rotating–The workpiece or tool turns.
• Reciprocating–The workpiece or tool moves back and forth.
• Linear–The workpiece or tool travels in a straight line.

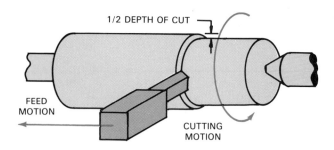

Fig. 11-15. Cutting and feed motions of a lathe.

All machines can be grouped by their cutting motion into basic classes. We will talk about these groups later.

Feed Motion

Cutting motion alone will not separate a material. New material must be constantly brought into contact with the tool. This movement, called feed motion, is usually in a straight line. It is created by either moving the workpiece into the tool or the tool into the workpiece.

The terms, *feed motion* and *cutting motion,* may be a little hard to understand. To see the difference between them, study the photograph of a bandsaw in Fig. 11-17. The cutting motion is created by teeth moving downward through the workpiece.

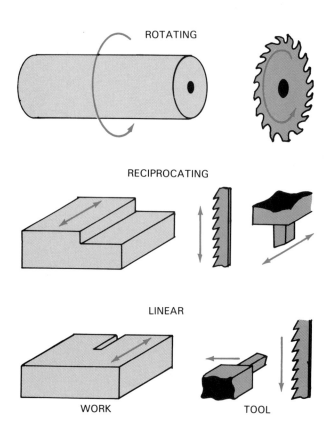

Fig. 11-16. Types of cutting and feed motion.

Imagine what happens when you place a board against the blade. If you turn the machine on, the first tooth will create a chip as it moves through the board. It would cut away wood fibers. However, the second tooth will follow the exact path of the first one. There would be no more wood to cut. However, if the board were pushed forward, new material would be there for the second tooth to cut. The forward movement of the workpiece is the feed motion. This action brings the new material into contact with the tools.

Depth of Cut

Depth of cut is another important term in separating activities. It is related to feed. The **depth of cut** is the difference between the original surface and the newly machined surface. The depth of cut and the rate (speed) of feed will determine the amount of material removed in a minute.

Clamping Devices

Most separating processes use devices to hold both the tool and the workpiece. These devices give the support necessary for accurate cuts.

The type of cutting motion dictates the tool clamping devices used. Linear cutting motion can be produced by a band that rotates around two large wheels. The wheels tension the blade to give it support. Guide blocks keep the blade cutting in a straight line, Fig. 11-17.

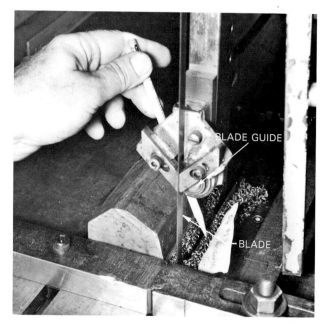

Fig. 11-17. Guide blocks guide the blade of a bandsaw. (DoAll Co.)

Fig. 11-18. A–A three-jaw chuck grips round stock. B–A four-jaw chuck can grip square stock or hold round stock off center. (LeBlond Makino Machine Tool Co.; Cushman Co.)

Rotating workpieces can be clamped between lathe centers. The work is held on a chuck or a faceplate. Jaws hold the workpiece. A center holds the other end of the material and allows it to rotate. Chucks and faceplates hold and rotate various shaped parts as seen in Fig. 11-18.

Vices, clamps, and magnetic tables can also hold workpieces during machining. Special jigs and fixtures, Fig. 11-19, are built when many similar parts are to be machined. Generally, all these devices are attached to the table or bed of the machine. They are then moved to produce feed motion.

SEPARATING MACHINES

There are six basic types of separating machines. These machines, as shown in Fig. 11-20, are:

- Turning machines.
- Drilling machines.
- Milling and sawing machines.
- Shaping and planing machines.
- Grinding and abrasive machines.
- Shearing machines.

In addition to these basic machines, there is special equipment for nontraditional separating and flame cutting.

Turning Machines

Most turning machines rotate (turn) the workpiece against a tool. The tool generally has a single cutting point. Some industrial wood turning operations use a rotating multipoint tool.

Fig. 11-19. These parts are being held in a clamping fixture. (Cincinnati Milacron)

The rotating workpiece is the cutting motion. The feed motion is developed by slowly moving the tool along or into the workpiece (linear motion). These movements are shown in Fig. 11-21.

Common turning machines are wood lathes, metal lathes, and potter's wheels. The latter are used for ceramic forming.

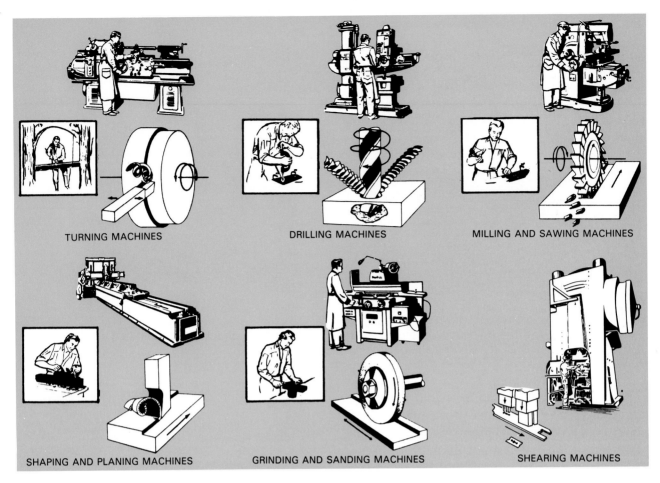

TURNING MACHINES

DRILLING MACHINES

MILLING AND SAWING MACHINES

SHAPING AND PLANING MACHINES

GRINDING AND SANDING MACHINES

SHEARING MACHINES

Fig. 11-20. These drawings show the six basic types of machines. (DoAll Co.)

Drilling Machines

Drilling rotates a pointed tool (drill) to create a hole. The movement of the drill produces *both* the cutting and feed motion. The drill is held in a chuck and rotated. This action produces the cutting motion. The rotating drill is moved into the workpiece, thus creating the feed motion, Fig. 11-22.

The drill press is the most common drilling machine. A number of hand tools and portable electric tools also perform drilling operations. These include hand drills, braces, and portable electric drills.

SAFETY WITH SEPARATING PROCESSES

1. Do not attempt a process that has not been demonstrated to you.
2. Always wear safety glasses or goggles.
3. Keep your hands away from all moving cutters and blades.
4. Use push sticks to feed small pieces of stock into wood-cutting machines.
5. Use all machine guards.
6. Stop machines or equipment when making measurements and adjustments.
7. Do not leave a machine until the cutter has stopped rotating.
8. Clamp all work when possible.
9. Unplug machines from the electrical outlet before changing blades or cutters.
10. Remove all chuck keys or wrenches before starting machines.
11. Remove all scraps and tools from the machine before turning on the power.
12. Remove wood scraps with a push stick. Use a brush to remove metal chips and particles.
13. Keep your hands behind the cutting edge of chisels and punches and behind screwdriver points.
14. Obtain the instructor's permission before using any machine.
15. Keep all work areas clear of scraps and unneeded tools.
16. Use only sharp cutting tools for separating operations.

Fig. 11-21. A lathe operation, showing the cutting and feed motions.

Fig. 11-22. The cutting and feed motions of a drill press. The bit rotates and can be moved down by the machine operator. (Inland Steel Co.)

Some common hand drilling tools are shown in Fig. 11-23.

Drilling machines and tools use a number of drills and bits. Some of these are shown in Fig. 11-24. They include auger bits, twist drills, countersinks, plug cutters, hole saws, and special-purpose bits.

Milling and Sawing Machines

All early saws had teeth arranged on a straight piece of metal like a handsaw. Later the teeth were arranged on discs that rotated. These two arrangements make up the milling and sawing tools.

A number of machines use rotating cutters. Among them are the milling machine, table saw, jointer, surfacer, wood shaper, and router. All of the machines have three things in common:
• They use a multiple tooth or knife cutter.
• The rotating cutter generates the cutting motion.
• The feed motion is produced by moving the workpiece into the cutter in a straight line.

Look at the two pictures in Fig. 11-25. Notice the feed and cutting motions.

Other sawing machines use evenly spaced teeth on a band or strip. The cutting motion is created by passing the teeth over the stock in one direction. Some machines use reciprocating (forward and backward) motion. The cut, however, is in only one

Fig. 11-23. Common drilling tools include hand drills. (Stanley Tools)

direction. The backward stroke simply returns the blade for the next cutting stroke. Machines that use this action are the hacksaw, Fig. 11-26, and the scroll (jig) saw. Handsaws and saber saws cut the same way. Files also work on the same reciprocating principle.

A bandsaw continuously feeds teeth past the workpiece. As the band travels around its track, the teeth are always on a downward path as they contact the workpiece, Fig. 11-27.

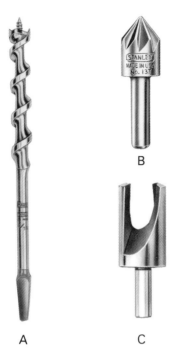

Fig. 11-26. Cutting and feed motions for a power hacksaw. (Armstrong-Blum Mfg. Co.)

Fig. 11-24. Some common cutting tools used for drilling. A–Auger bit. B–Countersink. C–Plug cutter.

Planing and Shaping Machines

The action of metal working planing and shaping machines is similar to that of a hand plane, shown earlier in Fig. 11-4. A single-point cutter is used to remove a continuous chip.

The metal shaper and hand plane operate exactly alike. The tool is moved forward, creating a chip. At the end of the stroke, pressure on the tool is released. It is moved back to the starting point. Then another cut is made. This reciprocating action is repeated until the surface is completely machined, Fig. 11-28.

The metal planer also uses reciprocating action. The cutter is stationary (stays in one place). The workpiece moves beneath it to create the cutting and feed motions.

Grinding and Abrasive Machines

Grinding and abrasive machines are adapted from other basic machines. An abrasive disc, drum, or belt is substituted for the cutter. Look at Fig. 11-29.

Sanding with portable electric tools and hand sanding use similar principles. The portable belt

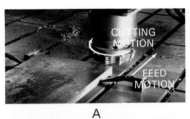

Fig. 11-25. Cutting and feed motions. A–Milling machine. B–Wood planer. (Inland Steel Co.; Delta International Machinery Corp.)

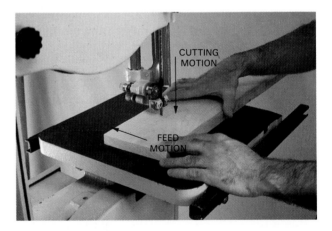

Fig. 11-27. Cutting and feed motions of a bandsaw. The blade is like a belt. It moves in only one direction.

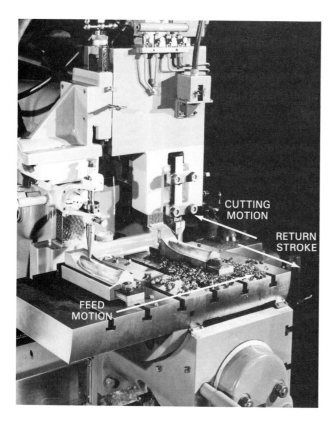

Fig. 11-28. Cutting and feed motions of a tracer metal shaper. Note the model on the left side. (Rockwell Machine Tool Co.)

sander is much like a stationary belt sander. Pad sanders and hand sanding are like the metal shaper. Abrasive paper is moved back and forth to machine the material.

Shearing Machines

The last major type of separating machine is the shearing machine. The other five types of machines use a tool to cut away a portion of the workpiece. Chips of material are cut from the stock. Shearing does not remove chips. It breaks material into parts. Shearing uses two opposing edges, like a pair of scissors, to fracture the material. In this process, material is not lost. The resulting parts weigh the same as the original piece. Also the sum of their lengths will equal the original length.

Most shearing machines have a moving blade or die and a stationary edge. A *die* is a blade designed to cut special shapes such as curves, circles, or whole outlines, Fig. 11-30. The material is placed between the shearing elements (blades or die). The movable element travels downward. The material is fractured (broken) as the two elements pass each other.

Typical machines that use this process are the squaring shear, corner notcher, and hole punch.

ABRASIVE MACHINE	RELATED MACHINE	CUTTING ACTION
Disc sander Grinder Drum sander	Milling machine	Rotating cutter Work fed into cutter (linear)
Belt sander	Band saw	Downward moving (linear) Cutting band. Work fed into abrasive belt (linear)
Surface grinder	Metal planer	Stationary rotating tool. Work reciprocates under tool

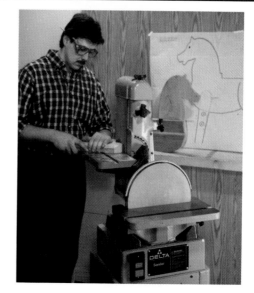

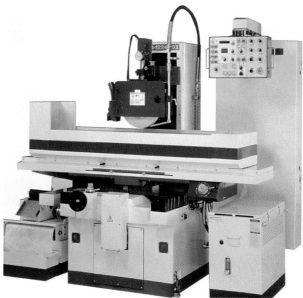

Fig. 11-29. Top. Comparing grinding with traditional machining. Middle. Combination disc and belt sander. Bottom. Surface grinder. (Chevalier Machinery Inc.)

Fig. 11-30. Special shapes can be cut using dies. (Strippit, Inc.)

Tin snips, scissors, chisels, and punches work on the same basic principle. Chisels and punches use the bench top or a back-up (scrap) board as an opposing edge.

SUMMARY

Separating is a very common process. All of the techniques use a tool or cutting element, movement between the tool and workpiece, and support devices for both workpiece and tool.

The tools are either single- or multiple-point. They are designed to provide a smooth cut with the least tool wear and power.

The movement in all separating acts can be classified as either cutting motion or feed motion. Cutting motion actually produces a chip. Feed motion brings new material into contact with the workpiece.

The workpiece and the tool are generally supported or held. Centers, chucks, or clamping devices are commonly used.

A combination of feed and cutting motions are built into six basic machines. These are turning, drilling, milling and sawing, shaping and planing, grinding and abrading, and shearing machines.

KEY WORDS

All of the following words have been used in this chapter. Do you know their meaning?

Cutting motion
Depth of cut
Die
Electrical discharge machining (EDM)
Feed motion
Flame cutting
Laser
Machine tool
Machining
Nontraditional machining
Rake
Relief angle
Separating
Shearing
Tool
Tooling

TEST YOUR KNOWLEDGE

Please do not write in this text. Place your answers on a separate sheet of paper.

1. Indicate which of the following are elements common to all separating processes:
   A. Tool or cutting element.
   B. Tool has a single point.
   C. Cutting element always uses a shearing operation.
   D. Movement occurs between the workpiece and the cutting element.
   E. Tool and workpiece are either clamped or held in place.
2. Describe cutting motion, feed motion, and depth of cut.
3. A _____ point tool has one cutting edge.
4. Which of the following are examples of multiple-point cutting tools or machines:
   A. File.
   B. Lathe.
   C. Tap and die.
   D. Chisel.
   E. Jointer.
   F. Saw.
   G. Abrasive paper.
5. What is rake and why is it important in a tool?
6. What do the following have in common: flame cutting, hot wire for cutting plastic, electrical discharge machining, and laser machining?
7. A die is a specially shaped blade for cutting various shapes. True or false?

ACTIVITIES

1. Design a drill press using a simple hand drill as the basic machine component.

2. Make a series of 35 mm slides and write an accompanying script to demonstrate safety with separating processes.
3. Prepare a list of cutting tools and machines in the technology laboratory. Group them according to their type: turning, drilling, sawing, etc. Indicate the type of tool they use: single-point or multiple-point.

Turning machines can be used to make large parts such as this roll.

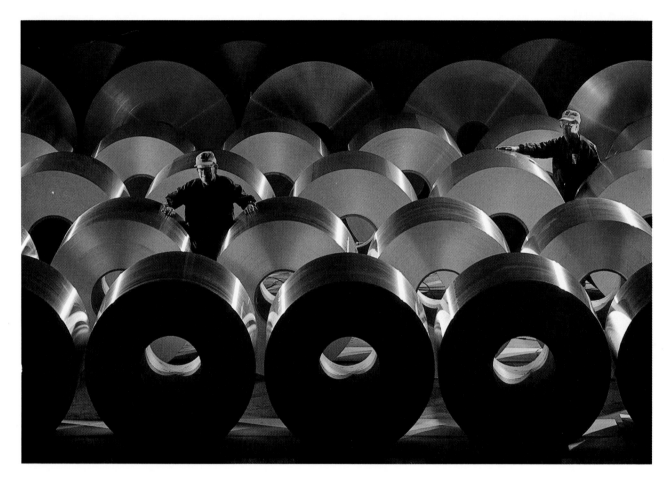

How a material is conditioned will affect how it is used in a manufacturing process.
(Ira Wexler, Reynolds Metals)

CHAPTER 12

CONDITIONING PROCESSES

After studying this chapter, you will be able to:
☐ Explain what conditioning does to a material and give at least one simple example of a conditioning method.
☐ State three reasons why manufacturing materials are conditioned.
☐ List and explain the three types of material conditioning.

Casting and molding, forming, and separating processes only change the size and shape of a workpiece. They change the outside of the product but not the inside.

Sometimes, however, the material itself needs changing to make it better suited for its purpose. Think of what happens when someone in your family makes cookies. After the flour, sugar, butter, eggs, and other materials are mixed into a dough, it does not taste like cookies. Bake the dough for a few minutes and it becomes crunchy and tastes very good. What has happened is that the heat of the oven changed the internal structure of the dough. The cookie now does its job. Its taste pleases you and it satisfies your appetite.

When you do the same thing to an industrial material, it is called *conditioning.* Look at Fig. 12-1. Before curing, the rubber on the tire is very soft and will wear out quickly. As with the cookies, heat changes the internal structure of the rubber. It makes the rubber tougher so it does its job better.

HOW WE CHANGE MATERIALS

Most often, conditioning is needed to change the physical or mechanical properties of a material. In Chapter 4, it was stated that:
• Physical properties mean the size, weight, or condition of a material. They describe what the

Fig. 12-1. These tires were conditioned using heat. They have been vulcanized (heat cured). (Goodyear Tire and Rubber Co.)

material is like when no outside forces are making changes in it.
• Mechanical properties describe a material's ability to support a load. Common mechanical properties are: strength, elasticity, plasticity, hardness, toughness, and fatigue resistance.

STEPS IN CONDITIONING

Before any conditioning is done, a manufacturer must consider the three things shown in Fig. 12-2.

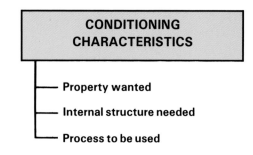

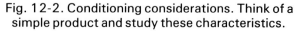

CONDITIONING
CHARACTERISTICS

— Property wanted

— Internal structure needed

— Process to be used

Fig. 12-2. Conditioning considerations. Think of a simple product and study these characteristics.

Let's go back to the cookie. What properties do you want in a cookie? What should the inside of the cookie be like? What process will change the cookie dough to what you want?

The cookie should be tasty and crunchy, not mushy as it is before baking. The inside should be hard but not so hard that it will not crumble when you bite into it. The way to process the cookie is to put the dough into a hot oven and bake it for a few minutes.

Other Examples

Any number of physical properties can be improved by conditioning. An important physical property for wood products is moisture content. Lumber cut from newly harvested logs (called green lumber) may have from 30 to 300 percent more moisture than dried lumber. Green lumber is not a good material for making furniture. The furniture would soon fall apart as the wood begins to lose moisture and shrink.

Air drying and kiln drying are conditioning processes that reduce the moisture content and makes the wood better for furniture making. Shrinking and warping would be slight compared to the green wood. Strength is one of the mechanical properties often changed in a material. This is the ability to withstand a load without breaking. Conditioning is used to improve the tensile (pulling), compression, shear, and torsion strength of a material.

Conditioning can also make a material harder. Internal changes will help it resist wear and denting. However, in making the material harder you also increase its brittleness. A hard material fractures more easily under load.

Plasticity can also be changed by conditioning. A material can be made softer and easier to form. Its ability to be hammered into form (malleability) can be improved. So can its ability to be stretched or rolled (ductility) to shape.

These are some examples of the properties that can be affected by conditioning. Other properties include elasticity, stiffness, fatigue resistance, and toughness.

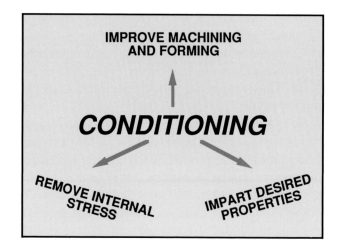

Fig. 12-3. Reasons for conditioning manufacturing materials.

SAFETY WITH CONDITIONING PROCESSES

1. Do not attempt a process that has not been demonstrated to you.
2. Always wear safety glasses or goggles.
3. Wear protective clothing, gloves, and face shield when working around hot metal or other materials.
4. Do not leave hot products or parts where other people could be burned.
5. Constantly monitor material temperatures during conditioning processes in which heat is used.

6. Use care when working with chemicals used for conditioning.
7. Use a holding tool such as pliers or tongs to hold metals that are being heat treated.
8. Use a spark lighter to light a heat-treating furnace.
9. Stand to one side of the quench solution when quenching hot metals.
10. Place a "Hot Metal" sign on any parts that are air cooling.

Structure of Materials

The properties of materials are directly related to their chemical structure. For example, some plastics are strong and rigid because of the way the molecules are linked together. Other plastics, whose molecules are loosely linked, can be reformed any number of times.

Round and widely spaced grains make a metal more ductile. A strong steel has flat, packed crystals. Also, fine-grained metals are harder and stronger than coarse-grained metals.

The length and arrangement of wood fibers also affect the strength. Longer fibers make for stronger wood. Hardwoods usually have longer fibers and are generally stronger than most softwoods.

TYPES OF CONDITIONING

A manufacturing industry conditions a material for a number of reasons. Three main reasons are shown in Fig. 12-3.

These goals may be met using one of three types of conditioning. These are thermal conditioning, chemical conditioning, and mechanical conditioning, Fig. 12-4.

Thermal Conditioning

Thermal conditioning uses heat to change the physical or mechanical properties of a material. There are a number of different thermal conditioning techniques. Three important ones are:
• Drying.
• Heat treating.
• Firing.

Drying

Drying removes moisture from a material. It is used to solidify clay slip. It changes a liquid suspension into a solid. The physical property of the material is changed.

A widely-used drying sequence reduces moisture in wood. Wood expands, contracts, and warps (twists or bends) as its moisture content changes. The wood is often stabilized by drying it. This process is called *seasoning.*

Two types of seasoning are used. One is natural, or *air drying*. The lumber is carefully stacked. Stickers (spacers made from strips of wood) are placed between each layer, Fig. 12-5, so air can circulate. The wood will naturally lose some of its moisture content this way. The lowest level that can be obtained with air drying is about 15 percent.

Air-dried lumber is suitable for some construction applications. However, it is not good for interior construction, cabinets, or furniture. Lumber for these uses is *kiln dried,* Fig. 12-6. The stacks of lumber are placed in a large oven called a kiln. Air circulation, heat, and humidity are carefully controlled as the lumber is dried. Kiln-dried lumber will have a moisture content of 6 to 12 percent.

Fig. 12-5. Lumber being air dried uses spacers between boards for good air circulation.

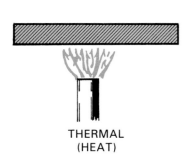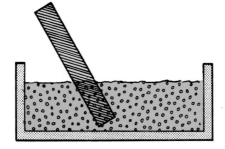

Fig. 12-4. Methods of conditioning materials.

THERMAL (HEAT)

CHEMICAL

MECHANICAL

Fig. 12-6. Lumber awaiting its turn at a drying kiln.

Heat treating

Heat treating is thermal conditioning of metals. It is a process of heating and cooling solid metal to produce certain mechanical properties. Heat treating includes the three major groups shown in Fig. 12-7. These are:

- *Hardening*–Increasing the hardness of a metallic material.
- Tempering–Removing internal stress.
- Annealing–Softening a material.

Hardening steel. As shown in Fig. 12-8, in order to harden a steel it is necessary to:

- Have a proper carbon content (0.08 to 1.5 percent) in the steel.
- Heat the metal to a proper temperature of 1400° to 1500°F (760° to 816°C) in a furnace like the one shown in Fig. 12-9.
- Cool the hot steel rapidly to obtain a fine grain structure, Fig. 12-10.

Other hardening processes produce a layer of hard metal on a soft core. Low-carbon steels are soaked in special material. The steel absorbs a layer of carbon from the other material. The metal is then heated and quenched. This process is called *case hardening,* or surface hardening. It is used for gears, shafts, and other parts that must be tough and long-wearing.

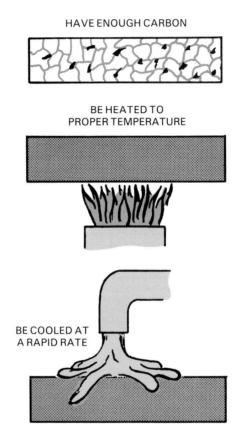

HAVE ENOUGH CARBON

BE HEATED TO PROPER TEMPERATURE

BE COOLED AT A RAPID RATE

Fig. 12-8. Conditions necessary to harden steel.

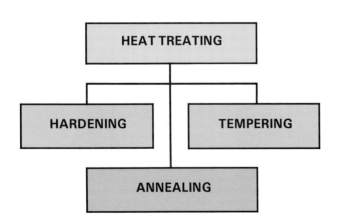

HEAT TREATING

HARDENING TEMPERING

ANNEALING

Fig. 12-7. Types of heat treating.

Fig. 12-9. These hot parts leaving a heat-treating furnace. (Bethlehem Steel)

Fig. 12-10. Hardened and tempered alloy steel magnified 400 times. Note the fine grain structure of the metal. (Bethlehem Steel)

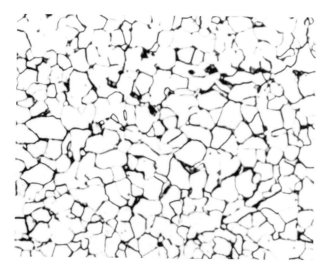

Fig. 12-11. Annealed, cold rolled steel magnified 400 times. Compare this grain structure with the grain structure shown in Fig. 12-10. (Bethlehem Steel)

Tempering. Fine-grained steel is hard but has internal stresses. It is very brittle and fractures easily. Therefore, after hardening, metals must be put through a *tempering* process. The parts are heated to a temperature between 300° to 1200°F (149° to 649°C). (The actual temperature depends on the type of steel and the hardness needed.) Then the heated metal is allowed to cool slowly. The result is a slightly softer but stronger metal.

Annealing. Metals can also be softened. This process is called *annealing.* The material is heated to its hardening temperature. Then, it is slowly cooled. The result is a stress-free metal with larger grain size as shown in Fig. 12-11.

Firing

Firing is a thermal conditioning process used in ceramics. It melts the glassy part of the ceramic. Upon cooling, the product will be clay particles held together by the glassy material.

The products are loaded on carts or conveyors, Fig. 12-12. The loaded carts are then moved into the kiln, as shown in Fig. 12-13. The material is heated to between 1650° and 2550°F (899° to 1399°C) then cooled. The result is a very hard material.

Chemical Conditioning

Materials can be changed using chemicals. This type of conditioning is called *chemical conditioning*. Catalysts (materials that start chemical actions) can be added to cause internal change. For example, a catalyst called a hardener, added to

Fig. 12-12. Workers are loading dinnerware on kiln cars. Note the refractory molds (right) that keep plates from warping during firing. (Lennox China)

Fig. 12-13. Loaded cars ready to enter the kiln. (Syracuse China)

Fig. 12-14. The concrete in this slab sets by chemical conditioning.

liquid polyesters, causes the liquid to become a solid. In scientific terms, this is called polymerization. Crosslinks form between the polymer chains.

Water added to plaster of paris or Portland cement starts a chemical conditioning process. The material will set (harden), Fig. 12-14.

Chemicals are also used to treat animal hides. Their organic fibers are made to change. The tanned leather is a more usable product than was the hide.

Mechanical Conditioning

Using physical force to modify the internal structure of a material is called *mechanical conditioning*. Cold forming operations change the internal structure of metals. The pounding or squeezing action changes the basic grain structure. Round, soft grains are changed into long, flat, hard grains, Fig. 12-15. This action is called *work hardening*.

Shot (steel pellets) may be sprayed against a part to mechanically condition it. The surface is purposely hardened. The result is a part that can withstand constant flexing. Its fatigue resistance is improved.

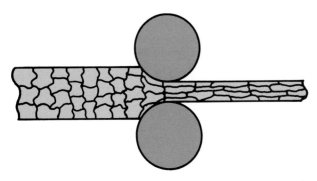

Fig. 12-15. Effects of work hardening on the grain structure.

SUMMARY

Not all processes change the external characteristics of material. Some change the material's internal structure. These processes are called conditioning. They use heat, chemicals, or mechanical forces to change the physical and mechanical properties of materials.

KEY WORDS

All of the following words have been used in this chapter. Do you know their meaning?
Air drying
Annealing
Case hardening
Chemical conditioning
Conditioning
Drying
Firing
Hardening
Heat treating
Kiln drying
Mechanical conditioning
Seasoning
Tempering
Thermal conditioning
Work hardening

TEST YOUR KNOWLEDGE

Please do not write in this text. Place your answers on a separate sheet of paper.
1. State, in your own words, what the word "conditioning" means.
2. Which of the following are not a reason for conditioning a product?
    A. Changing the shape of a product.
    B. To improve mechanical properties (strength, hardness, fatigue resistance, etc.)
    C. To remove internal stress and strain.
    D. To make a material easier to shape or cut.
    E. To make the material or product more attractive.
3. Conditioning is done by three processes. What are they?
4. Drying is one of the conditioning _____ processes.
5. Hardening, annealing, and tempering are chemical conditioning processes. True or false?

6. Sometimes, shot is sprayed against a part to harden the surface of the metal. The purpose of this conditioning is to _____.
   A. improve the appearance of the surface
   B. make the surface resistant to corrosion
   C. increase the ability of the part to withstand flexing
   D. improve fatigue resistance

ACTIVITIES

1. Working with a partner, cast several parts from plaster of Paris using various water-to-plaster mixes. Plot the curing (conditioning) time for the mixtures.
2. Identify ten items around your home that you think were conditioned during manufacture. Divide these items into groups based on whether you feel they were thermally conditioned, chemically conditioned, or mechanically conditioned. State reasons why you placed them in that particular group.

Heat treating processes are widely used to condition metallic materials.

Automated systems, such as the robots shown above, allow for products to be made with higher quality at a lower cost. (SI Handling, Inc.)

CHAPTER **13**

ASSEMBLING PROCESSES

After studying this chapter, you will be able to:
☐ Demonstrate an understanding of the importance of assembling processes in manufacturing products.
☐ List the two major assembly processes and cite examples of each.
☐ List and describe methods of bonding.
☐ Define three types of mechanical fastening and describe the process for each.
☐ Recognize and name five different types of joints.

Almost every product you use was put together out of several parts. The action of putting things together is called *assembling.*

If you have a lead pencil, look at it. How many parts are there? The simplest pencil, Fig. 13-1, has at least five parts. In addition there is a layer of glue holding the wood together. A layer of paint and some printing finish it off. Even the simple pencil is an *assembly* (a group of parts that form a unit).

Assembling is the manufacturing process that permanently or temporarily fastens parts together.

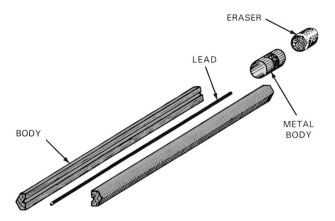

Fig. 13-1. A simple pencil has at least five different parts that must be assembled.

There are two major ways to assemble parts into products. These, as shown in Fig. 13-2, are:
• *Bonding*–Permanently fastening parts together using heat, pressure, and/or a bonding agent (like glue).
• *Mechanical Fastening*–Permanently or temporarily holding parts together using mechanical devices (like screws) or mechanical force.

ASSEMBLING BY BONDING

Bonding can be used with metals, plastics, wood products, and ceramics. In each bonding process, three basic things must be considered:
• The *bonding agent* (substance) to be used to hold the parts together.
• The method used to create the bond.
• Kind of joint used at the bonding point.

Bonding Agents

Bonding requires "atomic closeness" between two parts. *Atomic closeness* means the atoms of matter across a joint must be very close together. In fact, they must be as close together as are atoms inside each part.

Two basic types of bonding elements are used for bonding: self-bonding and bonding materials. These are shown in Fig. 13-3.

Heat and/or pressure can be used to make the two parts flow together. The material becomes liquid or plastic. When the parts cool, they appear as one. Fig. 13-4 shows two parts that were bonded by friction welding. The disc was held still. The ball-shaped part was rotated against the disc. The rubbing action created heat and atomic closeness. The parts were welded by self bonding.

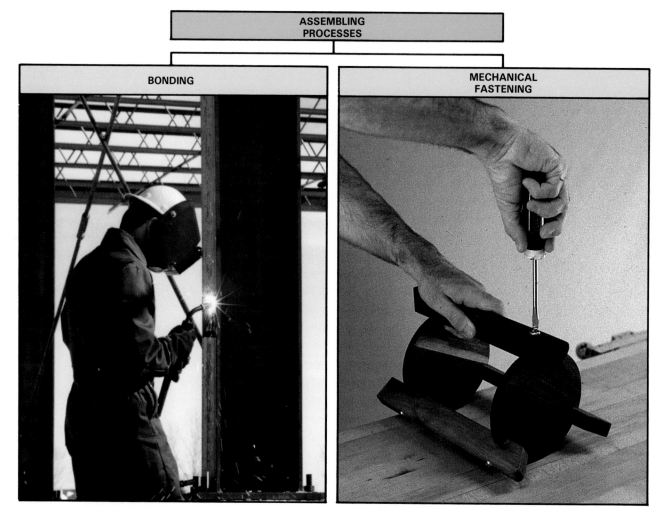

Fig. 13-2. There are two basic ways of assembling parts. Welding uses heat for a permanent assembly. A screw is a temporary type of fastener. (Miller Electric Mfg. Co.)

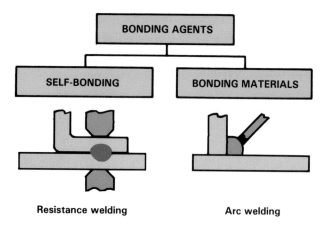

Resistance welding   Arc welding

Fig. 13-3. Self-bonding or bonding materials are used as bonding agents.

Fig. 13-4. Self-bonding uses no additional fillers. This photo shows an inertia (friction) welded part. (Caterpillar, Inc.)

Bonding materials are often used as bonding agents. These bonding materials may be:
- The same material as that being bonded. For example, using a mild steel rod to weld mild steel parts.

- The same type of material, but a different composition. For example, using solder (tin-lead alloy) to bond copper sheets.

• A totally different material with bonding properties. For example, using an adhesive (glue) to bond wood parts.

Methods of Bonding

There are hundreds of different bonding techniques. They can be grouped into five basic types:
• Heat bonding.
• Heat and pressure bonding.
• Pressure bonding.
• Solvent bonding.
• Adhesive bonding.

These methods differ both in the bonding agent used and the techniques for applying the agent.

Heat bonding processes

Several major techniques use heat for bonding. These processes use no pressure. Welding is an example. Heat bonding processes melt the edges of the parts to be joined. The molten material flows between the parts. Often, additional material from a filler rod is added to the weld area. Upon cooling, the part is a solid metal.

Heat bonding processes include two groups. One is fusion bonding, the other flow bonding.

Fusion bonding. *Fusion bonding* can use the base metals themselves to create the weld. However, if the part is thicker than 1/8 in., a filler rod is used. This rod is made of the same material as the base metal. It simply provides more metal to produce a strong weld, Fig. 13-5.

The common fusion welding methods get their names from their heat source. Heat to melt the base metal and filler material comes from one of two basic sources.
• Burning gases.
• Electric arc (spark).

The most common burning gas welding uses oxygen and acetylene. Fig. 13-6 shows a typical oxyacetylene welding outfit. The oxygen and acetylene are kept in separate tanks. Gauges on the tank regulate the pressure and flow of gases to the torch. The torch mixes the gases. The gas mixture flows out the tip where it is ignited. The burning gases will produce temperatures up to 6300°F (3482°C).

Most fusion welding techniques in industry use an electric arc as a heat source. The source of energy can be either alternating current (AC) or direct current (DC). One lead from the welder is attached to the work. The other goes to the electrode (rod) holder, Fig. 13-7.

When the electrode is brought close to the workpiece, a spark will jump. This electric spark generates about 11,000°F (6093°C) of heat. The heat from the spark melts both the base material and the electrode. These form a puddle of molten metal. As the puddle cools, the base metals are bonded together.

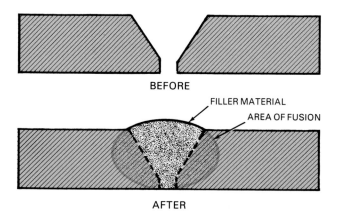

BEFORE

FILLER MATERIAL

AREA OF FUSION

AFTER

Fig. 13-5. Fusion bonding creates a part that appears to be one piece.

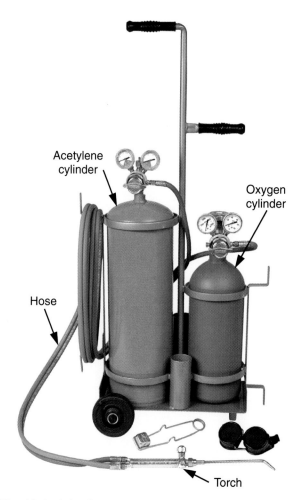

Acetylene cylinder

Oxygen cylinder

Hose

Torch

Fig. 13-6. A basic oxyacetylene welding outfit can be used for gas welding and flame cutting. (Uniweld)

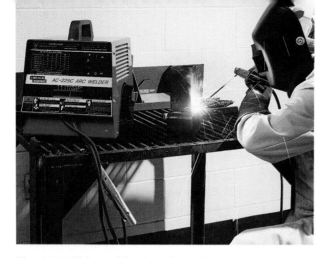

Fig. 13-7. This welder is using a fusion welding technique that uses an electric arc as a heat source. (Lincoln Electric Co.)

It is often necessary to keep oxygen away from the weld arc. This is the case when welding aluminum or other nonferrous metals. The heat from the arc and the oxygen in the air causes the metal to burn (vaporize). To weld these metals, an envelope (cloud) of inert gas is used to shield the weld area. The base metal and filler rod are melted in this cloud to form the bond, Fig. 13-8. The processes that use this type of system are Gas Tungsten Arc Welding (GTAW) and Gas Metal Arc Welding (GMAW).

Flow bonding. *Flow bonding* heats, but does not melt, the base metal. The heated metal is bonded by melting a different material into the joint.

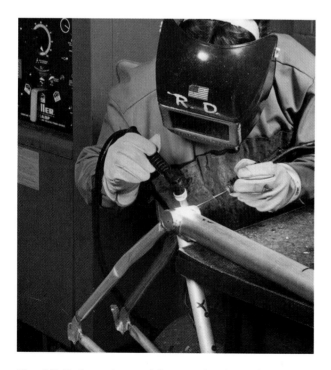

Fig. 13-8. A worker welding an aluminum frame with an inert gas system. (Miller Electric Mfg. Co.)

The two common methods for flow bonding are *brazing* and *soldering.* Both work on the same principle. A close-fitting clean joint is first prepared. Then the base metals are heated. Flux is applied to remove oxides. Flux also helps the bonding material to flow. The bonding material is then melted on the joint area. Capillary action (the same action that causes water to soak uphill through a paper towel) draws the bonding agent into the joint. There it hardens and bonds the parts together. This action is shown in Fig. 13-9.

The main difference between soldering and brazing is the material used as a bonding agent. Soldering uses a tin-lead alloy that melts below 800°F (427°C). Brazing is done with copper, silver, and aluminum alloys. These melt at temperatures above 800°F.

Heat and pressure bonding processes

Bonding processes that use heat and pressure do not use filler materials. The base materials form the bond themselves. There are several processes like this; the most common is resistance welding.

Resistance welding. This process is based on a material's ability to resist the flow of electric current. *Resistance welding* uses resistance to melt the material. The material is then squeezed and held to form the weld. A widely used resistance welding technique is *spot welding.* It uses a special welding machine, Fig. 13-10. A transformer (device to change voltage) delivers electric current to the copper electrodes (terminals). The metal to be welded is

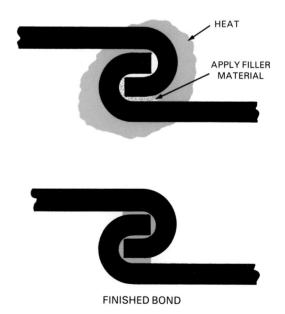

Fig. 13-9. The flow bonding process. Filler is drawn into the joint by heated metal.

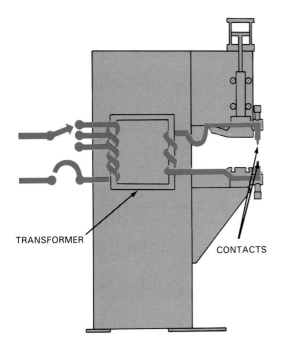

Fig. 13-10. A diagram of a spot welder.
(Taylor Winfield)

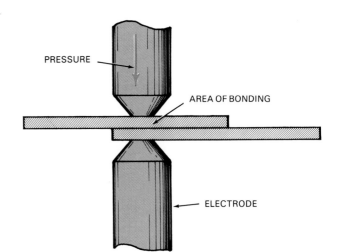

Fig. 13-11. The spot welding process. Material is placed between the electrodes.

placed between the electrodes. Then a four-stage cycle begins:

1. Pressure is applied to the metal parts.

2. Electricity flows between the electrodes. The electrical resistance of the metal parts causes them to heat up. A spot (kernel) of molten metal forms between the two parts, Fig. 13-11. The kernel forms at the point of maximum electrical resistance.

3. The current is stopped, but the pressure is held. The melted kernel cools.

4. The electrodes release the work.

One spot welding process uses rolling electrodes. The rolls perform the same four steps as a regular spot welder. The process produces a continuous weld, Fig. 13-12, called a *seam weld.*

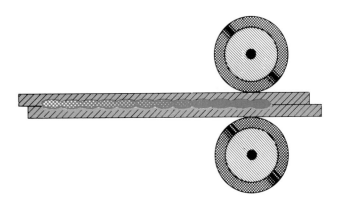

Fig. 13-12. A diagram of a seam welding process. Rollers act as electrodes. (Taylor Winfield)

Resistance welding is used to assemble sheet metal parts. The home appliance and automotive industries, Fig. 13-13, are major users of this process.

Impulse sealing. A special type of resistance welding–*impulse sealing*–is used on plastic films. It

---

SAFETY WITH ASSEMBLING PROCESSES

1. Do not try to complete a process that has not been demonstrated to you.
2. Always wear safety glasses.
3. Wear gloves, protective clothing, and goggles for all welding, brazing, and soldering operations.
4. Always light welding torches with spark lighters, never matches or lighters.
5. Handle all hot materials with gloves and pliers.
6. Perform welding, brazing, and soldering operations in well-ventilated areas.
7. Use proper tools for all mechanical fastening operations. Be sure screwdrivers and hammers are the proper size for the work being performed.
8. Carefully follow instructions for lighting welding torches. Light the gas (acetylene, etc.) first; then turn on the oxygen.
9. When shutting off a welding torch, first turn off the oxygen, then the gas.

Fig. 13-13. Automobile bodies at an assembly plant move through a robotic welding line. (Daimler-Benz)

is used to seal packaging films for bags and shrink packs. The films are held between two pressure bars. A wire recessed in one bar is heated by a pulse of electricity. The hot wire softens the plastic sheets. The pressure bar causes them to bond.

Pressure bonding processes

Pressure or cold bonding uses great pressures to get the necessary atomic closeness, Fig. 13-14. This method works only on very ductile materials such as copper and aluminum. Pressures from 50,000 to 200,000 psi (pounds per square inch) are needed.

Solvent bonding processes

Solvent bonding uses a chemical to soften the material. The parts are then pressed together. The solvent evaporates or is absorbed into the materials. The material hardens into a permanent bond. Solvents are used to bond plastics. Also, ceramics are assembled using liquid slip as bonding material, Fig. 13-15.

Adhesive bonding processes

Adhesive bonding uses a material that has "tackiness" or "stickiness." The parts are held together by an adhesive or glue, Fig. 13-16.

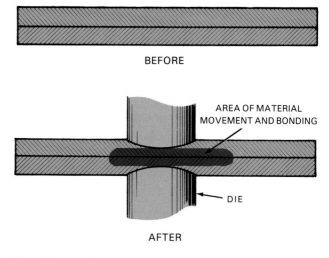

BEFORE

AREA OF MATERIAL MOVEMENT AND BONDING

DIE

AFTER

Fig. 13-14. Cold bonding uses heavy pressure to bond ductile materials.

These materials can be natural or synthetic. Early glues were natural. They were made from animal parts, fish, and milk (casein). Most modern adhesives are synthetic polymers. Like all plastics, they can be either thermoplastic or thermosetting.

Thermoplastic adhesives are usually resins suspended in water. They form a bond when the solvent evaporates or is absorbed into the material.

Thermoplastic adhesives cannot withstand water or high temperatures. They do absorb a great deal of shock before failing. Most thermoplastic glues are for home and school use.

Thermosetting adhesives are powders or liquids that cure by chemical action. Adding water or a catalyst starts the curing action. Heat will often speed the curing of the glue. Thermosetting glues

Fig. 13-15. A worker attaches cup handles to bodies with liquid slip. (Syracuse China)

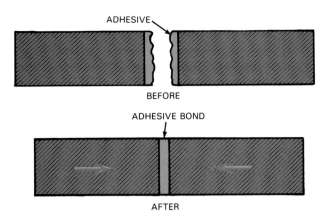

Fig. 13-16. Adhesive bonding uses a tacky substance to hold parts together.

resist heat and water. They are good for cabinet and furniture work.

A third type of adhesive is an *elastomer.* This glue, often called contact cement, is a polymer. Elastomers have low strength. They work well for attaching plastic laminates to panels.

Applying Adhesives

Adhesives can be applied by brush, roll coaters, and spraying. Each adhesive has a set life (pot life). The adhesive must be used within this time. Also, there is a maximum time, called open time, between applying the adhesive and clamping the parts together. Finally, the parts must be clamped for a minimum period of time (called clamp time). These characteristics vary with each glue. A technical data sheet from the manufacturer provides this information.

MECHANICAL FASTENING

The two major techniques using mechanical means are mechanical fasteners and mechanical force.

Mechanical Fasteners

Mechanical fasteners hold two or more parts in a specific position. There are many types of fasteners. Some are designed for general use; others are very special. Fasteners can be divided into groups by their permanency (how long-lasting they are). As shown in Fig. 13-17, these groups are:
- Permanent.
- Semipermanent.
- Temporary.

Permanent fasteners

Permanent fasteners are meant to be installed and not removed. If removed, the fasteners are destroyed.

Rivets are the most common permanent fastener used on engineering materials. When properly installed, the rivet is enlarged at both ends, Fig. 13-18. The parts are held by the force created when setting (forming the straight end) the rivet. When correctly installed, the rivet is destroyed when removed. Several head shapes are made for industrial application. As in Fig. 13-19, these are button, countersink, flat, and truss head.

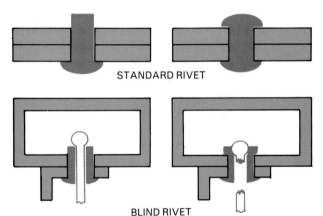

Fig. 13-18. Types of rivets—standard rivets and blind rivets.

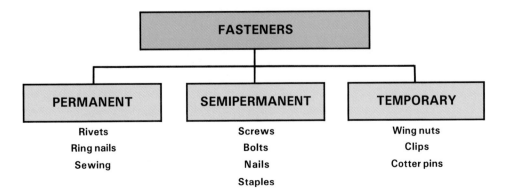

Fig. 13-17. There are three general types of fasteners.

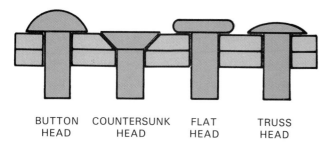

Fig. 13-19. Typical head shapes for rivets.

Rivets are widely used for attaching sheet metal to frames. Aircraft and trailer companies are major users of rivets.

Semipermanent fasteners

Two major types of fasteners can be classified as semipermanent fasteners—threaded fasteners and wire fasteners.

Both types depend on friction to hold them in place. Nuts are held on bolts because of friction between the nut and the surface it rubs against. Screw threads create friction with the fibers of wood. Nails are held in wood by friction.

Threaded fasteners

The three major threaded fasteners are wood screws, machine screws, and bolts. **Wood screws** are used to attach a metal, wood, or plastic part to a wood member.

Two different hole sizes are required when installing screws. One hole is drilled through the first part. It should be the size of the shank of the screw. A smaller diameter hole—the pilot hole—is drilled

into the second member. Also, countersinking or counterboring may be required for the screw head. The screw slips through the first part. The screw threads grip and draw the second part against the first one, Fig. 13-20.

Similar to the wood screw is the **sheet metal screw.** Its threads extend the full length of its shank. A sheet metal screw, as the name implies, is designed to hold two pieces of sheet metal together. The screw should fit easily through the hole in the first member. It will cut threads (self-threading) in the second part.

Screws are sold by their head shape, gage (diameter), and length. The material and finish are also specified. If a special slot is needed it must be listed. A screw might be described as "1 1/4 x 10 flat head cadmium-plated steel wood screw." A catalog will show the typical lengths and diameters available. The larger the gage number the greater the diameter. Fig. 13-21 shows the common screw head shapes.

Machine screws are threaded fasteners used to assemble metal parts. They have round, flat, or

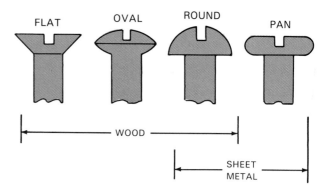

Fig. 13-21. Common screw heads.

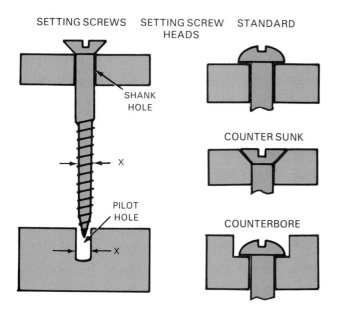

Fig. 13-20. Proper setting of a screw.

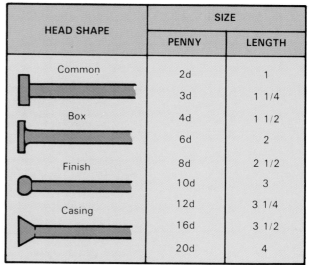

HEAD SHAPE	SIZE	
	PENNY	LENGTH
Common	2d	1
	3d	1 1/4
Box	4d	1 1/2
	6d	2
Finish	8d	2 1/2
	10d	3
Casing	12d	3 1/4
	16d	3 1/2
	20d	4

Fig. 13-22. Common nail lengths and head shapes.

oval heads. The shank has a uniform diameter and threads along its full length. Machine screws may fit through two parts and be secured by a nut, or they may fit through one part and into a threaded hole in the second part.

Machine screws are sold by diameter, number of threads per inch, and length. The head shape and material must also be listed. A common machine screw size is "10-32 x 1 flat head steel screw." It has the diameter of a No. 10 wire, 32 threads per inch, and is 1 in. long.

Bolts are larger threaded fasteners. They are used to assemble heavier parts.

Wire fasteners.

Wire fasteners are basically nails and staples. Nails are the most widely used. They have two basic head shapes:
- Flat heads designed to stay on the surface.
- Ball or tapered head designed to be set (driven) below the surface.

Nails are sold by diameter and length. Small-diameter nails (wire nails and brads) are sized by their actual diameter and length. For example, a 1 1/2-19 is a common wire nail. The 1 1/2 stands for the length and the 19 represents the gage number. A smaller gage number means a larger diameter. A No. 16 wire nail has a larger diameter than a No. 18.

Larger nails are gaged by the penny (d). This is a standard that gives both diameter and length. The greater the penny size the larger the diameter and the length. Fig. 13-22 shows the length and head shapes of some common nails.

Temporary Fasteners

Some assemblies must be quickly and easily taken apart. They require temporary fasteners. Wing nuts on bolts, quick-snap clips, and cotter pins are often used. Also, machine screws and bolts can serve as temporary fasteners.

Fastening by Mechanical Force

Parts may be connected without bonding or fasteners. Mechanical forces can be used to hold them in place.

One fastening technique using mechanical force is *seaming,* Fig. 13-23. It is used widely to fasten sheet metal parts. The parts are bent so they lock together.

Other parts are forced together. The friction between the two pieces keeps them assembled. A shaft may be pressed into a hole. This type of fit is called

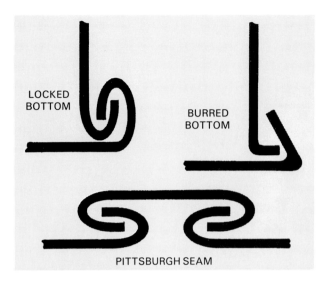

Fig. 13-23. Examples of common sheet metal seams.

a *press fit.* Also a part with a hole may be heated. The part and the hole diameter expand. A shaft may be placed in the enlarged hole. As the heated part cools, it contracts. A *shrink fit* is produced between the shaft and the hole.

JOINTS

All assembly operations require joints. The parts must come together at a point called a *joint.* There are five basic types of joints, as shown in Fig. 13-24.

However, additional modifications (changes) have been made to these basic joints. Special cuts have been added to increase strength. Compare the joints in Fig. 13-24 with those in Fig. 13-25. Can

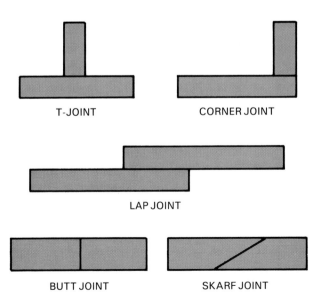

Fig. 13-24. Common types of joints used for many different types of materials.

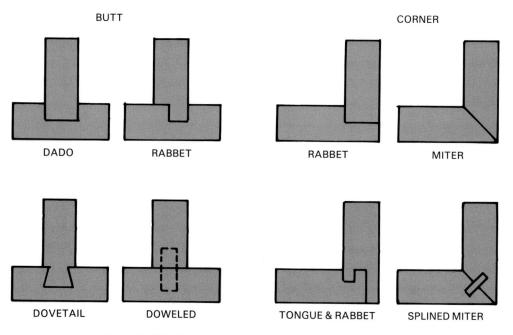

BUTT   CORNER

DADO   RABBET   RABBET   MITER

DOVETAIL   DOWELED   TONGUE & RABBET   SPLINED MITER

Fig. 13-25. Common types of woodworking joints.

you see how they could be stronger? Also, would the parts be easier to line up? These are but a few of the many joints that can be made.

SUMMARY

Assembly involves attaching two or more parts together. Two common ways of assembling parts is bonding and fastening.

Bonding uses heat, pressure, and/or adhesives to hold the materials. Bonds are created by:
- Melting the parts together without pressure.
- Melting a dissimilar (unlike) material that bonds (adheres) to both parts.
- Using heat and pressure.
- Applying high pressure.
- Dissolving the bond area.
- Applying an adhesive.

Parts may also be assembled using mechanical means. Mechanical fasteners may be used to hold parts in place. Self-assembly may use seams or press and shrink fits.

All assembly requires picking a proper joint. It must withstand stress and be attractive.

KEY WORDS

All of the following words have been used in this chapter. Do you know their meaning?

Assembling
Assembly
Atomic closeness
Bonding
Bonding agent
Brazing
Elastomer
Flow bonding
Fusion bonding
Impulse sealing
Joint
Machine screw
Mechanical fastening
Press fit
Resistance welding
Seam weld
Seaming
Sheet metal screw
Shrink fit
Soldering
Spot welding
Thermoplastic adhesives
Thermosetting adhesives
Wood screws

TEST YOUR KNOWLEDGE

Please do not write in this text. Place your answers on a separate sheet of paper.

1. The two types of assembling processes are _____ and _____ _____.
2. Describe each of the methods in Question No. 1.
3. When the atoms of matter across a bonded joint are very close together, they have _____ _____.

4. Which of the following are examples of bonded joints:
   A. Mild steel used to weld mild steel parts.
   B. A hide glue to bond wood parts.
   C. Rivets of mild steel holding tin sheets together.
   D. Solder used to bond copper sheets.
   E. None of the above.
   F. All of the above.
5. List and briefly describe the five methods of bonding.
6. Indicate whether each of the following fasteners is permanent, semipermanent, or temporary:
   A. Nail.
   B. Screw.
   C. Bolt and nut.
   D. Staple.
   E. Rivet.
   F. Bolt and wing nut.
   G. Cotter pin.
7. List the five basic types of joints.
8. Make a sketch of a dado joint and a miter joint.

ACTIVITIES

1. Look around your home. Identify four major joints used in products. Sketch the joint and describe how each is used.
2. Prepare a panel that displays samples of the mechanical fasteners described in this chapter.
3. Devise a test method that will determine the strength of various adhesives.
4. Develop a way to safely and attractively attach wooden wheels to a toy.
5. Invite a professional welder to the school shop to demonstrate fusion welding.

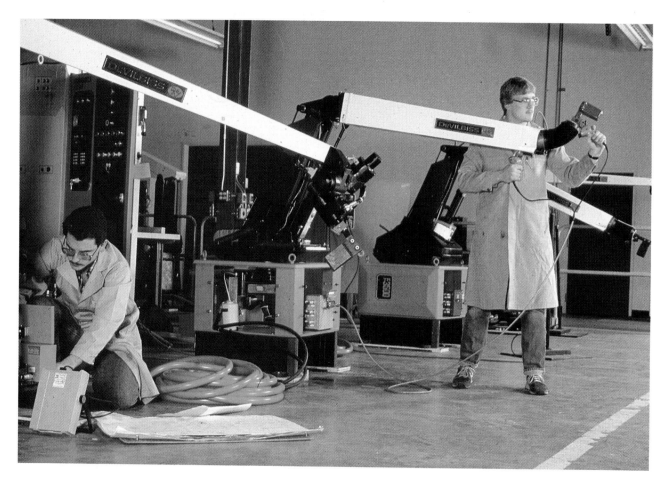

These painting robots can apply finishes to products without putting humans at risk from harmful fumes. (DeVilbiss)

CHAPTER **14**

FINISHING PROCESSSES

After studying this chapter, you will be able to:
- Explain the two purposes of finishes.
- Classify finishes under their main types.
- Describe methods of surface preparation before application of finishes.
- Give brief descriptions of application methods for each type of finish.

Almost every product you use is surface finished. Some products have a coating that makes them more attractive. They are more colorful or glossy than the base material. Such products have more value.

However, finishing is not just for looks. Many engineering materials are attacked by the environment. Metal rusts; wood rots; and clay crumbles. These materials must have a protective coating.

Finishing, then, is a surface treatment that protects or decorates a material. Finishing involves three steps:
1. Selecting a finishing material.
2. Preparing the surface to accept the finish.
3. Applying the finish.

FINISHING MATERIALS

There are a great number of different finishes. However, they fall into two major classes–converted finishes and coatings. See Fig. 14-1.

Converted Finishes

The surface of a material may be converted (changed) by chemical action. *Converted finishes* add no material as a coating. Instead, the surface molecules are changed to make a protective skin or layer. This layer resists the effects of a normal environment. Chemicals in the air and water will not damage the material.

Anodizing is a common converted finish. This process is shown in Fig. 14-2. It uses an electrical current and an electrolyte. An electrolyte is a solution that conducts electricity.

Aluminum parts are placed in an acid bath. The part becomes positive as electricity is run through the tank. Oxygen in the electrolyte solution is drawn to the part. The oxygen combines with the aluminum. This creates an oxide layer that resists corrosion.

The thickness of the coating is controlled by the current and the length of time the parts are in the bath. The pure aluminum develops a "converted" oxide layer. This layer can be colored with dye. The result is colorful aluminum products like automotive trim and bicycle parts.

Surface Coatings

Surface coatings are a protective layer of material. This material is designed to seal the surface

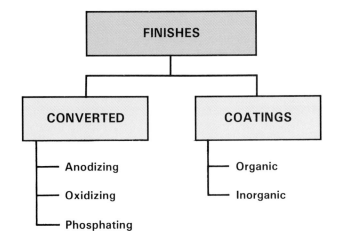

Fig. 14-1. Finishes are either converted finishes or coatings.

Fig. 14-2. The aluminum parts move through a series of cleaning and treatment tanks in this modern anodizing process. (Mirro Aluminum Co.)

against the environment, Fig. 14-3. In many cases, it also adds color and improves the appearance. Coatings are of two basic types–organic or inorganic.

Organic coatings

Organic (once living matter) *coatings* are the most widely used. They are natural or synthetic polymers (chain-like combinations of molecules of organic materials). Organic finishes are classified into a number of groups. Four important ones are paint, varnish, enamel, and lacquer.

Paint is a class of materials containing a liquid that forms a coating by polymerization. (This is a linking of molecules into strong chains.) Many paints have a coloring agent added. Special types of paints are *varnish* (a clear oil-based paint) and *enamel* (a colored paint).

Lacquer is a material containing a polymer coating and a solvent. A lacquer dries as the solvent evaporates.

Organic coatings are used as undercoats and top coats. Undercoatings improve the bond between the base material and the top coat. They may also smooth the surface. Top coats produce a long-lasting, attractive surface.

Inorganic coatings

Inorganic (never living matter) *coatings* are made up of metals or ceramic materials. Metal

Fig. 14-3 Coatings are a protective layer on top of the base material. This dishwasher case is receiving a dip coating of porcelain.
(White Consolidated Industries)

coatings are often applied to other metals or plastics. Chrome-plated automobile trim is an example. Others are zinc and tin applied to steel to prevent rust. Zinc coating, as shown in Fig. 14-4, is called *galvanizing.* Tin-coated steel, called tinplate, is used for food containers (tin cans).

Fig. 14-4. A large steel structure is being dipped into zinc. (American Galvanizers Association, Inc.)

Ceramic coatings are glasslike substances applied to metal or ceramic base materials. These include glaze used on dishes and porcelain enamel applied to ceramic and metal products, Fig. 14-5. The coating is cured by firing at temperatures above 1500°F (816°C). The heat melts the coating and fuses it to the product.

PREPARING MATERIALS FOR FINISHING

A surface generally must be cleaned before it will accept a finish. Therefore, industry has special cleaning methods. Two cleaning procedures are mechanical cleaning and chemical cleaning.

Mechanical Cleaning

Mechanical cleaning requires abrasives, wire brushes, or metal shot to remove dirt and roughness. This cleaning may involve simple hand grinding or polishing with an abrasive wheel, Fig. 14-6, or the parts may be tumbled with metal shot or abrasives as shown in Fig. 14-7. In more complex processes, parts may be cleaned or polished with automatic sand blasters or wire brushing machines.

Chemical Cleaning

Chemical cleaning uses liquids or vapors to remove dirt and grease. Chemical cleaning is a basic part of many finishing processes. All plating and surface conversion finishes use cleaning (pickling) steps, Fig. 14-8.

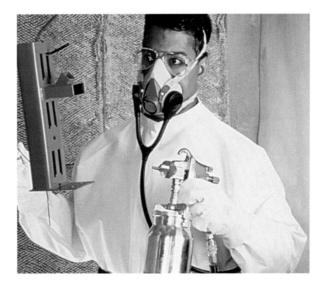

Fig. 14-5. A worker sprays an inorganic coating on a metal part. (3M Company)

Fig. 14-6. The surface of this metal structure is being prepared for its finish. (ARO Corp.)

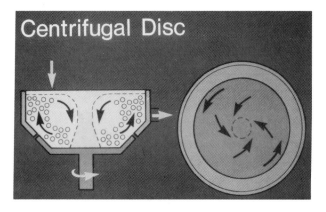

Fig. 14-7. A diagram of one type of tumbler. A part is placed on the disc and spun. Shot tumbles over the part's surface to polish it. (Ransburg Corp.)

Fig. 14-8. This row of tanks contains chemicals used to clean parts then coat them with finishing material.

APPLYING FINISHING MATERIALS

Applying finish often means adding a coat of material to a surface. This definition is too narrow for our purposes. Converted surface finishes are also applied. They produce a chemical change in the material being finished. A chemical or electro-chemical (combination of electricity and chemistry) process is used. Therefore, applying finish involves two basic technologies:
• Conversion finishing.
• Surface finishing.

Applying Conversion Finishes

Conversion finishes result from chemical action. Each finish has its own process. Basically, the processes expose the metal to chemicals. The chemicals react to change the metal. Its outer surface becomes a protective layer. The basic surface conversion finishes are:
• Phosphate coatings–Used as primers for organic coatings and chrome plating.
• Chromate coatings–Provides a decorative or paint-adhering surface.

• Oxide coatings–Provides an oxide of the metal. A common oxide coating is black iron oxide.
• Anodic conversion coatings–Electrochemical process that produces an oxide coating on aluminum.

Applying Surface Coatings

Coatings are the most commonly used finishes. They may be applied by a number of processes. The typical methods include brushing, dipping, rolling, spraying, and electroplating.

Brushing
Brushing is seldom used as a manufacturing process. It is slow and requires skilled painters. However, brushing surface finishes (painting) is a common practice of the construction industry.

Rolling
Rolling is also a little-used process in manufacturing. Its primary use is in coating sheet stock like steel, hardboard paneling, etc. These techniques first coat a roller with a finishing material. The

SAFETY WITH FINISHING PROCESSES

1. Do not try to complete a process that has not been demonstrated to you.
2. Always wear safety glasses when performing finishing processes.
3. Always apply finishes in well-ventilated areas.
4. Do not apply finishing materials near an open flame.
5. Always use the proper solvent to thin finishes and clean finishing equipment.
6. Avoid splashing or flipping finish onto other people or surfaces when you are using a brush.
7. Dispose of all waste finishes and solvents in the proper manner.

stock is fed under the roller. The finishing material is then transferred from the roller to the stock. Rolling can coat large areas very quickly.

Spraying

Spraying is a widely used method of applying finish material. Common spraying methods include hand spraying, automatic spraying, electrostatic spraying, and plasma spraying.

In hand spraying, a gun mixes finishing material with air, Fig. 14-9. Air under pressure carries the material to the surface where it sticks and dries. Hand spraying can apply both organic and ceramic material, Fig. 14-10. Modern techniques replace humans with robotic arms. The robots mimic the hand motions needed to spray coat the product.

Automatic spraying can be used for high-volume production. The spray heads mount in a fixed position. The parts to be coated move along on a

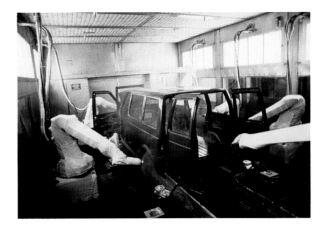

Fig. 14-11. Automatic spraying equipment is used in high-volume production work. (DeVilbiss Co.)

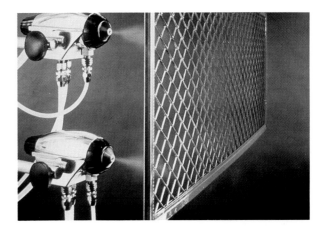

Fig. 14-12. Automatic electrostatic spray guns coat both sides of a metal grate. The paint has a magnetic attraction to the part. (DeVilbiss Co.)

Fig. 14-9. A general-purpose spray gun. Air under pressure mixes with fine particles of finish. (DeVilbiss Co.)

Fig. 14-10. A worker spraying a finish coat. (DeVilbiss Co.)

conveyor or turntable. They are automatically coated as they pass the spray heads. This process is shown in Fig. 14-11.

A big disadvantage of automatic spraying is overspray. *Overspray* is finishing material that misses the product. It is wasted and pollutes the air. *Electrostatic spraying* uses static electricity to overcome this problem. The part is given an electric charge. The paint receives the opposite charge. Since unlike charges attract, the paint is drawn to the part. It is mostly used for metal parts. Paint will actually wrap around the product. It will even blow past the part, then be drawn back. It is possible to paint the whole product while spraying from one side, Fig. 14-12. Note that all sides of the grate are being coated.

Plasma spraying uses a gun that vaporizes metal or ceramic materials, Fig. 14-13. Hot gases carry the particles to the workpiece. This process deposits a thin, even coating on metal, plastic, and ceramic parts.

Dipping

Dipping is a common way to coat materials. The product is dipped in a vat of finishing materials. The excess material is allowed to drip from the part. Examples of dip coating were shown earlier in Figs. 14-3 and 14-4.

Electrocoating, Fig. 14-14, is a type of dipping process. It uses unlike charges in parts and finishing materials just like electrostatic spraying. The charged part is dipped in a tank of charged finishing materials. The material is attracted to the part. When the part is removed from the tank it is rinsed with water. Then the paint is usually baked (dried) in a continuous oven. (This is an oven that surrounds a moving assembly line.)

Another process like dip coating is *curtain coating.* The surface of the material is flooded with finishing material. The excess runs off into a collecting pan. Curtain coating is often used to coat flat parts or sheet stock.

Electroplating

Electroplating, Fig. 14-15, deposits a layer of metal on a base material, usually steel. This process should not be confused with anodizing, which changes only the surface of the part. No material is added in anodizing.

Electroplating adds material. Often, layers of different metals are applied to obtain the desired

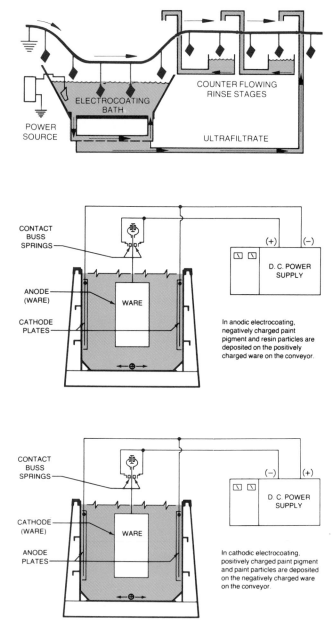

Fig. 14-14. Diagram of the electrocoating process. (George Koch and Sons)

result. For example, a coat of copper may be applied for adhesion. Then a layer of chromium may be added for appearance.

The electroplating process, like anodizing, uses a tank of electrolyte, Fig. 14-16. An electrical lead is attached to the part. The other lead (opposite charge) is attached to a piece of plating metal. The part and the plating metal are lowered into the tank. The direct current charge causes molecules to leave the plating metal. They move across the electrolyte and stick to the part. When the plating is thick enough, the power is turned off. Then the plated part is removed and rinsed. Electroplating is used on automotive trim, jewelry, and tinplate.

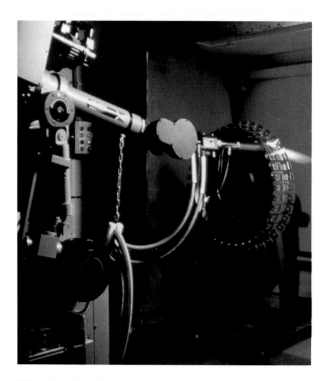

Fig. 14-13. A plasma spray gun in action sprays vaporizing metal or ceramics. (Metco)

Fig. 14-15. Automobile trim parts are lifted from a plating tank. (General Motors)

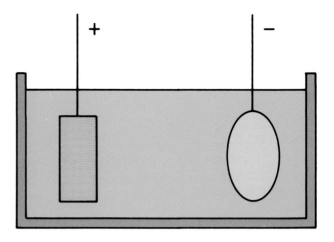

Fig. 14-16. Diagram of a basic electroplating circuit. The process causes new material to coat the part.

SUMMARY

Finishing processes protect and/or improve the appearance of materials. The process may change (convert) the outside layer of a material, or it may deposit a protective layer (coating) on top of the base material.

Coatings can be inorganic or organic. They are applied by brushing, rolling, spraying, dipping, or electroplating.

Careful attention to the selection, preparation, and application of finishes produces beautiful and durable products. These products are attractive and serviceable.

KEY WORDS

All of the following words have been used in this chapter. Do you know their meaning?

Anodizing
Chemical cleaning
Converted finishes
Curtain coating
Electrocoating
Electroplating
Electrostatic spraying
Enamel
Finishing
Galvanizing
Inorganic coatings
Lacquer
Mechanical cleaning
Organic coatings
Overspray
Paint
Plasma spraying
Surface coating
Varnish

TEST YOUR KNOWLEDGE

Please do not write in this text. Place your answers on a separate sheet of paper.

1. Finishing of products only makes them look better. True or false?
2. The three basic steps for finishing a product are:
   A. Pick a finishing material.
   B. Roughen the surface of the part to accept the finish.
   C. Do what is necessary to prepare the part to accept the finish.
   D. Apply the finish.
   E. Cure the finish.
3. If the finishing process does not add material to the part, it is called a _____ finish.
4. An electrolytic process that uses chemicals and electricity to change the material on the surface but does not add material is known as _____.
   A. painting
   B. electroplating
   C. anodizing

5. A(n) _____ contains a polymer coating and a solvent.
6. A conversion finish is the result of _____ action.
7. Which of the following finishes are conversion finishes?
   A. Paint.
   B. Lacquer.
   C. Phosphate coating.
   D. Oxide coating.
   E. Anodic coatings.
8. Explain what happens in electroplating.

ACTIVITIES

1. Visit an art museum that has a collection of pottery. Find out the techniques used to finish and decorate the various pieces.
2. Look around your community. Find and list two items which were primarily finished for protection, beauty, or protection and beauty.
3. Make a series of 35 mm slides and write an accompanying script to demonstrate safety with finishing processes.
4. Working in a team, apply several finishes to a piece using a brush, rag, and roller. Compare and contrast the quality of each finish.

Electrocoating uses electricity to attract paint to the product. The paint and the part are given opposite charges.

Secondary manufacturing processes are used to make all kinds of products, from large aircraft to small vacuum bottles. (Mc Donnell Douglass, Zojirushi)

ESTABLISHING A MANUFACTURING ENTERPRISE

CHAPTER 15

INTRODUCTION TO MANAGEMENT

After studying this chapter, you will be able to:

☐ Identify the roles of managers in companies formed to manufacture products and construct structures.

☐ Define at least 12 management terms.

☐ List the functions of management.

☐ Explain and give examples of management functions.

☐ List five kinds of activities carried on by management.

☐ Explain the kind of work done in each management activity.

There are many types of manufacturing systems. They produce a great variety of products. However, these systems have the same seven components, Fig. 15-1.

Every manufacturing system must be managed. *Management* coordinates (brings together to do one thing) the basic inputs of *people, machines,* and *materials.* These inputs are paid for with *finances.* Materials and machines are purchased. People receive wages or salaries for their work. These resources are brought together by *methods.* These are "ways of doing things." Workers use machines to change the form of material. They produce products. The products are sold in the *market.* People pay money to own these products.

The money the company gets from sales is called income. The income must pay for the cost of producing the products. This cost is called *expenses.* Any income above the expenses and taxes is called *profit.*

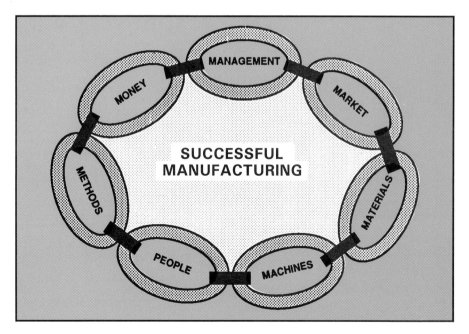

Fig. 15-1. These are the parts of successful manufacturing. Each "link" of the company must be strong to produce useful products.

The average manufacturing enterprise earns about 6 percent profit. This means that for every dollar of sales, the company earns about 6 cents.

Profit is used in two ways. Some is kept by the company to invest in additional productive capital. It pays for such things as new machines and new buildings. This money is called *retained earnings*. Profit is also used to pay *dividends*. These are payments made to the owners. It rewards them for

Fig. 15-3. Managers use many techniques to guide and direct company activities. (IBM)

investing their money in the company. Dividends are usually paid to the owners quarterly (every three months). How income and profits are used in a company is shown in Fig. 15-2.

Management is the process of guiding and directing company activities. The goal is efficient use of company resources, Fig. 15-3.

An understanding of management can be developed by studying three factors. These, shown in Fig. 15-4, are the: functions of management (what managers do), levels of management, and areas of activity.

FUNCTIONS OF MANAGEMENT

Anyone who manages has four functions. These functions, shown in Fig. 15-5, can be described as follows:
- Planning–setting goals and the course of action to be followed.

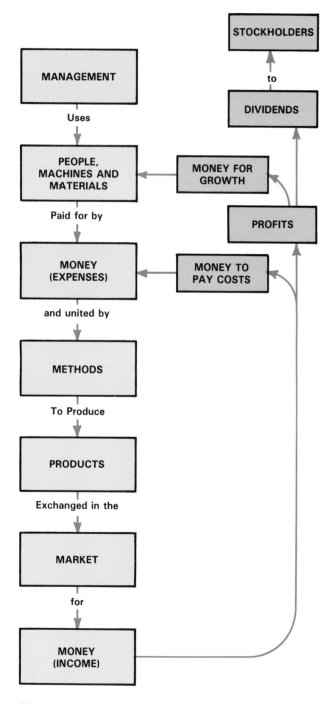

Fig. 15-2. The left side of the flowchart shows how management uses resources to produce products. The right side shows the ways income is used.

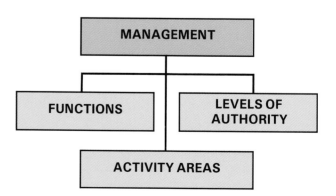

Fig. 15-4. Aspects of management.

PLAN

CONTROL

ORGANIZE

DIRECT

Fig. 15-5. Managers plan, organize, direct, and control company activities. (Rohm & Haas)

- Organizing–dividing tasks into jobs and establishing lines of authority (who gives orders to whom).
- Directing–assigning your employees to the jobs, and encouraging them to complete their work efficiently.
- Controlling–comparing the results of employees' work with the company plan.

Planning

Planning, Fig. 15-6, is the first function of management. Planning sets the goals for the company or for one of its activities. Basically, planning means to:
- *Gather* information about the task or problem.
- *Arrange* the information so you have a "picture" of the task or problem.
- *Identify* several solutions or courses of action.
- *Decide* on the best solution or course of action.

Planning is used in all parts of the company. It may be done to establish goals for the entire company. It can also be used to set smaller goals, such as: production goals, financial goals, or training goals. These goals can be short term–daily or weekly. They may also be part of long-term goals. Goals can cover one or more years.

Organizing

Organizing is the process of ranking the importance of and assigning resources to complete tasks. Each task uses human, material, and capital resources. People must also be given authority to complete the work. They must understand how their job fits within the overall company activity. Individuals need to know who answers to them. Likewise, they need to know to whom they must answer. In short, people should understand who works for them and who is their boss.

Fig. 15-6. A product planning session allows employees to exchange and evaluate product plans. (Motor Vehicle Manufacturers Assoc.)

Organizing involves three decisions:
- Who is to do each task.
- How much authority is needed to complete each task.
- How many resources are needed to complete each task.

Directing

Directing begins when goals are set and tasks are organized. Now people must be assigned to do these tasks. However, more is needed. They must be trained and motivated (given a reason) to work efficiently, Fig. 15-7.

To be successful, the directing phase must let employees know:
- *Why* each task is important.
- *How* to complete the task.
- The *rewards* (pay and recognition) for doing the job well.

Managers who direct employees will provide proper training. They will also let each worker know he or she is important to success. *Each task, large or small, is a step toward moving a product idea to the marketplace.*

Controlling

As work is completed, it must be checked and measured. The results of human effort must be compared to the company's goals. This task is called **controlling**. It means several things. The quality of the product must be controlled.

Fig. 15-7. These employees receive training as part of management's directing role.

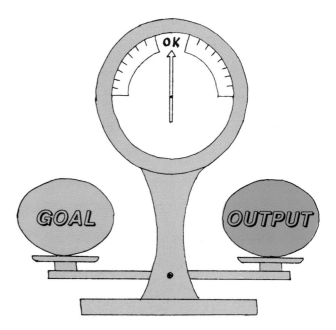

Fig. 15-8. Control compares results with the goal (plan).

Raw and finished goods inventories (lists of what is on hand) are controlled. The financial resources, hours worked, and cost of production are also controlled. Hundreds of things about the company operation must be watched.

The manager must see that the results are in balance with the goals, Fig. 15-8. To do this, managers:
- Gather performance data (such as records of sales, production, and payroll).
- Compare performance to the plan.
- Determine if changes are needed.
- Decide what action should be taken.
- Begin the right action to correct any problem.

A plan may work fine the first time. The performance may match the goals. However, management does not stop there. Plans are constantly changed. They challenge the company to become more efficient. New organizing and directing activities are encouraged. These improvements help a company increase its productivity (output per amount of labor). A more productive company can pay its workers more. It can also sell its products for less. Then it can compete better with other companies. A healthy company can finance new products and plants. It can grow larger and employ more people.

Without good management practices, a company soon dies. Its products become out-of-date. Other companies take away its customers. Workers must take less pay. In short, the company becomes a poor business citizen.

LEVELS OF MANAGEMENT

Managers must organize the company. They will establish **levels of authority**. Some people are given more responsibility than others. Some employees have greater decision-making powers than other people in the company. There is a "pecking order" within the company. This is true of all kinds of organizations.

Think about the school you are in. There are many citizens in your school district. They probably do not have the time or ability to run the schools. Thus, the voters elected a school board. The board then hired a superintendent. He or she manages the day-to-day operation of the school district. Larger districts have several assistant superintendents. Each manages an area such as curriculum, personnel, and business affairs.

Principals are hired to manage individual schools. Often, people are assigned to oversee (supervise) departments. Typical departments are technology education, mathematics, art, science, and history. Teachers conduct the classes offered by the departments. The students are offered a chance to learn.

How Companies are Organized

A company is organized much like a school, Fig. 15-9. There are levels of responsibility. Let us look at a corporation, a type of business organization.

(The different types of businesses will be discussed in Chapter 16.)

Most corporations have stockholders. They are like the citizens of the school district. **Stockholders** are the owners of a corporation. They buy a portion of the company. However, they do not run the company. They probably live all over the country. Many have their own jobs. They may not know how to manage an enterprise. They elect a group to represent them. This group is called the **board of directors**. The board gives the company direction. They form policy. The board hires a full-time manager called a **president**. The president is the top manager. She or he has several **vice-presidents**. They are in charge of a major part of the company. There may be vice-presidents for sales, marketing, engineering, manufacturing, personnel, and so on.

Let us look at the manufacturing side of the company structure. The next level is the **plant manager**. This individual is in charge of an entire production facility. He or she manages all activities at a single plant. The plant is usually divided into departments. These departments may be the machining, shipping, accounting, assembly, or welding departments. They are run by **department heads**. They are aided by **supervisors**. These individuals assign and supervise the production **workers**.

Employees at each level have work to do. Each person is important. One job should not be viewed as better than another. They are only different.

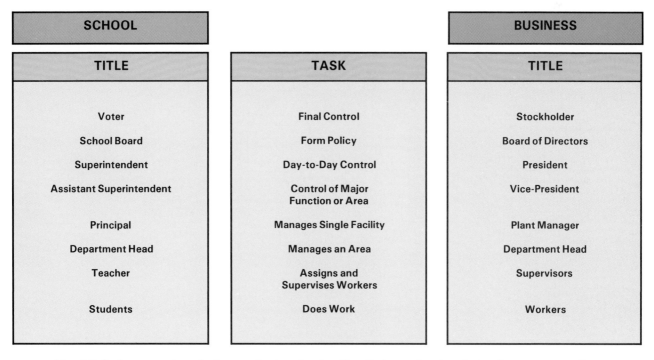

SCHOOL	TASK	BUSINESS
TITLE	**TASK**	**TITLE**
Voter	Final Control	Stockholder
School Board	Form Policy	Board of Directors
Superintendent	Day-to-Day Control	President
Assistant Superintendent	Control of Major Function or Area	Vice-President
Principal	Manages Single Facility	Plant Manager
Department Head	Manages an Area	Department Head
Teacher	Assigns and Supervises Workers	Supervisors
Students	Does Work	Workers

Fig. 15-9. A comparison between the levels of authority in a school and a business corporation.

Production workers are essential. A company cannot survive without them. However, they have different responsibilities than do the vice-presidents. This division of responsibility and authority is essential. It allows a company to be managed efficiently.

AREAS OF ACTIVITY

Managers have functions to carry out. They are given a certain amount of authority to do their job. They also work in certain areas. These areas move a product from the idea stage to completion. When all the work is done, an idea becomes a product. It is sold to customers for a profit.

There are five major managed areas of activity. These are shown in Fig. 15-10:

- Research and development–discovers, designs, develops, and specifies new and improved products.
- Production–engineers, designs, and sets up manufacturing facilities that produce products to the company's quality standards.
- Marketing–identifies the people who will buy the products. Then marketing promotes, sells, and distributes the products.
- Industrial relations–operates programs to find and train the company's workforce. It also does things that make the public and workers feel good about the company.

- Financial affairs–raises and controls the company's money.

These five areas of activity cause a product to evolve. These activities will be discussed more fully in Chapters 16 through 32.

SUMMARY

Management directs and controls company activities. A view of management requires some basic knowledge. This involves an understanding of functions, levels of authority, and areas of activity for managers.

Managers plan, organize, direct, and control. They manage single tasks or entire companies. They perform these functions in a structured way. The structure extends all the way from the owners down to the workers. Managers work in five areas of activity. These areas are research and development, production, marketing, industrial relations, and financial affairs.

KEY WORDS

All the following words have been used in this chapter. Do you know their meaning?

Board of Directors
Controlling
Department Heads
Directing

Fig. 15-10. The five managed areas of activity. When you go to work, where will you fit into this picture?

Dividends
Expenses
Levels of authority
Management
Organizing
Planning
Plant manager
President
Profit
Retained earnings
Stockholders
Supervisors
Vice-presidents
Workers

TEST YOUR KNOWLEDGE

Please do not write in this text. Place your answers on a separate sheet of paper.
1. What are the three factors you must study to understand management?
2. From the following list, select those activities that are the functions of management.
   A. Planning (setting goals and courses of action).
   B. Identifying markets.
   C. Organizing (assigning tasks to certain jobs and establishing lines of authority).
   D. Directing (assigning employees to jobs).
   E. Controlling (comparing employees' work with company plan).
   F. All of the above.
3. Stockholders (do, do not) run the company.
4. List the five major managed areas of activity. Describe what is done in each area.

ACTIVITIES

1. Study the organization of a church, school club, or other group. List the officers (managers) of the group according to the level of authority.
2. Organize a group to perform a community service such as picking up litter. Plan the activity, organize the group, direct the group, and control the activity.

The better a company is organized the better it will run. The employees must work together for a company to be a success. (General Electric)

CHAPTER 16

ORGANIZING AND FINANCING AN ENTERPRISE

After studying this chapter, you will be able to:
- ☐ List different ways companies are owned.
- ☐ Describe three methods of ownership.
- ☐ Discuss advantages and disadvantages of each type of ownership.
- ☐ Identify steps required by law to form a company.
- ☐ Describe three kinds of company organization.
- ☐ Describe how a company determines its money needs.
- ☐ List ways of financing (getting money) for starting a company.

Enterprises are organized by a person or group of people. As the company is organized, decisions are made. The main ones are:
- What type of ownership will be used?
- What local or state rules must be met?
- What type of management will work best?
- How will the finances (money or capital) be raised?

Each new company faces the same questions. Let us look at these elements one at a time.

FORMS OF OWNERSHIP

Most companies are publicly owned. That is, they are owned by one or more individuals. The government does not own them.

Most companies are formed to make money for the owners. They are said to be *profit-centered*.

There are three forms of public, profit-centered ownership. These are shown in Fig. 16-1. The type of ownership will depend on several things.

Proprietorship

The proprietorship is the simplest and oldest form of ownership. A *proprietorship* is a business enterprise owned by one person. Many service

PROPRIETORSHIP

FRED'S ''Hand Made'' Bird Houses

PARTNERSHIP

FRED and JAN'S Custom Bird Houses

CORPORATION

F&J Aviaries, Inc.

Fig. 16-1. These are the three forms of ownership.

stations, antique shops, farms, and retail stores are owned by a single individual. The owner is called the "proprietor."

The proprietorship is used for enterprises that are small and need little capital. They have several advantages, Fig. 16-2. Proprietorships are easy to form. A simple business license is all that is usually required. The management structure is simple. The owner directly controls all operations. This gives the company flexibility (ability to change easily). It can react quickly to changes in the market. Finally, the owner has the right to all after-tax profits.

However, proprietorships have certain disadvantages. See Fig. 16-3. Often the enterprise cannot easily raise more money. Thus, its growth is sometimes held back.

Also, few individuals have all the talents needed to run a company. Limited management talent can cause the enterprise serious problems.

Finally, the owner is responsible for all debts of the company. If the company fails, the owner must pay the debts with his or her own money. This is called *unlimited liability*.

Partnership

A partnership overcomes some of the disadvantages of a proprietorship. The *partnership* is an association of two or more people to run a legal business. Such businesses usually are easy to start and end. They can offer more management talent. Also, the owners have more ways to raise money for the company.

The partners must still accept unlimited liability for the company debts. Also, the owner-managers

Fig. 16-3. Proprietorships also have disadvantages.

might have arguments. They must share responsibilities as well as profits, Fig. 16-4.

Corporation

Most manufacturing companies are organized as corporations. A *corporation* is a legally created business unit. It is an "artificial being" in the eyes of

Fig. 16-2. A proprietorship has some advantages.

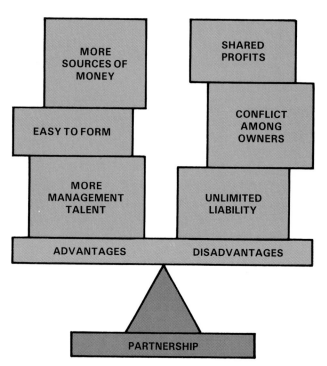

Fig. 16-4. Two or more people can form a partnership. It has both advantages and disadvantages.

Fig. 16-5. A corporation is an artificial being in the eyes of the law.

the law, Fig. 16-5. It is created in one state and can operate in all states.

Like all beings, corporations can own property. They can sue or be sued and enter into contracts.

Corporations have long lives. Their owners (stockholders) can sell their holdings without causing a change in management. Generally, the owners are not the managers. Individuals with special skills are hired to manage the enterprise.

Corporate owners have a definite advantage. They have limited liability. The corporation, not the owners, is responsible for all debts. Owners can lose their original investment if a corporation fails. They do not, however, have to furnish additional money to pay outstanding debts.

Of course, corporations have some disadvantages. The owners generally have little interest in the daily operations of the company. Their main interest is in dividends. This interest often causes management to work toward high short-term earnings. Long-term growth may not be given proper attention by the management.

Also, corporations must file many government reports. This makes their operations more public. Competing can be more difficult. Corporate profits are heavily taxed. Stockholders' dividends are also taxed.

FORMING A COMPANY

All enterprises must become a legal company. Most manufacturing companies are corporations. Therefore, we will limit our discussion to forming a corporation.

As we said before, a corporation is an artificial being. Therefore, it must be born. This birth process must follow steps shown in Fig. 16-6.

Articles of Incorporation

A corporation is controlled by three major things. These are:
• The laws of the state where it is formed.
• The corporate articles of incorporation.
• The corporate bylaws.

The laws vary from state to state. However, all provide basic rules for ownership and financing of a company.

The company must select a state where it wants to incorporate. It prepares an application form. This form is called the *articles of incorporation* or application for a charter. It is filed with the proper state official. The certificate usually requires:
• Name of the company.
• Purpose for forming the company.
• Names and addresses of those forming it.
• Location of the company office in the state.
• Type and value of the stock to be sold.
• Names of principal officers of the company.

Other information may be requested. The kind of information will vary from state to state.

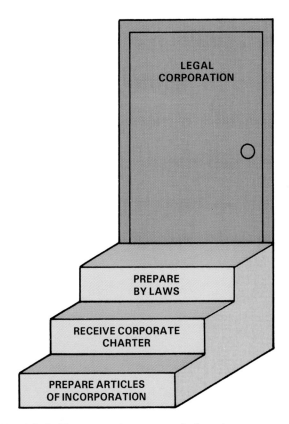

Fig. 16-6. There are three steps in forming a corporation.

Fig. 16-7. Articles of Incorporation mark the ''birth'' of a corporation. (Boise Cascade Corp.)

Corporate Charter

The state officials review the articles of incorporation. Also, they determine the filing fee. This fee is generally based on the number and value of the shares of stock to be sold.

When the articles are approved and the fees are paid, the state issues a *corporate charter*, Fig. 16-7. This charter authorizes the company to do business in the state. It is the corporate "birth certificate." All states recognize charters from other states. A charter from one state allows a company to conduct business in all states.

Corporate Bylaws

The corporate charter is very general. It does not give many directions for running the company. More detailed information is spelled out in the company *bylaws*, Fig. 16-8. Most bylaws outline:
- Date and location of the annual stockholders meeting.
- Date and place of periodic board of directors meetings.
- List of corporate officers with their duties, terms of office, and method of appointment.
- The number, duties, and terms of office of the directors.
- Types of proposals that must have stockholder approval.
- Method to be used to change the bylaws.

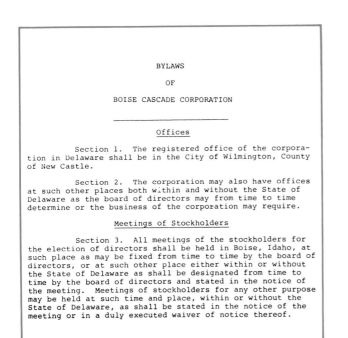

Fig. 16-8. Bylaws provide general rules for operating a corporation. (Boise Cascade Corp.)

The stockholders have the power to develop and change the bylaws. Often they delegate this power to the board of directors. In the end, the stockholders have little control over the company. This power rests with the major corporate managers and the board of directors.

DEVELOPING A MANAGEMENT STRUCTURE

Running a corporation properly takes a team of persons who will manage it. For each important function (task) of the company there will be a manager. There may be several levels of managers each with additional managers and staff. This is called a *management structure*. So that everyone knows who is her or his boss, the lines of authority are sketched into a chart. A management structure must be developed early in a company's life.

The main officers, managers, and work force were presented in Chapter 15. These included:
- President–responsible for all company activities.
- Vice-president–manages a major segment of the company.
- Plant manager–manages a single production facility.
- Department head–manages a major activity within the production facility.
- Supervisor–directs the work of production workers.
- Workers–complete the work outlined by the management.

This listing follows the production activity right down to the production worker. However, there are other areas of activity. Marketing, industrial relations, research and development, and financial affairs also have levels of authority, Fig. 16-9.

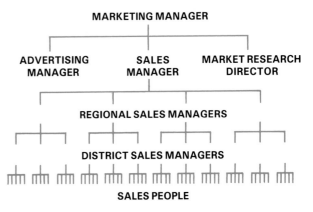

Fig. 16-9. A structure of a nonproduction area of activity. Their task is to sell the corporation's products.

These various areas of activity and levels of authority must be organized, too. Responsibilities must be fixed. Lines of authority are drawn, Fig. 16-10. The result is an organizational structure.

There are a number of organization models (charts). The three common types are:
• Line organization.
• Line and staff organization.
• Line and function staff organization.

Fig. 16-10. Everyone in the company should know who is responsible for each job.

Line Organizations

Line organization is the simplest. A single line of authority flows from the president to the vice-presidents, Fig. 16-11. From there, authority flows directly through various levels to the workers.

All information and direction flows vertically up and down the structure. There are no horizontal connections between different tasks. This type of organization is also called a military structure. It can work well only in very small organizations.

Line and Staff Organizations

In line organization a single person oversees all operations. This person manages sales, public relations, research, distribution, manufacturing, and many other operations. In larger companies, this becomes an impossible task. Therefore, the line and staff organization is used. It is shown in Fig. 16-12. The major line managers have staff people to advise them. The line managers still have the authority over operations. Staff advice helps them manage more effectively.

Line and Functional Staff

The third organizational structure is line and functional staff. The main change is in the staff function. They are given authority over their area. They move from advice giving to decision making. The staff, such as quality control, has authority over its activities until conflict occurs. Then higher management must resolve the differences. For example, the quality control staff may not agree with the production planning director. The vice-president for production must then decide who is right. See Fig. 16-13.

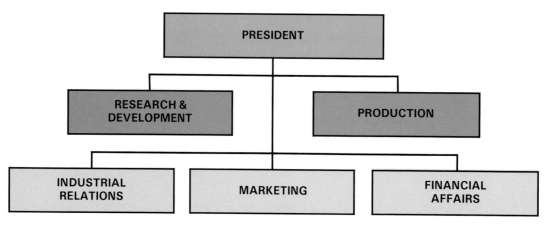

Fig. 16-11. Typical areas under the control of the company president. She or he is the immediate superior of managers of all these departments.

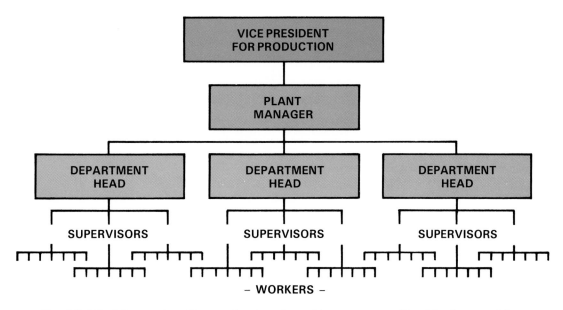

Fig. 16-12. A line and staff organization chart. Line managers like this vice-president have other managers to advise them.

DETERMINING FINANCIAL NEEDS

All companies need money to operate. Established companies can obtain most of their money from sales. New and expanding companies must raise finances from outside sources.

Companies find out how much money they need by making up a budget. *Budgets* are estimates of income and expenses. They detail the costs of operation and sources of income. There are six major types of budgets, Fig. 16-14:

- A sales budget estimates sales for a specific period.
- A production budget estimates the number of products to be produced to meet the sales budget.
- A production expense budget estimates production costs. They include material, labor, and overhead (equipment, utilities, rent, etc.) costs.

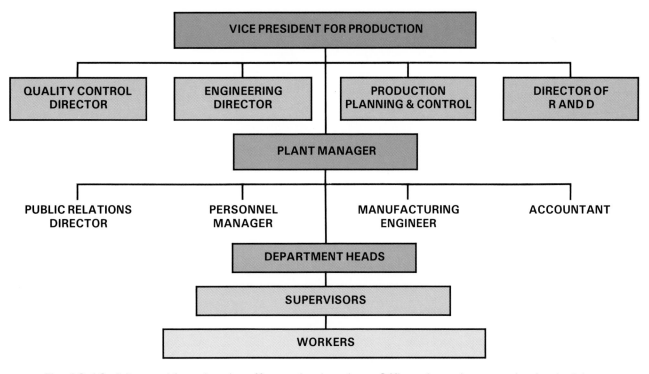

Fig. 16-13. A line and functional staff organization chart. Officers in each area make the decisions in their own departments.

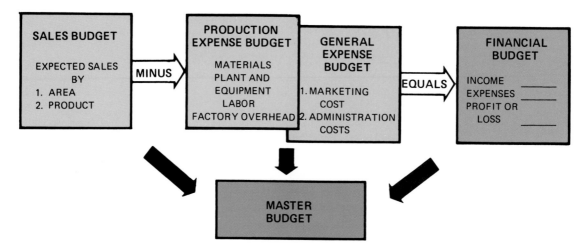

Fig. 16-14. Flow chart shows how a master budget draws information from other budgets.

- A general expense budget estimates cost not directly related to the manufacture of products. This includes marketing and administrative costs. Research and development, financial affairs, industrial relations, and top management's expenses are often considered administrative costs.
- A master budget summarizes all other budgets.

GETTING FINANCING

Budgets help managers determine their company's need for money. Often this money must be raised from outside the company.

There are two main ways to raise outside finances. Ownership rights to the company can be sold. This technique is called *equity financing*. Peo-

Fig. 16-15. A sample stock certificate. Study it and note the space for the owner's name and number of shares owned.

ple are sold *stock*, Fig. 16-15. They become part owners, or shareholders, of the company.

Companies can also borrow money. They can use *debt financing*. Basically they agree to "rent" some money. Someone will provide money for a period of time. This money is called a *loan*. The company must repay the money plus interest (rent).

SUMMARY

All beginning companies must be organized and financed. They become a legal business by meeting certain state requirements. They may be formed as proprietorships, partnerships, or corporations.

The company must establish a managerial structure. Responsibilities and lines of authority for managers must be developed.

Finally, money must be raised to run the company. Budgets are developed to determine financial needs. Money is obtained through equity or debt financing.

KEY WORDS

All of the following words have been used in this chapter. Do you know their meaning?

Articles of incorporation
Budget
Bylaws
Corporate charter
Corporation
Debt financing
Equity financing
Loan
Management structure
Partnership
Profit-centered
Proprietorship
Stock
Unlimited liability

TEST YOUR KNOWLEDGE

Please do not write in this text. Place your answers on a separate sheet of paper.

1. Name and describe the three profit-centered types of company ownership.

2. The _____ _____ _____ is an application form for a state charter.

3. Most bylaws outline six basic directions by which companies run. What is included in these directions?

Matching questions: Match the definition on the left with the correct term on the right.

4. _____ Manages a major activity within the production facility.

5. _____ Manages a major segment of the company.

6. _____ Directs the work of production workers.

7. _____ Single line of authority flows from president to vice-presidents; from them to workers.

8. _____ Major line officers have staff officers to advise them.

A. Line organization.
B. Supervisor.
C. Line and staff organization
D. Department head.
E. Vice-president.

9. _____ are estimates of income and expense.

10. A master budget estimates production costs including labor, material, and overhead. True or false?

ACTIVITIES

1. Study the organization of a church, school, or other group. Prepare an organization chart for the group.

2. Visit a local company and obtain their organization chart. Share it with your class.

3. Work with your parents to set up categories for a household budget. DO NOT include dollar values for each category.

4. Assume you and two friends are going to start a lawn care service. What type of ownership would you use and why?

DESIGNING AND ENGINEERING PRODUCTS

CHAPTER 17

ESTABLISHING PRODUCT NEEDS

After studying this chapter, you will be able to:
- ☐ Define and describe two approaches manufacturing companies use in developing new products.
- ☐ Explain how companies can identify good product ideas.
- ☐ Describe several processes companies might use in developing new product ideas.
- ☐ Appreciate the role product development plays in the success of a manufacturing enterprise.
- ☐ Develop some methods of your own for finding products your class can mass produce and sell.

All products must start with an idea, Fig. 17-1. Ideas usually start with needs. Someone thinks of a product that people need. Companies use two basic systems in developing products. These are pictured in Fig. 17-2.

PRODUCTION APPROACH

The production approach to product design stresses producing products. A design staff develops a product. It is then produced in quantity. Major advertising campaigns try to convince people they need the product.

Many high-volume consumer goods are developed by the production approach. Cosmetics, toiletries, soaps, toothpaste, and designer clothing are examples of products using this approach. It is doubtful that large numbers of people were asking for CD players or electric pencil sharpeners to be developed. They were first designed and produced. Then we were told, through advertising, that we needed them.

CONSUMER APPROACH

The consumer approach first identifies products people need. Then the products are designed and produced. This approach is widely used in developing industrial goods, Fig. 17-3.

For example, the Boeing Airplane Company carefully collects data from airlines before they design a new aircraft. They try to include all the features requested by the many different airlines.

Another company asked boat builders and casket makers "What kind of sander do you need?" Their answer was "A small machine that will sand curves and small surfaces." This research led to the hand-held oscillating sander.

Fig. 17-1. All products start with an idea.

Establishing Product Needs   157

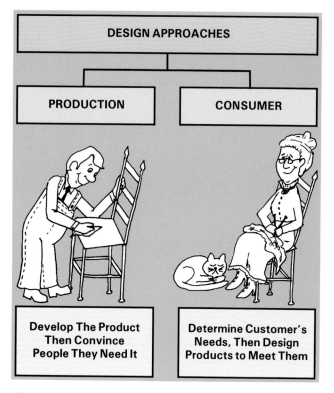

Fig. 17-2. These common design approaches are used by companies.

Until recently most products you bought were designed using the production approach. Growing competition has caused more companies to use the consumer approach.

IDENTIFYING PRODUCT IDEAS

Developing products is hard. New products must balance the needs of the customer with the strengths of the company. Customers must need or want the

Fig. 17-3. This machine was developed using a consumer approach. (Caterpillar)

products. Likewise, the company must have the resources to design, produce, and market the product.

A company cannot produce a product just because it is a good idea. It must fit the company's area of operation. A metal machining company will not be very interested in an idea for a wood desk. See Fig. 17-4.

DETERMINING CONSUMER NEEDS AND WANTS

Each of us has needs and wants. You may want a new bicycle. Your best friend may want a stereo system. This difference causes a problem for companies. They cannot manufacture a product just for you. They need to produce products many people want (mass appeal).

The company must decide what product a group of people will buy. The way this is done varies. It will depend on how the company develops products.

Fig. 17-4. Products must be designed to meet customer needs and use company strength.

Some companies are imitators. They produce a product much like those of other companies. They let someone else identify and build the market. The basic information they need is sales figures. Assume Company D (developer) is selling lots of widgets. Then Company I (imitator) will also want to make widgets. **Imitation** is a common product development technique. Think of products that are widely imitated. How about home computers, stereo receivers, clothing styles, and toys?

Another technique is **adaptation**. This means a product is "improved" by changing it. The manual typewriter was adapted to be an electric typewriter.

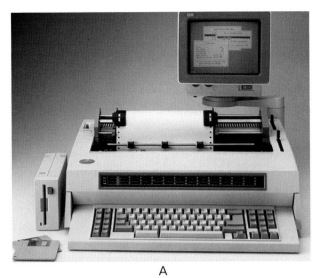

A

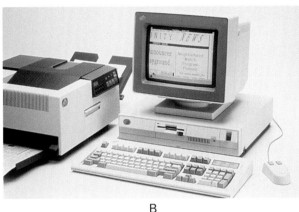

B

Fig. 17-5. A–The electronic typewriter was the precursor to the personal computer. B–Today's personal computer allows the user to go beyond typing to integrate text and graphics to produce high-quality documents. (IBM Corp.)

The electronic typewriter was a further adaptation, replacing the electric typewriter. Today's personal computer loaded with word processing software has replaced the typewriter in most workplaces and many homes. See Fig. 17-5.

The last technique is *innovation* (creating something new). A totally new product is developed. The video recorder, CD player, microchip (Fig. 17-6), and polyester fibers are recent innovations.

SOURCES OF PRODUCT IDEAS

Each of the methods for product development starts with ideas. These ideas come from both inside and outside the company. They basically arise from studying three sources shown in Fig. 17-7.

Market Research

Market research is used to study people's thinking about products. It may tell the company what

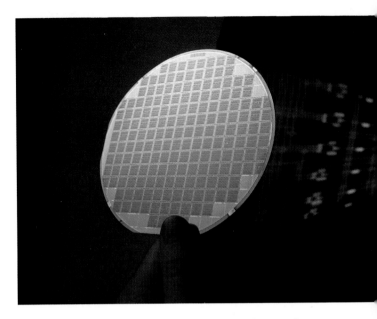

Fig. 17-6. The silicon wafer is a recent innovation. Each small square on the wafer contains a custom designed integrated circuit. (AT&T)

products people want. It may test people's feelings about a product the company already makes. The information gathered is used for either product development or product improvement.

Market research gathers information in three major areas as seen in Fig. 17-8. It gives the maker information about people's choice of product size, color, style, and function. This information is the starting place for good product design or redesign.

Some kinds of research collect information about the market itself. A company learns things

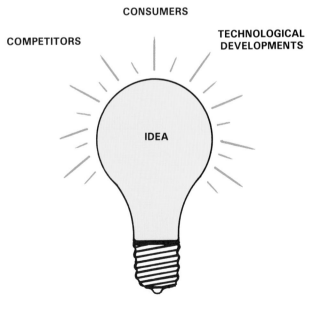

Fig. 17-7. New product ideas come from many sources.

Fig. 17-8. Market research helps identify product ideas by gathering information about the product, the market, and the marketing system.

about its customers: their age, gender, where they live, their occupation, and income.

Finally, a company gathers data on how good its marketing activities are. Information is obtained on types of stores where the product is purchased.

More detailed information about the product is obtained by surveys. Individuals are often asked to use or taste the product, Fig. 17-9. Then they are questioned. The actual questions try to bring out the following information:
- Feelings about the product.
- Evaluation of product quality.
- Whether the person would like to own or use the product.
- Reaction to product color, size, and function.
- Expected selling price.
- Number of products that would be purchased in a year.
- Use for the product–gift or personal.
- Improvements that could be made.
- Comparison to other similar products on the market.
- Type of store in which the product would be expected to found.

Often the warranty card, Fig. 17-10, is used to gather this data. Basic information is usually needed on:
- Name and address of purchaser.
- Gender and age of the new owner.
- Income of customer.
- How the customer heard about the product.

- Type of store in which the product was purchased.
- Whether the product was purchased for a gift or personal use.

Competitive Analysis

All companies carefully study the products of their competitors. From this study a company can determine the need to improve its own products. This is called *competitive analysis*.

Product imitators can determine trends in product development. They can identify areas where they want to develop similar products.

Of course, each company must ensure that they do not break patent laws. They must either:
- Develop their own technology.
- Pay to use someone else's ideas.
- Use technology that is not patented.

There are thousands of ideas not patented. The patents of many other products have expired.

Technological Developments

The last source of product ideas is *technological developments*. Advancements in science and technology can give designers product ideas. New materials may suggest new products. The development of composites gave us fiberglass fishing poles and lightweight aircraft parts. The invention of the laser and glass fibers gave us fiber-optic communication systems.

Fig. 17-9. Some product ideas are tested through consumer surveys. (American Woodmark)

OWNER INFORMATION CARD

Seal card here

Model
0234351 (4600 EFU)

IMPORTANT: Please complete the information below and mail this card right away.

1. ☐ Mr. 2. ☐ Mrs. 3. ☐ Ms. 4. ☐ Miss   **41D**

Name (First/Initial/Last)

Street

City   State   Zip

Date of Purchase: ___/___/___
Mo Day Yr

Serial Number _____

A) Where was this product purchased?
1. ☐ Camera store
2. ☐ Department store
3. ☐ Discount store
4. ☐ Mail order
5. ☐ Military (PX, etc.)
6. ☐ Catalog showroom
7. ☐ Received as gift
8. ☐ Other (specify: _____)

B) This product will primarily be used for:
1. ☐ Commercial/Industrial/Govt.
2. ☐ Scientific/Medical
3. ☐ Photo journalism
4. ☐ Creative hobby
5. ☐ Family/Travel

C) Who/What was the greatest influence in your final decision to purchase this product?
1. ☐ Advertising
2. ☐ Noko brand name
3. ☐ Product features
4. ☐ Friend/relative
5. ☐ Price
6. ☐ Product brochure/literature
7. ☐ Salesperson
8. ☐ Other (specify: _____)

D) Check the one which is appropriate:
1. ☐ This is the first time I have owned a product of this type.
2. ☐ I own another Elite product of this type.
3. ☐ I own another product of this type, but not an Elite
4. ☐ I already own other products of this type—both Elite and other brands.

E) User's highest level of education completed:
1. ☐ High school
2. ☐ Some college
3. ☐ College graduate
4. ☐ Post graduate

F) Which of the following do you read/see/listen to regularly?
1. ☐ Newspaper
2. ☐ Television/Radio
3. ☐ Modern Photography
4. ☐ Petersen's Photographic
5. ☐ Playboy Magazine
6. ☐ Popular Photography
7. ☐ Readers Digest
8. ☐ Sports Illustrated
9. ☐ Special Interest magazines
10. ☐ Time/Newsweek/U.S. News
11. ☐ TV Guide

G) What brand of 35mm SLR do you own?
1. ☐ Conar   4. ☐ Xbrand
2. ☐ Mito   5. ☐ Mbrand
3. ☐ Noko   6. ☐ Other

H) What model do you own? _____

I) Which of the following have you done in the past 6 months? (check all that apply)
1. ☐ Redeemed a product coupon
2. ☐ Ordered an item from mail order catalog
3. ☐ Sent in product inquiry card from magazine
4. ☐ Bought item from offer received in mail
5. ☐ Entered sweepstakes/contest

J) Month and Year of your birth:
☐☐   [1][9]☐☐
Month   Year

K) Do you have any children in any of the following age groups who are living at home?
1. ☐ Under age 2   5. ☐ Age 11–12
2. ☐ Age 2–4   6. ☐ Age 13–15
3. ☐ Age 5–7   7. ☐ Age 16–18
4. ☐ Age 8–10

L) Marital status:
1. ☐ Married   2. ☐ Unmarried

M) Which group best describes your family income?
1. ☐ Under $10,000   6. ☐ $30,000–$34,999
2. ☐ $10,000–$14,999   7. ☐ $35,000–$39,999
3. ☐ $15,000–$19,999   8. ☐ $40,000–$44,999
4. ☐ $20,000–$24,999   9. ☐ $45,000–$49,999
5. ☐ $25,000–$29,999   10. ☐ $50,000 & over

N) Do you:
1. ☐ Own your home?
2. ☐ Rent your home?

Fig. 17-10. Study the questions on this warranty card. How would the information help a product designer? An advertising person?

Companies must never stop gathering information about new developments. They may produce the advancement in their own research labs, Fig. 17-11. Other data are obtained by outside sources. These sources include:

- Other companies.
- Government agencies.
- Universities.
- Private research centers.
- Private inventors.

Company Profile

Product ideas, as mentioned, must be matched to the company strength. These strengths are often contained in a list called a company profile. Five

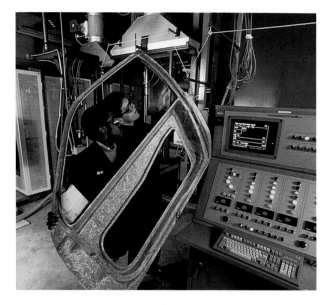

Fig. 17-11. These engineers are developing a new composite door frame. (Du Pont)

main elements are included in a company profile. These are:

• Market the company knows.
• Type of products the company produces.
• Sales volume the company expects from each product.
• Cost to develop and engineer the product.
• Financial resources available.

SUMMARY

Companies may develop products using either production or consumer approaches. They start the development process with product ideas. The ideas may be imitations (copies) of other products. Some ideas adapt or improve on existing products. A few ideas are truly new. They are called innovations.

Product ideas are generated by studying consumers, competitors, and technological developments. All ideas must fit the company. They must fall within a profile of the company's strengths.

KEY WORDS

All of the following words have been used in this chapter. Do you know their meaning?

Adaptation
Competitive analysis
Imitation
Innovation
Market research
Technological developments.

TEST YOUR KNOWLEDGE

Please do not write in this text. Place your answers on a separate sheet of paper.

1. Explain the difference between a consumer approach and a production approach to product development.
2. Adaptation means producing a new product by (select best answer):
   A. Improving an old design so the product does the job better.
   B. Changing a product so it looks different.
   C. Making a product of cheaper materials to make more profit.
   D. Stealing another company's product ideas.
3. _____ _____ is studying people's thinking about products.
4. List the three sources of ideas for product development.
5. Describe two methods of getting information from users of a company's product.
6. When a company studies the products of its competitors to see how it can or should improve its own products, the method is called:
   A. Comparison shopping.
   B. Competitive analysis.
   C. Technological development.
   D. Patent search.

ACTIVITIES

1. Working in a group, identify ten new product ideas that people in your age group need or want.
2. Visit a company and interview a product designer. Find out how she or he finds new product ideas.
3. Interview a retail store manager. Ask him or her to discuss products which:
   A. Were designed to meet a basic customer need.
   B. Were first designed and then the need was developed by advertising.
4. Do you have a new product idea? Make a sketch of the product and market it to your friends. Do they want to buy it? Why or why not?

CHAPTER 18

DESIGNING PRODUCTS

After studying this chapter, you will be able to:
☐ List and describe the objectives of design.
☐ Explain factors of industrial design.
☐ List and describe steps in a design process.
☐ Explain different types of models used in presenting designs.

Product ideas must be developed to meet product needs. Product designers must change words into products. They convert statements of need into product ideas.

Designers use a process called *ideation*. They sketch many ideas. Then the best ones are selected.

Fig. 18-1. Products are designed to meet three factors. They must fill a need (function), be easy to make (manufacture), and customers must want them.

The ideas are refined. They move ideas-in-mind to ideas-on-paper.

Product design has objectives and a process. It also has goals and a method (way of doing).

DESIGN OBJECTIVES

All product design activities are aimed at meeting a goal. They have a purpose. The major goals are to develop products that:
• Customers want.
• Meet or beat the competition.
• Are profitable to make.

Successful designers always keep three major factors in mind. They design for function, manufacture, and selling, Fig. 18-1.

Designing for Function

All products are designed to do a job. A train or truck must move freight, Fig. 18-2. A picture must decorate a wall. A washer must wash clothes.

The ability to do a job is called *function*. Designers consider the product's purpose, operation, and safety. These are the factors in designing for function.

For example, a designer of toy trucks must consider many things. Several of these are related to function.
• Where is the toy going to be used? Will it be an indoor or outdoor toy?
• Is it designed for educational purposes?
• What type of surface must it roll on?
• What age of child will use it? What safety features are required for this age group?

Every product's worth is measured in terms of function. It must operate under typical conditions.

Fig. 18-2. Trucks and trains are designed to move freight. This is their function.
(Freightliner Corp., Norfolk Southern)

Fig. 18-3. Designers considered manufacturing when they designed this airplane. Design for manufacture allows the skin to be easily mated with the frame. (Boeing)

Designing for Manufacture

It is not enough to have a functional product. The company must be able to build it efficiently. Designers consider ease of manufacture, Fig. 18-3.

Designers will also consider the number of parts needed. Usually, the fewer parts the better. Moreover, they will use standard parts and materials whenever possible. Why make a bolt if you can buy it cheaper?

In addition, the number of different parts are considered. A designer would not use a 1 x No. 8 screw in one place and a 1 1/4 x No. 8 screw in another. They are the same diameter. The number of threads per inch is the same. There is only a slight difference in their length. Using only one size reduces inventory costs.

The ability to process the part is another consideration. Look at Fig. 18-4. The part on the left would be more difficult to cut out and sand. The shape on the right is a better design for manufacture.

Designing for Selling

Product function and manufacture are important. But the product must also sell. Customers must want to buy it. They must see it as meeting their needs. These needs include function, appearance, and value, Fig. 18-5.

We buy products because they do a job for us. But we also want them to be attractive. Even a table saw is designed to look good. Finally, the product must have value. We must feel that it is worth the price.

Generally we are first attracted to a product by its looks. We then decide if it will do the job. The final decision is related to its cost. Is it worth the money it costs?

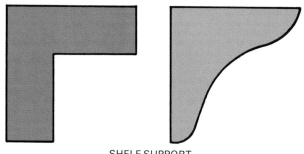

SHELF SUPPORT

Fig. 18-4. The part on the right would be easier to manufacture than the one on the left.

Fig. 18-5. Consider the simple spoon. Was it designed for selling? Does it have a function, beauty, and value? (INCO)

DESIGN PROCESS

Product designers follow a few basic steps in developing product ideas. These steps, shown in Fig. 18-6, include:

- Developing preliminary (beginning) designs.
- Refining designs.
- Preparing models.
- Communicating designs.
- Obtaining approval for designs.

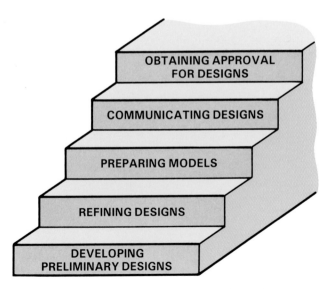

Fig. 18-6. There are five steps in product idea development.

Preliminary Designs

Generating ideas is the first step in product design. Designers quickly sketch as many ideas as they can, Fig. 18-7. Often these sketches are simple "doodles." They record what the mind dreams up.

These first sketches are often called *thumbnail* (or *rough*) *sketches*. They serve the same purpose as notes do for writers. They are assorted pieces of information. Later, they will be sorted and organized into more complete pictures.

You might think of the rough sketches as a "library of ideas." A large "library" is more likely to have good ideas. Therefore, it is important for a designer to develop many rough sketches.

Refining Designs

During refining, the designer selects the best ideas from the many rough sketches. These ideas are improved. Details are added. Several sketches may be fused (put) together to form a better idea. The sketches, as seen in Fig. 18-8, become more complete. This type is called a *refined sketch*.

The refined sketch shows shape and size. It gives a fairly accurate view of the designer's ideas.

Fig. 18-7. Designers develop rough sketches for their ''library'' of product ideas. (RCA)

Fig. 18-8. This designer is working on a sketch for a new toy. (Ohio Art Co.)

Many designers now use computers to develop sketches, Fig. 18-9. Computer systems allow the designer to quickly change lines and details. The stroke of a "wand" changes the computer picture. These pictures can be stored for later use. They can also be used to create a drawing. The computer will direct a pen to draw a sketch. These systems are called *CAD* (**c**omputer **a**ided **d**esign) systems.

Preparing Models

Many times sketches do not show enough detail. They are generally two-dimensional (have width and height only). They do not show depth. People may have a hard time imagining this third dimension. Therefore, models are often built. *Models* are three-dimensional representations of the product.

There are two major types of models: mock-ups and prototypes. A *mock-up* is an appearance model, Fig. 18-10. It shows what the product will look like. Mock-ups are usually made of easily worked materials. Cardboard, balsa wood, clay, styrofoam™, and plaster are commonly used.

Prototypes are working models. They generally show the product in full size. Prototypes use the same material the product will use. Their purpose is to check the operation of the final product. Fig. 18-11 shows a typical prototype.

Models allow the design to be viewed more completely. It can be seen from all angles. The appearance and operation of the product can be checked carefully.

Communicating Designs

Developed designs must be communicated to management. Often, managers want to study the ideas for size, shape, color, and decoration.

Fig. 18-9. This 3-D CAD drawing allows the designer to see a car's suspension system. (Diamler Benz)

Fig. 18-10. This designer is working on a scale model of a new vehicle. (Ford Motor Co.)

Fig. 18-11. This engineer is testing a toy for safety and durability. (Ohio Art Co.)

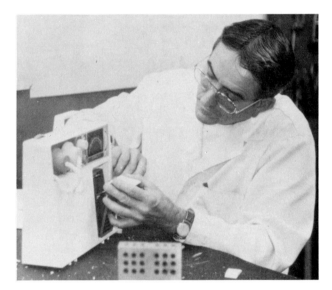

Fig. 18-12. A final model of a toy is built by a model maker. (Ohio Art Co.)

Typically, completed designs are shown in two ways: models and renderings.

The models are usually final prototypes or mockups. Earlier models were used for the designer to check ideas. Now, new models are made that include all design changes, Fig. 18-12. These models will look exactly like the finished product.

Renderings are also used to show final designs. These are colored pictorial sketches. They show the overall detail of the design. Fig. 18-13 shows a rendering of a new product.

Getting Management's Approval

The final step for a design idea is getting approval. Management must give its "OK" to continue developing the product.

Management evaluates the product design against several factors. These factors include: strengh of competing products, the cost to manufacture the product, the size of the market, the money that can be earned, and the resources required.

The managers usually receive preliminary cost estimates. They also review the design sketches and models, Fig. 18-14. They decide the fate of the product ideas. If approved, the designs will be sent to product engineering. There the product is refined, specified, and tested. These activities are the subject for the next chapter.

Fig. 18-13. This designer is developing a rendering of a possible new product. (Ohio Art Co.)

Fig. 18-14. A management team reviews sketches for a new automobile. (Ford Motor Co.)

SUMMARY

Designing products involves careful consideration of function, manufacture, and selling. Products must be designed to do a job. They also must be efficiently produced. Finally, they must sell.

Creating a successful design involves several steps. Ideas must be generated through rough sketching activities. These ideas are further developed. Refined sketches and models are prepared. The refined ideas are communicated to management for approval. Approved ideas are turned over to product engineering.

KEY WORDS

All of the following words have been used in this chapter. Do you know their meaning?

CAD
Function
Ideation
Mock-ups
Models
Prototype
Refined sketch
Rendering
Rough sketch
Thumbnail sketch

TEST YOUR KNOWLEDGE

Please do not write in this text. Place your answers on a separate sheet of paper.

1. Give the steps for the process of ideation.

2. Tell what is meant by:
   A. Designing for function.
   B. Designing for manufacture.
   C. Designing for selling.

3. Arrange the following steps for design in their proper order:
   A. Obtaining approval for designs.
   B. Developing preliminary designs.
   C. Communicating designs.
   D. Refining designs.
   E. Preparing models.

4. What are the two types of models used by product designers? What is the difference between them?

5. Using computers to draw up designs is known as _____. The term stands for _____ _____ _____.

6. A rendering is a:
   A. Final prototype.
   B. Colored pictorial sketch.
   C. Final mock-up that has been painted.

ACTIVITIES

1. Visit a product designer to see samples of product sketches. Ask about the design process (steps) used. Find out about the way products are designed and approved for manufacture.

2. Select three simple products in your home. Evaluate their designs in terms of function, manufacture, and selling.

3. Sketch three to five new products you would like someone to design.

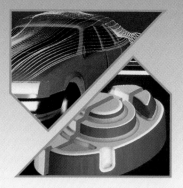

CHAPTER 19

ENGINEERING PRODUCTS

After studying this chapter, you will be able to:
☐ Explain how products are engineered.
☐ Define the terms: engineering modification and engineering specification.
☐ Recognize different types of engineering drawings and tell how they are used.
☐ Describe a bill of materials and explain its use.
☐ Discuss specifications and describe their form and contents.

Product designs show how the product will look and work. But the product is not ready to be produced. The design must be refined. This final preparation for manufacture is called *product engineering.*

Product engineering modifies and specifies the design. *Specifying* means to give the size, material, and quality requirements for the product. Product engineers also test the product. They check its operation and safety, as well as other important features.

SPECIFYING DESIGNS

Most products have several parts, Fig. 19-1. These parts must fit and work together. Often the product has parts from several sources. Standard items are bought from suppliers. Other companies may build special parts. Suppliers may bid to produce parts of the product. The company, itself, may produce many different parts. All of them must fit together to make the product, Fig. 19-2.

Each supplier must know the exact size, shape, and properties of the components they make. This information is found in the specifications. Product engineers specify product characteristics (features) in three ways using:
• Engineering drawings.

Fig. 19-1. The automobile is a product with many individual parts. (Ford)

• Bill of materials.
• Specification sheets.

Engineering Drawings

Engineering drawings tell how to make the product. The drawings include specifications for individual parts. Also given is information needed to assemble the product. This basic information is placed on three types of drawings:
• Detail drawings.
• Assembly drawings.
• Systems drawings.

Detail drawings

Engineering will prepare a detail drawing for each different part. *Detail drawings* give the exact size of the part as well as the size and location of all features. These features may include holes,

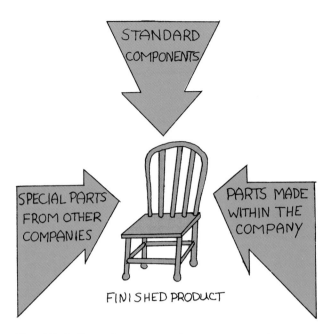

Fig. 19-2. Parts from several sources must fit together to make a typical product.

notches, curves, and tapers. The features give the parts their final form.

Detail drawings usually have two or more views. They show the part from several sides. These drawings use a system called **orthographic projection**. This system generally shows the part in two or three

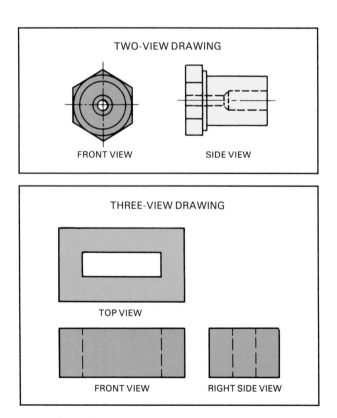

Fig. 19-3. Orthographic projections are "straight on" drawings of parts. Two types are shown.

views, Fig. 19-3. Round parts are shown by an end view and a side view. Other shapes are shown in three views: front, top, and right side. You see each view in two dimensions, height, and width. It is as though you are looking directly at that side of the part.

Many detail drawings are now prepared using CAD (computer-aided design) systems. These systems allow the drafter (a person who prepares drawings) to quickly draw and change a drawing while working at a computer. Fig. 19-4 shows a CAD drawing on a computer screen.

A detail drawing must give all the information needed about a part. The manufacturer (maker of parts and products) must be able to make the part from the drawing. Look at Fig. 19-5. Could you make the table leg from the information given? What additional information would you need? Remember we are talking about making many parts that are alike. Could you make the curves identical on each part? Does the drawing give you that information? You can easily see why the drawing must be complete. Without good detail drawings, parts cannot be accurately produced.

Assembly drawings

Parts must be put together to make many products. How these parts mate is shown on **assembly drawings**. These drawings identify the parts by a code (number, letter, etc.). They then show where each part goes.

Assembly drawings may be two dimensional (width and height) like the one in Fig. 19-6. This type of drawing shows the parts in their final assembled position.

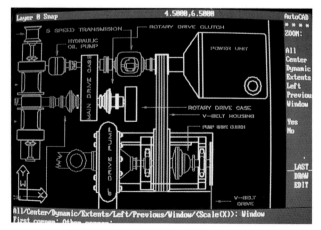

Fig. 19-4. Many drawings are first prepared and checked on a CAD system. They can be stored or printed out.

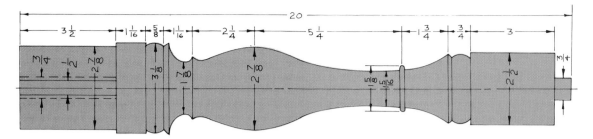

Fig. 19-5. This is a simple detail drawing.

Pictorial (picture) drawings are also used. These drawings represent the parts in a single three dimensional (has depth as well as height and width) drawing. Often the drawing is an exploded view, Fig. 19-7. The parts are pulled apart to show how they fit together.

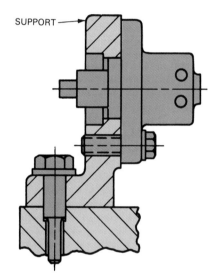

Fig. 19-6. A simple assembly drawing shows where each part belongs.

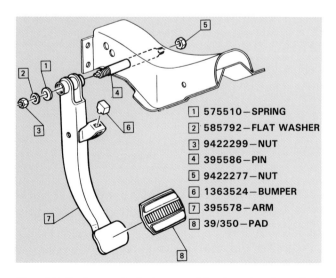

1	575510 – SPRING
2	585792 – FLAT WASHER
3	9422299 – NUT
4	395586 – PIN
5	9422277 – NUT
6	1363524 – BUMPER
7	395578 – ARM
8	39/350 – PAD

Fig. 19-7. An exploded assembly drawing is pulled apart so you can see better where each part belongs.

Fig. 19-8. This drafter is carefully checking a drawing for accuracy.

Assembly drawings, like detail drawings, must communicate. They must give all information needed to put the product together. Each assembly drawing must be checked, Fig. 19-8, to be sure that it:
• Identifies the parts by name or number.
• Shows the location of each part.

Systems drawings

Systems drawings are used to show electrical, pneumatic (air), and hydraulic (fluid) systems. They show the location of parts in the system, Fig. 19-9. Various connections are also shown.

Systems (also called schematic) drawings give information needed for assembly and servicing. Workers can easily see how components fit in the system. Most systems drawings do not show distances between components. Instead they show how the components relate to each other.

Bill of Materials

A second tool of the product engineer is the bill of materials. It is a list of all materials needed to

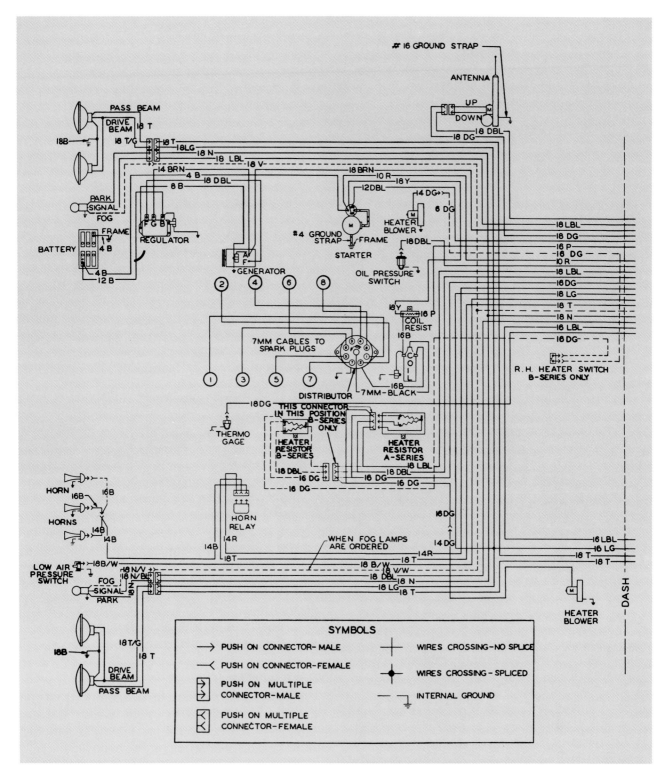

Fig. 19-9. An electrical systems drawing. (General Motors Corp.)

make one product. A **bill of materials**, shown in Fig. 19-10, includes:
• Part number.
• Part name.
• Quantity of each part needed.
• Size of each part.
• Material to be used.

The sizes are given in a logical order. The thickness is listed first. Then the width is given, then the length.

A bill of materials is a valuable form. It is used to determine the material to order. It is also used to estimate the cost of manufacture. However, a bill of materials, itself, does not list costs. It is used to

MASTER BILL OF MATERIALS							
PRODUCT:							
PRODUCT CODE NUMBER:							
Part No.	Part Name	Material	Qty.	Size T	W	L

Fig. 19-10. A bill of materials lists sizes and quantities of materials in orderly fashion.

determine quantities of materials. These are then multiplied by current prices. If a bill of materials did include costs, it would soon be out-of-date. Prices change often.

Specification Sheets

Some items and certain qualities cannot be shown on a drawing. How would you show adhesives on a drawing? A drawing of sheet steel would be of little value.

The important characteristics for these materials is not size and shape. The detail drawings show the final size and shape. They could describe size and shape of a note holder made from wood. However, the wood is chosen because of its properties. These properties are described on a specification sheet.

Product engineers need to know or specify these various properties. The material's strength, weather resistance, and other qualities must be determined.

Small manufacturers cannot afford to have materials developed for them. An adhesive (glue) may be needed to bond an aluminum sheet to plywood. A small manufacturer would call an adhesive manufacturer and describe the need. The adhesive company would provide *Technical Data Sheets.* These sheets describe adhesives that would do the job. They would give:
- Properties of the adhesives.
- Information on its application, clamping, and curing.

The product engineer reviews the data sheets. Then, she or he picks the best adhesive for the job.

Larger companies may specify the material characteristics they want. They prepare a "specification sheet" for the material. Suppliers offer to supply the material. It would be produced to meet the customer's specifications.

Fig. 19-11. This engineer is testing a cylinder head. (General Motors)

TESTING PRODUCTS

Product engineers also test designs. They make sure that the product works, Fig. 19-11. Just as important, they will test it for safety.

The product is put under actual conditions of use. Then it is closely watched, Fig. 19-12. The data gathered helps engineers to decide if the product works. Also, testing information is one source of ideas for product improvement.

Fig. 19-12. This technician is testing a new television. (Zenith)

One more use of product testing is to answer customer complaints. Broken products may be returned. They may have quit working. Testing can determine if the product design has flaws. It can find out if customer misuse caused the failure. If so, new instructions for use may be needed.

SUMMARY

All products move from design to engineering. Designers only develop products. Product engineers must specify their characteristics.

An engineering staff prepares detail drawings for each part. They describe the size, shape, and surface finish for the part. Assembly drawings show how the parts go together. Systems drawings describe electrical, pneumatic, and hydraulic systems.

A bill of materials lists all parts needed to make a product. The list is a guide for purchasing and cost estimating.

Finally, the properties of a material or product are specified. They are contained in technical data sheets and specification sheets.

Product engineers also test a product. They check its operation and safety. After these activities are completed, the product design is released for manufacture. The product has been designed and engineered. Now it needs to be produced and sold.

KEY WORDS

All of the following words have been used in this chapter. Do you know their meaning?

Assembly drawing
Bills of materials
Detail drawing
Orthographic projection
Product engineering
Specif ying
Systems drawing
Technical data sheet

TEST YOUR KNOWLEDGE

Please do not write in this text. Place your answers on a separate sheet of paper.

1. Three ways to specify characteristics (features) of a product are _____, _____ and _____.

2. Indicate which of the following types of drawings you would use to give the exact size of a part:
   A. Systems drawing.
   B. Assembly drawing.
   C. Detail drawing.

3. If you wanted to show all the features of a drawing (including features like holes, notches, curves and tapers) you would use a (an) _____ drawing.

4. An orthographic projection (select all correct answers):
   A. Allows you to see height, width, and depth in a single view.
   B. Generally shows parts in two or three views.
   C. Shows each view in two dimensions, height and width.
   D. Shows round parts in two views.
   E. Often shows three views: front, top, and right side.

5. A drawing which presents the parts as though it were a picture is called a _____ drawing. It shows the part in _____ dimensions, _____, _____ and _____.

6. List the information included on a bill of materials.

7. If a small company asked an adhesive manufacturer to supply information on a glue to meet the company's needs, would the adhesive manufacturer supply the information on a Technical Data Sheet or a Specification Sheet?

8. When are specification sheets used?

ACTIVITIES

1. A maple book rack has three major parts–a large end which is 3/4 x 6 x 8, a small end which is 3/4 x 6 x 3, and a shelf which is 3/4 x 6 x 14.
   A. Prepare a bill of materials for the product.
   B. Prepare a drawing for the large end.

2. Interview a drafter to find out:
   A. Types of drawings he or she prepares.
   B. Methods used to prepare the drawing.
   C. Basic requirements for the job.

3. Take apart something that has several parts and reassemble it.

4. Make a dimensioned sketch of a simple product you own.

The use of the computer as a design tool has allowed human creativity to be extended.

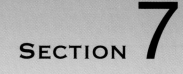

DEVELOPING MANUFACTURING SYSTEMS

CHAPTER 20
CHOOSING A MANUFACTURING SYSTEM

After studying this chapter, you will be able to:
- ☐ Recognize the differences between custom, intermittent, and continuous manufacturing.
- ☐ Compare these three types of manufacturing.
- ☐ Define terms used with each type.

Once products are designed they must be made. Materials are processed into usable goods. The company uses a manufacturing system to produce products.

Three basic types of manufacturing systems are used today. These are outlined in Fig. 20-1.

CUSTOM MANUFACTURING

Custom manufacture is used to make small numbers of products. Often they are one-of-a-kind items, Fig. 20-2. The company produces them to a customer's specifications. The buyer decides the features of the product.

Some people have clothing manufactured to fit them. Kitchen and bathroom cabinets are sometimes built to fit one house. Tooling, like that shown in Fig. 20-3, is custom manufactured. (*Tooling* is the

Fig. 20-2. This passenger ship was custom manufactured to the customer's specifications. (National Steel and Ship Building)

equipment a plant uses for production.) Tooling is built to order. The customer's specifications are used.

Custom manufacture generally requires skilled workers. They must be able to read plans (drawings and specifications). Such workers are often required to set up machines. They operate their own equipment. Each worker checks the quality of his or her own work, Fig. 20-4.

Custom manufacture is the most expensive system for manufacture. Workers are more skilled. Thus, they are paid more. Setting up and checking machines takes a long time. Only a part of the work time is spent in actual production.

Equipment use is also low. Part of the time it is idle. At other times it is being set up. The cost of each machine is charged against products. If it is not used often, more cost is charged to each product.

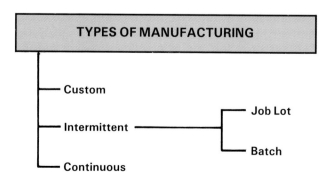

Fig. 20-1. All manufacturing is done by one of these systems.

TYPES OF MANUFACTURING
- Custom
- Intermittent
  - Job Lot
  - Batch
- Continuous

Choosing a Manufacturing System 177

Fig. 20-3. Most tooling for manufacturing processes is custom manufactured. (AT&T)

For these and other reasons, custom manufacture is not often used. It is chosen only when demand for the product is low but users are willing to pay the added cost.

INTERMITTENT MANUFACTURING

In *intermittent manufacturing,* products are mass produced. They are built in large quantities. Intermittent means starting and stopping at intervals (periods of time). The process starts, is completed, then stops. At a later time the cycle is repeated.

You may have seen intermittent manufacture in your home. A member of your family may have baked a batch of cookies. Perhaps a week later another batch was produced. The same process was used. The two baking activities were separated by a period of time.

Intermittent manufacture can be used for both primary and secondary processing. Steel, for example, is made in batches. The mill produces and pours a melt of steel, Fig. 20-5. Then another batch is produced. Intermittent manufacture in primary processing is called *batch processing*.

In secondary processing, intermittent manufacturing processes groups of items. A number of parts

move from station to station until they are finished. At each station the entire group, called a lot, is processed. For example, a hole may be drilled at one station. The entire lot is drilled before it moves to the next station. There the hole may be reamed. This type of manufacture is called *job-lot manufacture.* It is pictured in Fig. 20-6.

A company may do intermittent manufacturing for two purposes. Products may be made for the company's own use. The system may also be used to make products for other companies. The specifications, therefore, may be its own or another company's.

Fig. 20-4. Custom manufacturing requires highly skilled workers who are responsible for their own work. Here a potter forms a bowl.

Management must do more planning for intermittent manufacture. The job must be scheduled through the plant. Machines and workers must be assigned for each task. The lot must, somehow, be moved from station to station. Inspections must be scheduled.

Also, machines may need to be set up for each operation. Tooling must be installed and checked. The first parts produced have to be carefully inspected.

Intermittent manufacture is more efficient than custom manufacture. While skilled machine set-up

Fig. 20-5. A batch of steel is being poured. (American Iron and Steel Institute)

CONTINUOUS MANUFACTURING

Continuous manufacturing produces products in a steady flow. Materials enter the system to start the process. Parts are made from the materials. Products are assembled from the manufactured parts. The process continues at a steady rate without stopping.

This method depends heavily on *division of labor*. This means the task of making the product is divided into *smaller* jobs. Each worker is trained to do one job. Parts are produced as workers complete their individual jobs, Fig. 20-7. The product takes shape as it moves through the system.

Continuous manufacture is based on the movement of resources. Most often the worker stays in one place while the product moves to him or her, Fig. 20-8. As a worker completes one job, the product moves on to the next worker.

Not all products are easy to move. In these cases the product is not moved. The workers move to the product. Each worker completes a job. He or she then moves to the next product. There they do their job again. Different employees work on the product at each stage of manufacture. Large air conditioners, electric generators, locomotives, and aircraft are examples of products that are assembled in one spot. See Fig. 20-9.

people are needed, less skilled machine operators can run the equipment. They receive lower pay since they are less skilled. Also, the equipment can produce any number of like parts. Therefore, equipment is not idle as much.

Fig. 20-6. These cabinets are being produced in job lots. Note the stack of parts. (American Woodmark)

Fig. 20-7. A series of workers assemble a new toy. (Ohio Art Co.)

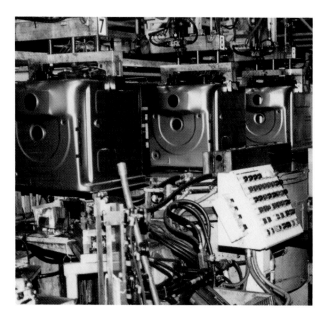

Fig. 20-8. Like these dishwasher cases, many products are moved from station to station during manufacture. (General Electric)

A new continuous system is now being used. It is called *flexible manufacturing*. This system uses computers to operate machines and material handling devices. These systems allow companies to produce small numbers of products using intermittent manufacturing techniques at continuous manufacturing costs.

Fig. 20-9. Large products may be assembled without being moved. Workers move to them to complete their jobs. (McDonnell Douglas)

Continuous manufacturing saves time. Since workers are trained to do one job, each becomes skilled in completing that one task, Fig. 20-10. Equipment is built or set up for a single operation. It is used over a long period of time.

Special tooling and trained workers waste less material. Also, equipment can be developed to perform routine tasks. Automatic equipment can spray finishes, machine parts, and weld assemblies, Fig. 20-11.

Fig. 20-10. This worker is trained to see defects in kitchen cabinets. (American Woodmark)

Fig. 20-11. This robot is automatically cutting a steel part. (Cincinnati Milacron)

	CUSTOM	INTERMITTENT	CONTINUOUS
Flexibility	High	←——————→	Low
Worker Skill	High	←——————→	Low
Unit Costs	High	←——————→	Low
Types of Machines	General	←——————→	Special
Equipment Cost	Low	←——————→	High
Use of Automation	Low	←——————→	High
Material Handling	Manual	←——————→	Automatic
Using of Tooling	Low	←——————→	High

Fig. 20-12. A comparison of manufacturing systems. As you can see, each has advantages.

SUMMARY

The system of manufacture is selected because of its nature. Custom manufacturing is suited for producing a few special products. Its cost of operation is high. A high degree of skill is required of workers in this type of manufacture.

Intermittent manufacture is used to produce set quantities of materials. The materials move through manufacture as a batch or lot. Materials measured by volume or weight, such as steel, are batch processed. Products that can be counted are processed in groups called job lots.

Continuous manufacture is generally the cheapest way to produce a product. However, a large quantity must be needed. Unsold products mean lost money.

The three major systems are compared in Fig. 20-12. These comparisons are general. They may not be true for all cases.

KEY WORDS

All of the following words have been used in this chapter. Do you know their meaning?

Batch processing
Continuous manufacturing
Custom manufacturing
Division of labor
Flexible manufacturing
Intermittent manufacturing
Job-lot manufacture
Tooling

TEST YOUR KNOWLEDGE

Please do not write in this text. Place your answers on a separate sheet of paper.

1. The three major manufacturing systems are:
   A. Assembly line manufacture.
   B. Custom manufacture.
   C. Job-lot manufacture.
   D. Batch processing.
   E. Intermittent manufacture.
   F. Continuous manufacture.

2. Describe each of the major manufacturing systems.

3. Suppose that you were employed in a factory where you received a part for a product at your work area in lots of a dozen. You made a saw cut in each part and then moved them to another person's station for different operation. What kind of manufacturing would you be doing?

4. If there is a steady and high demand for a product, what type of manufacture would normally be best?

ACTIVITIES

1. If you had an order for two book racks of the same design, which manufacturing system would you use? Which system would you use if your order was for 25 racks per month for two years?

2. Visit a local industry. Describe the manufacturing system being used.

CHAPTER 21
ENGINEERING MANUFACTURING FACILITIES

After studying this chapter, you will be able to:
☐ List the major engineering tasks in organizing a manufacturing operation.
☐ Describe how the manufacturing engineer performs these tasks.
☐ Demonstrate the use of forms such as the operation process chart and the flow process chart.

Manufacturing takes place in a factory. It is a carefully engineered facility. A factory's design and equipment permit efficient production.

Manufacturing engineers develop manufacturing facilities. They are responsible for five major tasks. These are shown in Fig. 21-1.

The tasks are important. They help the company produce its product at a *competitive price*. (This means it can be produced cheaply enough to sell at a price similar to like products on the market.)

SELECTING AND SEQUENCING OPERATIONS

Hiring good workers, buying materials at the right price, and getting the right kind of equipment all help a company compete with other manufacturers. However, these activities alone cannot do the job. The equipment and workers must be employed wisely. The work must be done in an orderly way. The right processes and machines must be used to shape and build the product.

Seeing to this is the job of plant engineering. The first task is called *selecting and sequencing operations*. Simply put, it means deciding what processes must be done (selecting) and putting them in the order that they must be done (sequencing). The *manufacturing engineer* is a person trained to this. She or he will use certain forms and methods to organize the manufacturing operations.

Operation Sheet

One of these forms is an operation sheet. Before she or he fills in the sheet, the manufacturing engineer must analyze (study parts to understand the whole) the product drawings. First the engineer decides what operations (processes) are needed to shape the product, Fig. 21-2. *Operations* are processes that shape the product. These processes are recorded on the *operation sheet*. This record gives the following information:
• Operation name.
• Machine to be used.
• Tooling needed.

Shaping of the product is not the only thing done during manufacture. Parts and whole products must be inspected. They are also moved from place to place. Sometimes they are held or delayed for

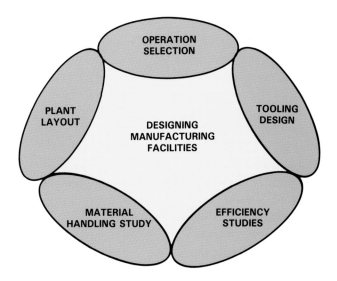

Fig. 21-1. These tasks are completed by manufacturing engineers in designing manufacturing facilities.

Engineering Manufacturing Facilities   183

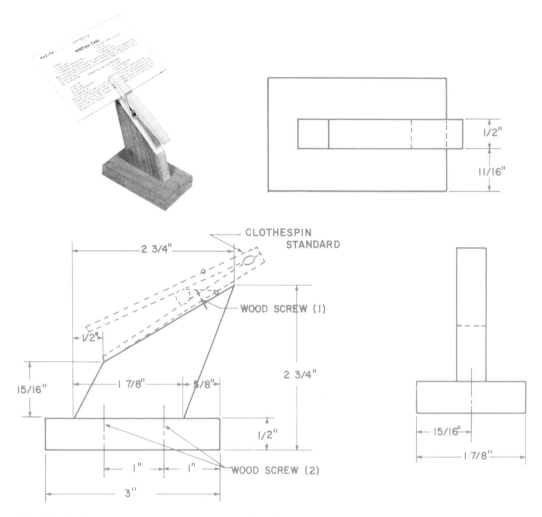

Fig. 21-2. An engineer must study a product's working drawings to determine the operations needed for making it.

further processing. Materials, parts, and finished products may even be stored for a while.

All of these actions must take place in orderly steps. These related tasks make up the total manufacturing process.

Placing tasks in logical order is done with two major forms. These are the:
- Flow process chart.
- Operation process chart.

Flow process chart

Look at the flow process chart in Fig. 21-3. It shows at a glance the sequence of tasks for producing a single part. (Sequence means the step-by-step arrangement of tasks to complete a part.)

A *flow process chart* often:
- Describes the tasks.
- Provides a code number for each task.
- Identifies the machines to be used.
- Lists tooling needed for the task.

A symbol identifies each task. These symbols are standard throughout industry. They were developed by the American Society of Mechanical Engineers (ASME). The five common flow chart symbols and their meanings are shown in Fig. 21-4.

The flow process chart lets engineers study the sequence of operations. It helps them find the best way to make a part, Fig. 21-5.

Operation process chart

A flow process chart is prepared for each part. The charts show how the individual parts are made. However, flow process charts do not let you view the whole system. The operation process chart does, Fig. 21-6.

It shows how each part is made. Then it shows how they are assembled into a product. The operation process chart also shows where operations and inspections fit into the sequence. Transportation, delay, and storage tasks are not included.

FLOW PROCESS CHART

PRODUCT NAME		FLOW BEGINS	FLOW ENDS	DATE
RECIPE HOLDER		Upright 0-1	Upright T-2	
PREPARED BY: A.B. COMBS			APPROVED BY: D.E. FRY	

PROCESS SYMBOLS AND NO. USED

◯ OPERATIONS __4__   ▢ INSPECTIONS __1__   ⬠ TRANSPORTATIONS __2__

⬭ DELAYS _____   ▽ STORAGES _____

Task No.	Process Symbols	Description of Task	Machine Required	Tooling Required
0-1	◯⬠▢⬭▽	Cut top angle	Back saw	Jig U-1
0-2	◯⬠▢⬭▽	Cut base angle	Back saw	Jig U-1
T-1	◯⬠▢⬭▽	Move to sanding		
0-3	◯⬠▢⬭▽	Face sand		
0-4	◯⬠▢⬭▽	Edge sand		
I-1	◯⬠▢⬭▽	Inspect		Gage I-1
T-2	◯⬠▢⬭▽	Move to assembly		

Fig. 21-3. The flow process chart for the upright part of the product shown in Fig. 21-2.

With the operation process chart the manufacturing engineer can analyze the overall manufacturing process. See Fig. 21-7.

The operation process chart is also used in scheduling production. It shows which parts must be

◯	Operation	Object is changed in its chemical or physical makeup; it is assembled (put together) or disassenbled (taken apart).
⬠	Transportation	Object is moved from one place to another.
▢	Inspection	Object is checked against quality standards.
⬭	Delay	Object is held for next operation.
▽	Storage	Object is placed in a protected location.

Fig. 21-4. A process flow chart uses symbols to indicate the type of manufacturing activity. Symbols save space and show process flow at a glance.

Fig. 21-5. Efficient production of parts like these computer chips can be studied with flow process charts. (Hewlett-Packard)

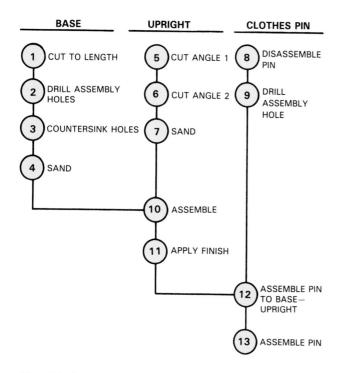

BASE	UPRIGHT	CLOTHES PIN

1 CUT TO LENGTH

2 DRILL ASSEMBLY HOLES

3 COUNTERSINK HOLES

4 SAND

5 CUT ANGLE 1

6 CUT ANGLE 2

7 SAND

8 DISASSEMBLE PIN

9 DRILL ASSEMBLY HOLE

10 ASSEMBLE

11 APPLY FINISH

12 ASSEMBLE PIN TO BASE— UPRIGHT

13 ASSEMBLE PIN

Fig. 21-6. This operation process chart was made for the recipe holder shown in Fig. 21-2.

finished first. Parts needed later may be produced later. This reduces the need to store some parts. The scheduling information is needed for a new manufacturing system: JIT (**Just In Time**). In this system each part is made or arrives at the plant "just in time" for assembly. The part does not have to be stored, thus reducing costs. The product is also made "just in time" to meet a customer's order.

Fig. 21-7. The total system of manufacture of products like these computer devices can be studied with an operation process chart. (Hewlett-Packard)

DESIGNING TOOLING

As you learned in a previous chapter, many operations cannot be done easily with standard machines. Often, special cutters are needed. In other cases, holders and clamps must be built. Sometimes a unique (one-of-a-kind) machine is required. At other times, molds and patterns must be made. All of these devices are called tooling.

Tooling helps the machine operator make parts better and faster. It reduces the number of machine adjustments. Tooling often fixes the position of the material. The part will be held, worked on, and released. Fig. 21-8 shows a worker stacking cabinet parts from a tooled-up operation. The machine feeds the wood automatically past shaped cutters.

Tooling is designed for three major purposes. For each operation, it should increase the:
- Speed.
- Accuracy.
- Safety.

Speed of manufacture increases when the operations run smoothly. The tooling can be designed to operate at a set speed.

The tooling in Fig. 21-9 is a good example. It moves the workpiece from station to station. Operators do not have to clamp, drill, and unclamp the part at each machining position.

Tooling also increases accuracy of the operations. Operators do not have to position materials. Lines and layout marks are not needed. Look at Fig. 21-9 again. Notice how each part is firmly held. The drill cannot help but produce a hole in the right spot.

Fig. 21-8. These cabinet parts are produced with the help of tooling. (American Woodmark)

Fig. 21-9. Tooling is used to increase the speed and accuracy of drilling operations. These vertical and horizontal CNC units can machine at either station, allowing for maximum cutting while parts are being loaded and unloaded in the alternate position. (Turmatic Systems, Inc.)

Finally, tooling increases safety. If the tooling holds the part, the operator's hands are out of the way and cannot be injured by the machine. Special devices may add more safety. Some machines will operate only when the operator holds switches with both hands, Fig. 21-10. Guards may come down. Straps may pull hands away from dangerous positions.

Well designed tooling helps people and machines produce accurate parts. Quality is improved. Scrap is reduced. In turn, production costs are lower.

PREPARING PLANT LAYOUT

Selecting operations and designing tooling is not all that manufacturing engineers do. They must also be concerned with *resource flow*. This means moving materials and people through the factory efficiently.

Workers need to get to their work stations easily. Movement to and from restrooms, cafeterias, and other support areas must also be considered. There must also be rapid movement out of the plant in case of fire, storm, earthquake, or accident.

All of these elements are considered in designing a factory. For good plant layout, manufacturing engineers must plan:
- Where to place machines.
- How to move material.
- Where to have aisles.
- Where to locate utility systems (electricity, water, gas, etc.).

There are two basic types of plant layouts: process layout and product layout.

Process Layout

Process layout groups machines by the process they perform. A furniture plant may group machines by the process they perform. Joint cutting machines may be grouped in one location, assembly operations in another place. All finishing equipment could be in still another spot.

Process layout is used for custom manufacturing. Also, many intermittent manufacturing plants use this system. These plants could produce a number of different products. Each product would have its own set of operations. Departments like machining, assembly, and finishing are created, Fig. 21-11.

Product Layout

Product layout places machines according to the sequence of operations. It is used in most continuous manufacturing plants. The machine needed for

Fig. 21-10. This machine will only close if the operator presses both switches at the same time. The orange boxes to each side of the press chamber produce a light beam that must be unbroken if the press is to operate. (Minster Machine Co.)

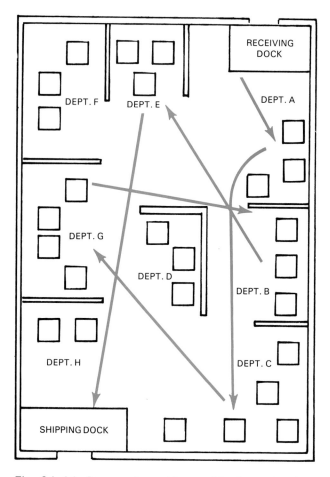

Fig. 21-11. Process layout is used for factories that make a number of different products. Each product is moved to different departments as needed for its manufacture.

the first operation is placed nearest the material storage area. The machine for the second operation is placed next, and so on, Fig. 21-12.

Communicating layouts

The manufacturing engineer puts his or her ideas about plant layout on paper or into a model. Plant engineers must be able to locate equipment in the correct places. Electrical power, air, water, and other utilities must be brought to where they are needed.

A drawing, Fig. 21-13, is one way of showing plant layout. The location of all equipment and features is shown in two dimensions.

In some cases, drawings are confusing. Lines showing different elements (machines, conveyors, utility lines) may cross. Overhead clearances are difficult to judge. To overcome these disadvantages, a model may be used, Fig. 21-14. All features are shown in three dimensions. Sizes are easier to judge. Clearance over aisles and under overhead conveyors are more visible.

Complex plant layout may use both drawings and models. Separate drawings may show equipment placement, utility runs, and conveyor locations. Models put all the features together. They provide a complete miniature view of the plant.

DESIGNING MATERIAL HANDLING SYSTEMS

The fourth part of a manufacturing system is a way to move materials. This is called *material handling.*

The materials must be moved from storage to the manufacturing area. During processing the material must be moved from work station to work station. Finally, finished parts and products must be moved into storage or to transportation (trucks, trains, ships, planes, etc.).

Material handling devices are of two major types: fixed path and variable (steerable) path.

Fixed Path Devices

Fixed path devices move a product from one fixed point to another. The item always travels on

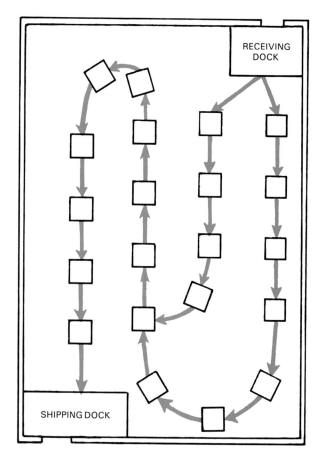

Fig. 21-12. Product layout uses the sequence of operations for a product to determine machine location.

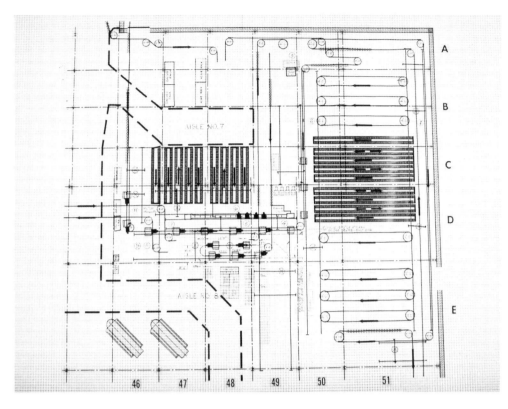

Fig. 21-13. A plant layout drawing shows equipment locations on a grid. (Oldsmobile)

the same path. It is like a train on railroad. Once it starts down a main line there is only one way to go. The train cannot decide to take a detour or make a turn.

Typical fixed path devices are conveyors, pipes, chutes, and elevators, Fig. 21-15. A new fixed path device is the "pick and place" robot, Fig. 21-16.

Variable Path Devices

Variable path devices can be steered. They can move in a number of directions. Common variable path devices are fork lifts, overhead cranes, tractors, and hand trucks. They require an operator to direct them, Fig. 21-17.

Fig. 21-14. A model of a plant layout uses blocks and parts that are scaled down to size. (Oldsmobile)

Fig. 21-15. These electronic components are moved from operation to operation by a conveyor. (GM Hughes)

Fig. 21-16. A ''pick and place'' robot is being tested for an assembly operation. It picks up a part in one location and delivers it to another. (Cincinnati Milacron)

Variable path robots generally follow wires buried in the floor. A computer can direct the robot to follow any path. Fig. 21-18 shows a robot vehicle. It can move through a 77 acre plant. Its path is directed by over 19,000 ft. of buried wire.

Variable path devices are used for two main purposes. They move materials and products in inter-mittent manufacturing plants. They also are used to load materials onto continuous manufacturing systems.

IMPROVING MANUFACTURING SYSTEMS

The last task of a manufacturing engineer is improving the manufacturing system. Like products, production lines can be improved. They can be

Fig. 21-17. A fork lift is being used to load logs at the start of a lumber manufacturing line.

Fig. 21-18. An automated guided vehicle. (FMC Corp.)

redesigned. Operations can be refined. New ones can replace older, inefficient ones. Better material flow can be introduced. New material handling devices can be installed. More efficient machines and tooling can be developed or purchased.

SUMMARY

Efficient manufacturing systems must be designed and engineered. This task is the responsibility of manufacturing engineers. They must select and sequence operations. Flow process and operation process charts are used.

Tooling is also designed. It includes special cutters, holding devices, molds, patterns, and machines. The tooling increases the speed, accuracy, and safety of operations.

The manufacturing plant must also be arranged for efficiency. Equipment is organized in process or product arrangements. The easy, safe flow of people and materials is always considered.

A material handling system is also needed. Materials, parts, and products must be moved through the factory. Fixed and variable path devices are used.

Finally, the system is always open for improvement. It is often redesigned and improved.

KEY WORDS

All of the following words have been used in this chapter. Do you know their meaning?

Competitive price
Flow process chart
Manufacturing engineer
Material handling
Operations
Operation sheet
Process layout
Product layout
Resource flow
Tooling

TEST YOUR KNOWLEDGE

Please do not write in this text. Place your answers on a separate sheet of paper.

1. What are the major engineering tasks?

Matching questions: Match the definition on the left with the correct term on the right.

2. _____ Selecting process tasks to be done and putting them in order they must be done.
3. _____ Person who organizes people and machines for efficient manufacture.
4. _____ Form listing operations, machine to use, and tooling needed.
5. _____ Shows at a glance the sequence of tasks for producing a single part.
6. _____ Movement of part through manufacture.
7. _____ Represented by a circle on the flow process chart.
8. _____ refers to special tools or devices which make manufacturing operations more efficient.
9. What does the term "resource flow" mean?
10. _____ layout groups machines by the process the machines perform.
11. _____ layout is used in most continuous manufacturing plants.
12. List and describe the two major material handling devices.

A. Operation sheet.
B. Flow process chart.
C. Manufacturing engineer.
D. Selecting and sequencing operations.
E. Transportation.
F. Operations task.

ACTIVITIES

1. Visit a manufacturing plant. Describe:
   A. Sequence of operations.
   B. Tooling being used.
   C. Type of layout used.
2. Prepare a flow process chart for a simple task such as washing a plate.
3. With a partner, design a piece of tooling for a drill press that will drill:
   A. One hole in the center of a 4″ × 4″ part.
   B. Two holes along a center line of a 2″ × 6″ part. The holes should be spaced 2″ apart.

People are the most important part of a manufacturing system.
(Hewlett-Packard)

CHAPTER 22

GETTING HUMAN AND MATERIAL RESOURCES

After studying this chapter, you will be able to:

☐ List steps for hiring workers and describe how hiring is done.

☐ List the six major steps for buying materials.

☐ Describe various personnel and materials forms and state their uses.

The product has been designed. Engineering drawings have been prepared. The product is approved for manufacture. The manufacturing facility has been engineered. Equipment is in place. Tooling has been built. Operations have been selected and sequenced. The material handling system is in place. Now what?

The product cannot be produced without more resources. Workers must be hired. Materials must be ordered. Securing these resources will complete the preparations for manufacture. Managers must employ workers and purchase materials.

EMPLOYING WORKERS

Employees are people hired to do a specific job. The company matches workers' abilities with its needs. Placing people in jobs is called *employment*. It requires the six major steps listed in Fig. 22-1.

Determining Needs

The employment or human ressources office must be told to hire a worker. Generally an employee requisition (request) form is prepared. This form tells the employment office:

• The job title.

• The skills required.

• The date the employee is needed.

Receiving a job requisition starts the employment process. It provides basic hiring information.

Recruiting Applicants

People must be found to fill job vacancies (openings). The employment office then begins to search for individuals who can do the job. This process is called *recruitment*.

There are four basic ways to recruit employees. These are shown in Fig. 22-2.

The technique used will vary with the job opening. General factory and office jobs may be filled by walk-ins. These are people who come to the company looking for a job. They seek out the company and the job.

Jobs requiring more skill are filled by other methods. These jobs may include managers, technical staff, and skilled operators. Recruiters may visit schools to interview prospective employees.

The company may advertise in newspapers and special technical magazines for trained people. They may also use employment agencies.

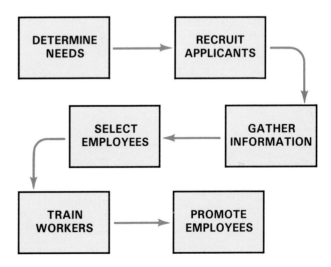

Fig. 22-1. Six steps are followed in the employment and advancement of workers.

Gathering Information

Employers need information about an applicant (person seeking a job). They will use the information to decide how well suited the applicant is for the job. These facts may be gathered in several ways, Fig. 22-3:

- Application blank. This is a form that provides basic personal data (facts) and work records.
- Interview. The applicant answers questions about his or her previous work experience, goals, and training.
- Test. An applicant takes a written or performance test to measure her or his ability to do the job.

Selecting Employees

It is in a company's best interest to choose the best applicant for each job. Information from the application blanks, interviews, and tests are used to arrive at the best choice. The best applicant is one who:

- Can do the job well.
- Will fit into the company.
- Is willing to accept training.
- Wants to advance (get ahead).

Suppose that the person selected is hired. What happens next? He or she will receive a job notice or an employment letter. It will tell the worker when to report for work. The job title and pay rate are included.

A

B

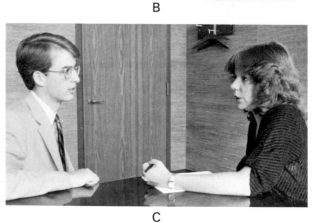

C

Fig. 22-3. Employment departments gather information about future employees using three methods. A—Application blank. B—Test. C—Interview. (Ball Corp.)

Fig. 22-2. These four methods may be used to recruit employees.

TRAINING EMPLOYEES

Few people can start a new job without some training. *Training* is the process of preparing workers to do their jobs. All newly hired workers need some basic information. They should learn something about the company itself. A knowledge of the company's products, competitors, and plant locations is also important. Basic rules about hours, pay rates, and work practices must be presented. This information is often given in an induction session for new employees.

They then receive any special training they need. Production workers may receive training through:

- On-the-job training. This is training at the work station. Actual products on the production line are used. A supervisor or another worker will do the training.
- Vestibule (off-line) training. This is training in a special training area. Workers produce actual products, too. However, the training location is away from the manufacturing line, Fig. 22-4. A special instructor is often used.
- *Apprenticeship*. Such work preparation combines on-the-job with classroom training, Fig. 22-5. This type is used to prepare skilled workers. An experienced worker provides the on-the-job training. Often the classroom instruction is provided by a special teacher.
- Cooperative education. The new worker gets training by attending school part-time and working part-time.

Fig. 22-5. These workers are receiving classroom training. (General Motors Corp.)

Employees also receive additional training during their working life. Individuals attend conferences and workshops. Special classes, Fig. 22-6, are offered. Employees are trained in new developments, methods, and equipment. This on-going employee development is essential for company growth.

ADVANCING

Employees often change jobs. They develop new skills and knowledge. They are given more responsibility. They advance to better jobs. These jobs are often more secure and pay higher wages.

Managers prefer workers who want to get ahead. Workers can show this by their willingness to accept new job and training opportunities.

Fig. 22-4. These workers are receiving training on new manufacturing equipment. (AC Rochester)

Fig. 22-6. Employees attend training on new technology. (Motoman, Inc.)

PURCHASING MATERIALS

Making products requires many parts and materials. Each of these may be bought. For example, raw materials must be purchased by steel mills. Their steel is bought by appliance manufacturers. Finished parts, like motors, are purchased by power tool manufacturers. Purchasing takes place at each step of manufacture, Fig. 22-7.

Purchasing brings suppliers and users together. This effort involves six major steps. These, shown in Fig. 22-8, are:
- Requisition (request) materials.
- Get bids or price quotes.
- Issue a purchase order.
- Receive shipment and invoice.
- Accept shipment.
- Pay for materials.

Each of these steps involves filling out forms. Paperwork records each activity. These forms are important for controlling purchasing activities. They ensure that the right material or equipment is ordered and received.

Material Requisition

The purchasing office buys materials when told what is needed. This may be done in a material requisition. This is a form that lists:
- The material needed.
- Quantity required.
- Date needed.
- Delivery location (plant, department, etc.).

Often production planners fill out the requisition form. It is their job to determine when material and human resources are needed.

Bids and Quotes

The purchasing staff must find out the cost of the requested materials. First, they must find suppliers (also called vendors). Then a request for a price is sent to each vendor selected.

The vendors submit their prices for the materials. Some prices must be guaranteed for a period of time. These are called *bids*. Other prices are current prices. They are the purchase price for that day. These prices are called *quotes*.

Purchase Orders

The purchasing staff reviews prices. They study the bids or quotes. Then they will choose the best

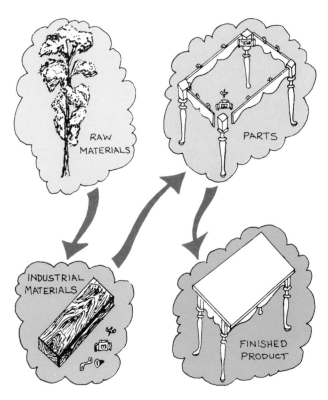

Fig. 22-7. Purchasing takes place at each step in manufacturing.

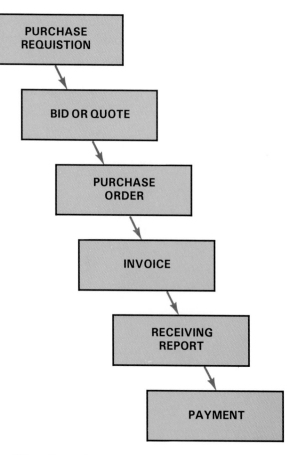

Fig. 22-8. Steps in the purchasing procedure. Filing of proper forms keeps track of each purchase.

supplier. The choice depends on several factors. These include:
- Price.
- Material quality.
- Delivery date.
- Vendor's reputation.

Then the purchasing people prepare a purchase order. It is sent to the selected vendor. The purchase order, Fig. 22-9, lists the quantity needed, material description, and price. It also tells where and when the order is to be sent.

The vendor signs a copy of the purchase order. This copy is returned to the company. The purchase order has become a legal, binding contract. The vendor must supply the materials. The purchaser must pay for them.

Invoice

When the ordered materials are shipped, a bill is also sent. This form is called an invoice, Fig. 22-10. The invoice indicates that:
- The order has been shipped.
- The company owes the vendor for the price of the materials.

Receiving Report

Often, materials ordered from one location are received in another. For example, an order may come from Detroit to deliver materials in Kansas City. The order and receipt of materials must be coordinated.

The receiving area receives, from Detroit, copies of the original purchase order. This tells the receiving area: "These items are ordered. Be ready to receive them." When the order arrives, Kansas City personnel check the shipment. They compare the purchase order with the materials received. They should match. If they do, Kansas City signs a copy of the purchase order. It becomes a receiving report that is sent to the purchasing office. The signed order tells purchasing officers in Detroit that the materials have arrived safely.

Payment

The receiving report and the invoice are compared. The materials and prices are checked. The invoice and the purchase order should match. If they do, the invoice is approved for payment. A check is written. The vendor is paid. The purchasing cycle is complete.

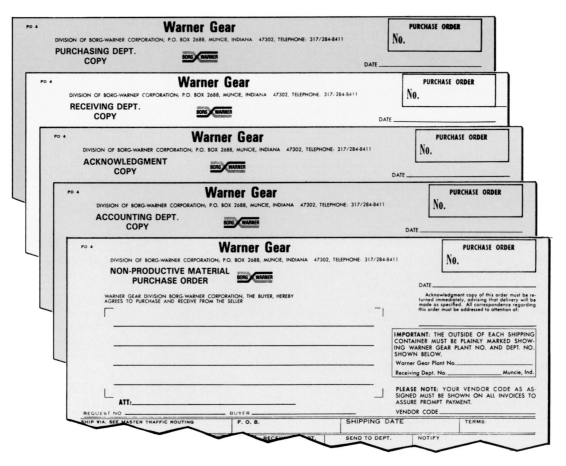

Fig. 22-9. Sample of a large company's purchase order. Note number of copies needed.

Fig. 22-10. A sample invoice. This is the bill that is included with delivery of an order. (Ball Corp.)

SUMMARY

Manufacturing depends upon human and material resources. People are hired to do work. Their abilities are matched with jobs. This is the task of employment. First the need for workers is determined. Then, applicants are recruited. Information about them is gathered and studied. The best applicants are hired. New employees receive training about the company and job. Sometime during their employment they are likely to receive additional training.

Materials for production are purchased. The best supplier is found. The material is ordered and received. The vendor receives payment for the materials. These tasks are the job of people in purchasing. They buy the correct materials at the correct price. They also see that they are received on time.

Obtaining the best human and material resources is very important. Qualified workers and managers are keys to success. Proper material must be on hand to produce quality products. Without these resources, a company will surely fail.

KEY WORDS

All of the following words have been used in this chapter. Do you know their meaning?
Apprenticeship
Employment
Purchasing
Recruitment
Training

TEST YOUR KNOWLEDGE

Please do not write in this text. Place your answers on a separate sheet of paper.

1. What are the major steps used to employ workers?

2. There are four basic ways workers can be recruited. Name them.
3. Which of the following are methods companies use to gather information about people looking for jobs with them?
    A. Have person demonstrate skills by giving them a test.
    B. Ask questions about their work experience, education, training, and goals.
    C. Have persons fill out a job application.
    D. All of the above.
    E. None of the above.
4. Training a person at an actual work station is called _____ _____ _____ training.
5. Apprenticeship training combines on-the-job training with special classes. True or false?
6. List the steps in a typical purchasing system.

ACTIVITIES

1. With a partner, design an application that could be used to gather information for job openings on your school newspaper (or other student position).
2. Brainstorm several questions to ask the applicant for the job in Activity 1. The questions should determine if the applicant can do the job well, will fit into the working environment, is willing to accept training, and wants to advance.
3. Role-play an interview between the supervisor and applicant for the position in Activity 1. Ask the questions you formulated in Activity 2.
4. Do some comparison shopping. Go to a store and choose an item, such as a CD-radio-cassette recorder. Compare the price, quality, stock availability, and manufacturer's reputation of three different models. Which do you think is the best purchase and why?

Control systems are needed for all types of activities, especially complex ones such as launching the space shuttle. (NASA)

CHAPTER 23

ESTABLISHING CONTROL SYSTEMS

After studying this chapter, you will be able to:
☐ Name the four phases involved in developing and using a resource control system.
☐ List the major resources used to manufacture a product.
☐ Discuss the three major factors that affect labor costs.
☐ Name and discuss the two tasks in a total quality control system.

Good managers know how to use resources to get the best results. Machines that the company owns must be used as much as possible. People need to be kept busy doing productive work. Materials should not be wasted. The word for this management task is *resource control.*

The outputs of the system must also be controlled. Waste, scrap, and pollution must be kept down. Product quality must be assured, too.

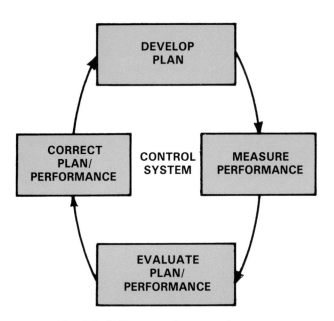

Fig. 23-1. Phases of a control system.

CONTROL SYSTEMS

As we can see, all manufacturing activities need controlling. They must be carefully managed. Managers develop control systems to do this. These systems, shown in Fig. 23-1, have four phases.

Planning Activities

There are two basic types of manufacturing plans: long-range and short-term. Long-range plans are usually three to five year projections (forecasts or guesses). They direct overall business activities. Long-range product development, marketing, and finance plans are common. Long-range plans are general in nature. They only give guidelines for policy decisions.

Short-term plans are more concrete (real). They outline performance goals (work to be done) for a set period. Short-term plans can be for a day, week, month, or year. They provide directions for daily activity.

Typical short-term plans include production schedules, budgets, and sales quotas. (A quota is a goal or amount to be done.) Goals guide day-to-day operations.

Manufacturing activities are guided by short-term plans. They include plans for using labor, materials, and machines. Also included are plans for controlling product quality.

Measuring Performance

Controlling requires measurement. The heat in your home is an example. Most houses have heating systems to keep them warm. Some homes also have air conditioning to cool them. These systems are controlled. Thermostats measure room temperatures and turn furnaces and air conditioners on and off.

Likewise, manufacturing activities are controlled. That is, their performance is measured. Some method is used to record the use of machines, labor, and material, Fig. 23-2. Records are kept of time worked, products produced, and material used. These measurements provide the basis for management decisions.

Evaluating Performance

Collecting data is not enough. To say, "It sure is hot today," is not very meaningful. "How hot is it?" compares today's temperature with some average and adds meaning. Maybe it is 10 degrees hotter than normal. This means more to us.

Manufacturing performance is also rated against some base. This base is often the company's plan. The number of products produced is measured against production plans. Scrap rates and rejected products are evaluated. Product quality, Fig. 23-3, and worker output (amount of work done) are always measured. Product function, reliability, and appearance are evaluated.

Corrective Action

Such measurement and evaluation often point out shortcomings. Performance may not live up to the plan. Then the company must correct the problems. Management must decide what action to take.

Fig. 23-2. The use of labor, material, and machines must be controlled. (Reynolds Metals)

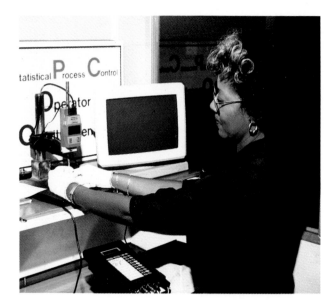

Fig. 23-3. This inspector is measuring the performance of automobile components. (AC Rochester)

A number of things could be done. Operations may need to be changed. Manufacturing engineers may redesign the task. The work station could be made more efficient. These actions could increase the worker's efficiency. Scrap rates could go down. Productivity could rise.

Materials may be changed. Another standard size could provide better cuts. The size of scrap at the ends of the material could be reduced. A different material may work better.

Whatever the corrective action, product quality must be maintained. Managers try to find the most efficient system to produce good products.

FACTORS TO CONTROL

Everything a company does is controlled. Sales are controlled. Raw material and finished goods inventories (stores) are controlled. Income and expenses are controlled. Control is the basis for success. Two major concerns of any company are: use of resources and quality of its products. These can be controlled.

Controlling Use of Resources

The major resources used to make products, Fig. 23-4, are:
- Human labor.
- Machine time.
- Materials.

These resources must be managed. They must be used efficiently.

Fig. 23-4. This worker is using a machine to form a steel part. The part, the machine, and the worker are resources of the company. (Cincinnati, Inc.)

Controlling human labor

Each job takes time to do. Thus, there is a labor cost for the job. This cost adds to the total product cost. Management must see that the labor cost stays within the plan's limits.

The actual labor cost is affected by several things. These include:
- How well the operations are planned.
- Worker efficiency. (How well the workers do their job).
- Wage rate paid to the workers.

Operations

These things can be changed through management action. The operations can be improved. Manufacturing engineers can study flow and operation process charts. Operations can be simplified and combined. Product design changes can do away with some assembly steps. New technology may make manufacturing more efficient. Any of these actions can reduce labor costs.

Worker efficiency

Operations can be studied from the worker's point of view. The task can be made more efficient. Machines can be modified (changed) to make them easier to use. Tooling can be improved. Machine controls can be located for greater convenience. The amount of reaching can be reduced by handier location of materials, Fig. 23-5.

Often, the efficient use of labor is improved by *automation*. Simple, routine jobs are given to machines, robots, and computers, Fig. 23-6. Depending on company policy, workers can be retrained and reassigned to more challenging jobs.

Wage rate

The final item in labor cost is *wage rates* (what the worker is paid). Generally, labor cost and worker skill are related. Difficult jobs require

Fig. 23-5. Note how the worker sits comfortably while working. All machine controls and parts are within easy reach. This is an efficient work station. (AC Rochester)

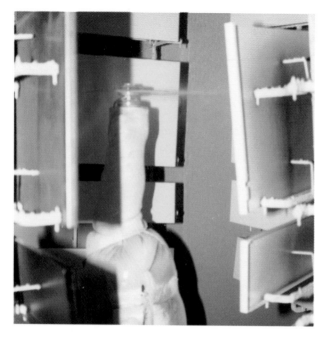

Fig. 23-6. This automatic spraying machine coats panels without putting a human operator at risk from paint fumes. (White Consolidated Industries)

skilled workers. Skills take time and ability to learn. This ability and training is rewarded with higher wage rates. Labor costs can be controlled by *deskilling* (making the job simpler).

The total skill of any operation, Fig. 23-7, includes:
• Skill built into the machine.
• Skill of the worker.

Manufacturing engineers always try to build skill into the machine. They can do this in several ways: better tooling, easier-to-use or self-adjusting controls. As a result, the operator needs less skill to run the machine. She or he can be hired at a cheaper wage.

Labor costs can only be controlled by studying results. Manufacturing information must be gathered.

Measuring labor

There are three major measurements used to control labor costs. These are:
• Time worked.
• Products produced.
• Productivity.

The simplest measure for labor is time worked. Everyday, employees record the times they start and end work. This time span is the workday. Often, a time clock and time card are used, Fig. 23-8. A *time clock* automatically prints the employee's starting and ending times on the card. At the end of the week, total time worked is added together.

Work completed at each station is another way to measure labor. This technique records quantities of work rather than time.

The time worked is important to the worker. Time is the basis for many people's pay. But, the number of good products made is the important measure for a company. Profits are made by

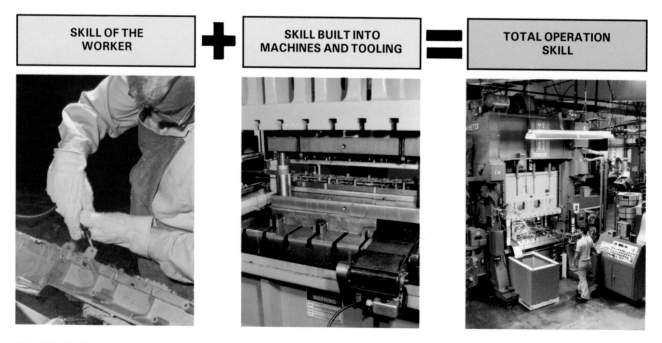

Fig. 23-7. The skill of the job equals the skill of the machine plus the skill of the operator. (ARO Corp., Minster Machine Co.)

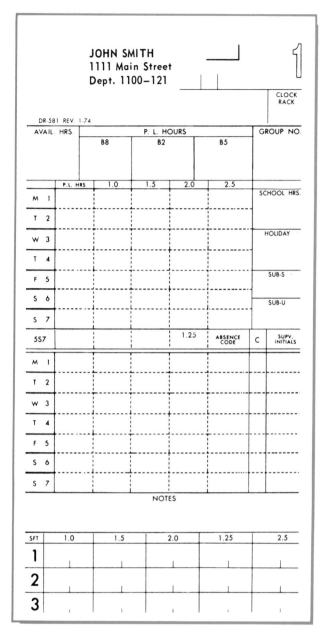

Fig. 23-8. A typical time card. When card is inserted into a time clock, time will be recorded.

Fig. 23-9. This worker is "punching" a job card. It records both the time she starts and completes a specific job. (ARO Corp.)

scheduled for use. Production planners must see that machines are not idle for long, Fig. 23-10. Similar operations should be scheduled on the same machine. This reduces set-up and tear-down times. Also, long runs should be scheduled whenever possible. Efficiency rises as the length of the run increases.

producing quality products. Production records, Fig. 23-9, are often kept. They will record the number of products produced. The time it took to produce them is also recorded.

The production and time data are the basis for the third measure of labor efficiency. It is called *productivity*. This is a measure of the output per unit of labor. Typically, it is measured in terms of products per worker hour (one person working one hour) or worker day (one person working one day).

Controlling machine time

Proper use of machines has an important effect on cost of production. Machines must be carefully

Fig. 23-10. This production planner schedules the use of machines in an intermittent manufacturing system. (AC Rochester)

Machine use can also be increased through careful operation design. All machine operations have at least three phases:
- Loading parts or materials into the machine.
- Processing the parts or materials.
- Unloading parts or materials from the machine.

Only the second phase is productive (makes products). It changes the form or shape of materials. The other phases contribute nothing to the form change. Loading and unloading time should be kept to a minimum.

At the same time, actual processing time should be studied. Correct machine speeds and feeds should be used. Drilling a hole at a speed slower than required is wasteful.

Controlling material use

The use of materials must be controlled. This activity is called *inventory* (materials on hand) *control*.

There are several materials that can be controlled. These, shown in Fig. 23-11, are:
- Raw materials–materials that will be processed during manufacture.
- Purchased parts–hardware and parts bought from other companies. They will become part of the product.
- Work-in-process–products that are being built but are not finished.

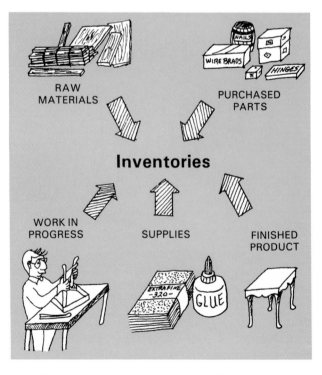

Fig. 23-11. Types of inventories. Companies keep careful records of these items.

- Finished products–completed products ready for shipment to customers.
- Supplies–materials, such as abrasives or paint, that are used up in the manufacture of the product.

These inventories are carefully kept. Often, computers are used to help keep the records. The record will list material by six categories:
- On order–items ordered but not yet received.
- Received–items received since the last update of the records.
- On hand–items in storage.
- Issued–items released from the stockroom to production or shipping.
- Allocated–items being held that are marked for production or shipping.
- Available–items in inventory that are available for use.

These records allow inventory control workers to keep track of material use. Also, the materials used can be compared with products produced. This will allow the manager to find areas of waste or theft.

Controlling Quality

Quality is important to everyone. Customers want products that work. Retailers want to sell good products.

Manufacturers also want quality. Returned products cost money to process. Sales can be lost by creating dissatisfied customers.

Quality is *everybody's* business. Every stage in manufacturing must be concerned with quality. Products must be designed with quality in mind. Facilities (space and equipment) must be engineered to turn out quality. Training programs must stress quality. Customer service must be alert to quality problems.

The success of a company will depend on its image. It must be seen by customers as a quality manufacturer.

The key to producing a quality product is *quality control*. It ensures that the product meets standards. This function of a company has two tasks. These are seen in Fig. 23-12:
- Motivating workers to produce quality products.
- Inspecting products to remove substandard items.

Motivation

Humans generally do what they think is important. For many years, production was emphasized by companies. Numbers of products manufactured was stressed. Quality was important, but took a back seat.

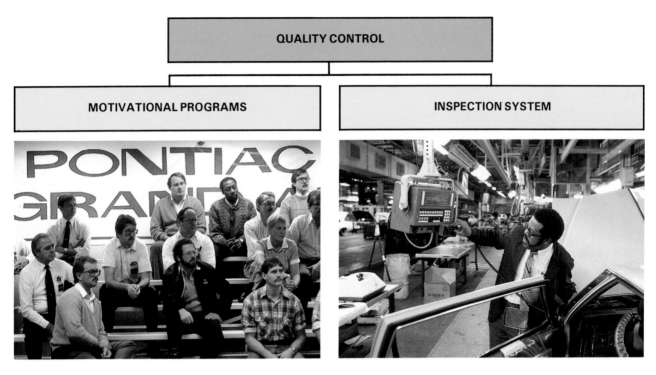

QUALITY CONTROL	
MOTIVATIONAL PROGRAMS	INSPECTION SYSTEM

Fig. 23-12. Quality control programs have two functions: motivation and inspection. (General Motors)

Workers reacted as expected. They produced products. Not all of them were good. But times have changed. Quality is now very important. It is in the "driver's seat." A number of programs have been developed to encourage quality. A few years ago "zero defects" was popular. Slogans, badges, and banners, Fig. 23-13, encouraged workers to produce good products. These programs were developed by managers. They talked to the workers.

These programs had mixed success. Many workers did not believe their work was important. To them, quality was just a slogan. Foreign competition has changed workers' minds. The automotive and steel industries were seriously hurt by the image of poor quality.

Now workers are asked to help improve manufacturing systems. They are invited to join *quality circles* and "quality of work life circles." These are voluntary groups that meet often. They discuss ways to improve the company and its operations, Fig. 23-14. New production methods, management activities, and other ideas are discussed.

The goal of quality circles is to improve quality of both products and work life. Workers who join these groups tend to feel they are important. They can help the company improve and compete. Also,

Fig. 23-13. Posters are used to encourage quality production. (ARO Corp.)

Fig. 23-14. These workers take time from their work to discuss ways to improve the company. (Brush-Wellman)

they have a better understanding of the importance of their job. They talk over problems with people in management.

Inspection

An old joke, known as "Murphy's Law," suggests that "if something can go wrong, it will." Of course this is not exactly true. But no person or machine is perfect. Either can produce a poor product or a bad part. Items are sometimes built that fail to meet standards. These items must be taken out of the manufacturing line. This is the responsibility of *inspection*.

Inspectors ensure that only quality products leave the plant. They check:
- Materials entering the plant.
- Purchased parts.
- Work-in-progress.
- Finished products.

Each of these items are compared with engineering standards, Fig. 23-15. They are often tagged to indicate the condition. Good items receive an "accepted" tag. Other parts are marked for either rework or scrap. A *rework* corrects defects. Parts are then inspected again before they leave the plant.

Inspectors also prepare inspection reports, Fig. 23-16. They report on their activity for a set period of time (hourly, daily, etc.). They record the number of parts:
- Inspected.
- Accepted.
- Rejected and the reason.

Fig. 23-16. The inspector enters inspection data into a computer. The computer will prepare an inspection report. (Whirlpool Co.)

This information will identify problems in the manufacturing system. Managers can then take proper corrective action.

SUMMARY

Resources must be used wisely. Materials must not be wasted. Machines must be used efficiently. People need to be assigned to appropriate work. They must be busy producing products. Production planners must schedule the use of these resources. They then need to evaluate their use.

Product quality must also be maintained. Employees need to understand their importance. Each worker should know that his or her job contributes to quality products. Everyone must be motivated to produce good products.

In addition, inspection activities must remove defective items. Materials and purchased parts must meet standards. The product must also meet standards. It must be inspected to ensure quality. Only through control of resources and quality can a company compete.

KEY WORDS

All of the following words have been used in this chapter. Do you know their meaning?
Automation
Deskilling

Fig. 23-15. This computerized inspection system checks automobile engines before they are installed. (Ford Motor Co.)

Inspection
Inventory control
Productivity
Quality circle
Quality control
Resource control
Rework
Time clock
Wage rates

TEST YOUR KNOWLEDGE

Please do not write in this text. Place your answers on a separate sheet of paper.

1. List the four phases in developing and using a control system.
2. The number of products or parts spoiled during manufacture is called the _____ _____.
3. Which three of the following are resources for making a product?
   A. The building that houses the factory.
   B. The workers' labor.
   C. Machine time.
   D. Materials.
   E. Capital (money for running business).
4. List the three factors (things) that affect labor costs.
5. Making an operation easier to perform to lower a wage rate is known as _____.
6. Industry uses three methods to measure labor costs. Indicate which of the following are included:
   A. Quality of the work.
   B. Time worked.
   C. Productivity.
   D. Number of products produced.
   E. Number of rest periods in a day.
7. Products that are being built are known as _____.

Matching questions: Match the definition on the left with the correct term on the right.

8. _____ Items in inventory available for use.
9. _____ Items being held in inventory that are marked for production or shipping.
10. _____ Items released from stockroom to production or shipping.
11. _____ Items in storage.
12. _____ Items ordered but not received.

   A. On order.
   B. Issued.
   C. On hand.
   D. Available.
   E. Allocated.

13. List the two tasks in a total quality control.
14. Indicate which of the following materials are checked by quality control inspectors:
   A. Materials coming into the factories.
   B. All parts purchased from other factories.
   C. Work in progress.
   D. Finished products.
   E. All of the above.
   F. None of the above.

ACTIVITIES

1. Design a poster to encourage quality work.
2. You have decided to manufacture track hurdles. What are the various elements that you will have to control? How would you control them?
3. With a partner, develop an inspection gage to determine if a board is 3/4″ (±1/32″) thick.
4. With a partner, develop an inspection gage to determine the location of a hole in the center of a 4″ × 4″ block. The hole should be within ±1/32″ of the center.

MANUFACTURING THE PRODUCT

CHAPTER 24

PRODUCING PRODUCTS

After studying this chapter, you will be able to:
☐ List and explain the three major steps in production.
☐ Define technical terms used in controlling production.
☐ Describe, in general terms, the method and sequence used in managing production.

Finally, when the manufacturing system is ready, actual production can begin.

Manufacture of products involves three major steps. These, shown in Fig. 24-1, are:
1. Scheduling production.
2. Producing products.
3. Controlling production.

SCHEDULING PRODUCTION

Scheduling production means organizing a manufacturing production line so products or parts are produced on time. It must be done efficiently: high quality products made with the least use of time and materials.

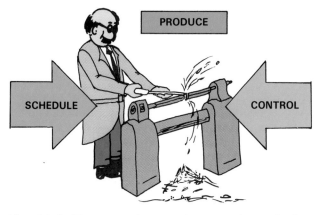

Fig. 24-1. There are three major steps in producing products.

People who do this kind of work are called **production planners.** To plan properly they must know:
• The number of parts or products that must be built.
• The deadline (when the parts and products must be ready).
Using this information, they organize the workforce, equipment, and materials to do the job.

Production Planning

The work of a production planner can be grouped into four parts:
• *Routing*–determining the production path for each product going through the plant.
• *Scheduling*–deciding when each production activity will take place and when it will be finished.
• *Dispatching*–giving orders for completing the scheduled tasks.
• *Expediting* (follow-up)–ensuring that the work stays on schedule.

Routing and scheduling

Routing is determined by the operations needed to make the product. If the part needs sawing, drilling, and sanding, it will be routed in that order to the saw, drill, and sander.

Routing is done using flow and operation process charts. You will recall that these charts were shown in Chapter 21. They outline the sequence (order) for making each part and product.

Since the purpose of scheduling is to have enough of the product at a certain time, planners must know how much product is needed. Using this information, they will set levels of production. (This is the amount of product that must be made in

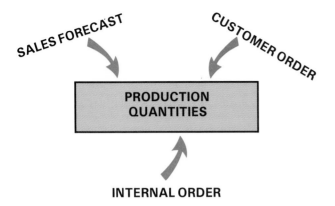

Fig. 24-2. Production levels (amounts) are set from orders or forecasts.

Fig. 24-3. Production scheduling insures efficient use of human, capital, and material resources. (Goodyear Tire and Rubber Co.)

a certain time period.) The schedule can be set up for a day, week, or month.

Planners never guess at how much product is needed. This information is gathered from three sources. As shown in Fig. 24-2, the sources include:

- *Forecasts* of needs. Forecasts are management's estimates of demand for products.
- Customer orders. These are sales orders from other enterprises such as stores.
- Internal orders (shop or stock orders). These are orders to produce parts or products that will be used by the enterprise itself.

Some companies produce products only when they have orders for them. Major industrial and military equipment are first sold. They are then manufactured. Aircraft, locomotives, and transit buses are also produced *after* being sold.

Other companies build to forecast. They first estimate their sales. Then, products are produced to the forecast. High-volume consumer goods are

examples of items produced using this technique. Television sets, jeans, and toothpaste are manufactured to forecast.

Many manufacturing plants produce parts and products for internal use. Automotive engines, bumpers, and alternators are produced in separate plants. They are then shipped to an assembly plant. At the plant these and other products are made into automobiles.

All of these activities must be scheduled so parts will be ready when needed. See Fig. 24-3. Quantities of products needed are written on a form like the one in Fig. 24-4.

Production schedules must consider *lead time*, Fig. 24-5. This is the time needed to get a product or

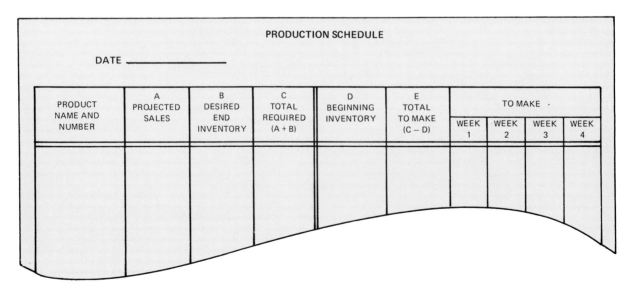

Fig. 24-4. Sample production schedule form.

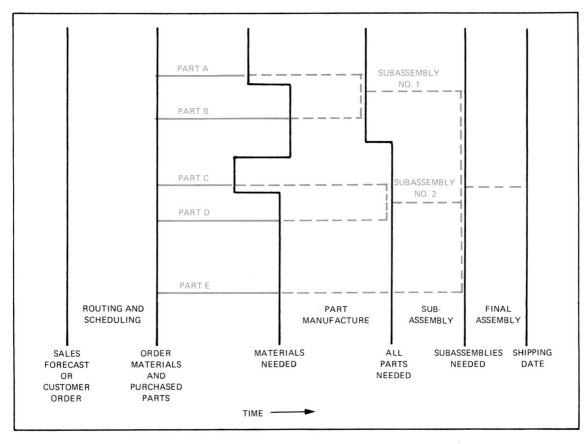

Fig. 24-5. A lead time diagram shows major tasks to be done. Spaces between vertical lines represent periods of time. They could be days, weeks, or months. Such a diagram tells a manager when to order materials and assign tasks.

part made. Not all parts take the same time to make. Parts are needed at different times. All these things affect the production schedule. Production scheduling is very important in manufacturing.

PRODUCING PRODUCTS

Once developed, the schedules are given to the production supervisors. These managers assign workers to complete specific tasks. They must also supervise and motivate the workers.

Line management must see that products are produced on time. This involves:
- Getting all parts manufactured.
- Making subassemblies.
- Making final assembly.

Pilot Run

Often, a production system is tried out to see if it works. The system is tested before full manufacture starts. This test is called a *pilot run*. It is designed to "debug" (correct) the system. The line runs for a short time. A few products are produced and evalu-

ated. Design errors are caught. Corrections can be made before high-volume manufacture starts.

The pilot run can turn up a number of problems. These could cause changes to be made in the:
- Product design.
- Tooling.
- Materials used.
- Plant layout.
- Material handling systems.
- Type and sequence of operations.

Full production starts after the pilot run. Various parts are put together into subassemblies. Various assemblies make up the final product. Look at Fig. 24-6.

CONTROLLING PRODUCTION

Once production is started it must be checked often for problems. This activity is called control.

Three basic types of data (information) are important for controlling production. These are:
- Product output data.
- Quality control data.
- Labor utilization (use) data.

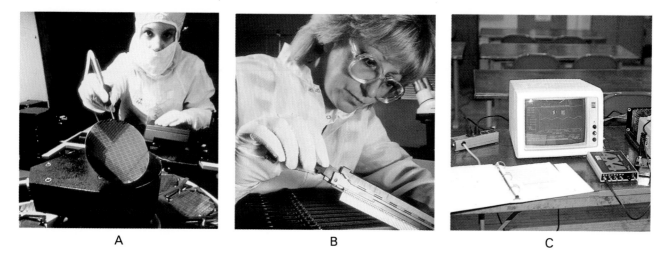

Fig. 24-6. Product manufacture involves making parts, putting together subassemblies, and assembling final products. A–This worker is making computer chips. B–The chips will become part of an electronic circuit. C–The circuit is used in a computer. (IBM)

Product Output Data

A production department schedules levels of product manufacture. Each plant, department, and worker is expected to complete certain tasks on time.

During manufacture, production data is collected. Various reports are prepared to tell whether production schedules are being met.

A production record may be kept for each worker. These records are often summarized on departmental production reports, Fig. 24-7. The plant manager will review each department report. Then she or he prepares a plant production report. This report usually goes to the corporate office.

Daily production reports show areas needing corrective action (change in plan). Overtime can be scheduled to keep from falling behind. More work-ers may be hired. New equipment or tooling may be installed. Training and motivational (reason to work harder) programs can be used.

Production reports are not just a record of what happened. They are also a record for future action.

Quality Control Data

Success or failure in producing quality products is shown by quality control reports. These reports tell about three major activities:
- Receiving material.
- Processing materials.
- Testing final products.

Inspecting materials

Since quality starts with good materials, inspectors must check incoming stock, Fig. 24-8. If the

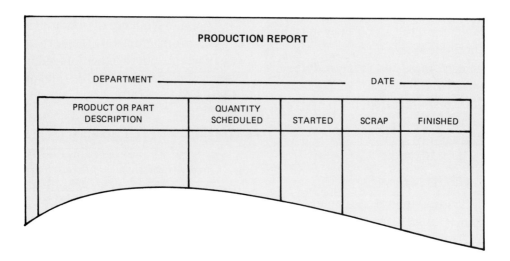

Fig. 24-7. A typical daily production report form.

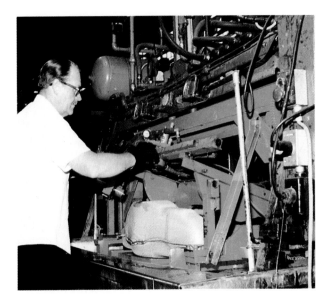

Fig. 24-8. This inspector is using a water test to check fuel tanks for leaks. (AC Rochester)

material fails to meet standards, the product will also fail. Each batch of material is inspected (compared to a set standard). The inspectors report all rejected material, Fig. 24-9.

Work-in-process inspection

As materials are processed they are inspected at various stages, Fig. 24-10. Work-in-process is divided into:

- Rejects–items failing to meet standards. These items cannot be repaired.

- Rework–items failing to meet standards. These items can be repaired.
- Accepted–items that meet standards.

The results of these inspections are reported to management, Fig. 24-11. The data will be used to decide what corrective action to take. The errors are first studied to see why they happened. The reject can be caused by:

- Material defects.
- Machine error.
- An operator making a mistake.

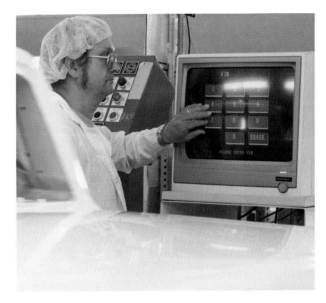

Fig. 24-10. This inspector is checking the quality of the paint finish on this automobile. (Chrysler Corp.)

MATERIAL REJECTION FORM

QUANTITY _____ DATE _____

DESCRIPTION _____

SUPPLIER _____

REASON FOR REJECTION:

AUTHORIZED BY: _____

Fig. 24-9. This type of form can be used to report rejected materials and purchased parts.

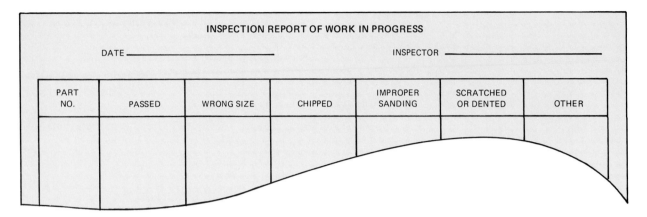

			INSPECTION REPORT OF WORK IN PROGRESS			
DATE				INSPECTOR		
PART NO.	PASSED	WRONG SIZE	CHIPPED	IMPROPER SANDING	SCRATCHED OR DENTED	OTHER

Fig. 24-11. An inspection report such as this one is used for work-in-process. Such reports will help managers decide what corrective actions need to be taken.

Material defects can be corrected by better material inspection. Machines and tooling can be adjusted to reduce machine error. Workers may need more training or supervision.

Product inspection

Final products must meet quality standards, Fig. 24-12. Some products may be visually (by eye) inspected. Their overall appearance may be checked. Other products are inspected by machines. Their size and performance may be checked. These tests are called nondestructive. Products are not damaged during such an inspection.

Some products, however, undergo destructive testing. A sample product is destroyed as it is checked. It may be operated until it breaks. Some parts are cut apart to check welds and other features. Other products are dropped to check durability.

Products that pass inspection are so marked. An "OK" may be stamped on them. Or a sheet saying "Inspected by _____ _____" may be placed in a pocket. The customer is thus shown that the product met company standards.

Labor Data

Workers expect to be paid for their work. Therefore, records for pay purposes are kept. The type of records maintained depends upon the pay system. The two basic systems are:

- Standard pay systems–workers are paid for time spent on the job.
- Incentive pay systems–workers receive a base pay for time worked. The company may pay a bonus for production beyond a set number of units called a quota. Workers are encouraged to be more productive. They receive additional pay for extra production.

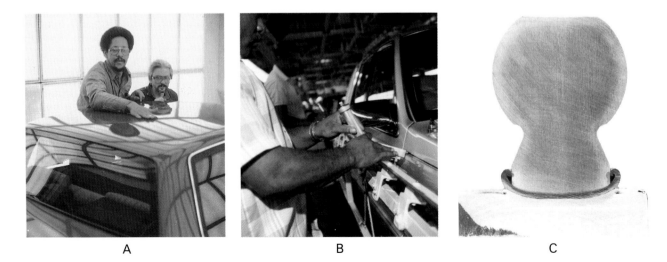

Fig. 24-12. Finished goods are inspected in many ways. A–Visually. B–A machine guides a striping applicator on a car. The striping will be checked visually later. C–Destructive testing. (GM, Chrysler, Caterpillar)

Standard pay systems generally require the worker to keep a time card. A time clock is used to automatically record starting and quitting times.

Incentive systems use time cards and production records. The workers' starting and ending times are recorded. Also, the output of each worker is recorded. Any reject parts produced are subtracted from the output. The result is then used to calculate the worker's pay.

For example, a worker may work for eight hours. The base production rate may be 300 parts per day. The worker produced 325 parts. Five of these were rejects. The worker receives pay for eight hours work. He or she also receives a bonus for producing 20 extra good parts.

Labor records are used to determine pay checks for each pay period. Hourly employees (paid by the hours worked) commonly receive a pay check each week.

SUMMARY

Products must be produced efficiently for a company to make money. This production must be scheduled, carried out, and controlled.

Production levels are set to match known or expected sales. They are based on orders or forecasts. People, machines, and materials are scheduled to meet production goals.

Parts, subassemblies, and products are manufactured. The output is controlled. The numbers produced are compared to the schedules.

Data is gathered to measure the success of the manufacturing activity. Product output, quality control, and labor utilization (use) information is kept. Reports are prepared. Corrective action is taken to keep the activities on schedule.

KEY WORDS

All of the following words have been used in this chapter. Do you know their meaning?
Dispatching
Expediting
Forecast
Lead time
Pilot run
Production planners
Routing
Scheduling

TEST YOUR KNOWLEDGE

Please do not write in this text. Place your answers on a separate sheet of paper.
1. What three steps are involved in manufacture of products?
2. One who schedules production is concerned with three major tasks. Indicate which of the following are included:
   A. Deciding how many of a product to make.
   B. Calculating how much the product will cost.
   C. Indicating when the parts/products will be built.
   D. Telling what numbers of workers, equipment, and amounts of materials are needed to produce the product or parts.
   E. Determining how much workers should be paid.
3. _____ is determining the path of production for each part or product as it moves through the plant.
4. What are internal orders?
5. Lead time is the amount of time it takes to produce a part once it is ordered. True or false?
6. Indicate what changes can be brought about after a pilot run.
7. Quality of the product is the responsibility of those who (schedule, control) production.
8. List the defects or errors that may cause a part to be rejected.

ACTIVITIES

1. In a team, develop a plan for and produce five kites. Keep a daily production report form.
2. Read a "how-to" book or follow a set of instructions that teach you how to make something you have never made before.
3. Help a child learn to do something. What incentives are there for doing things besides earning money?

Safety is important whether you work on the factory floor or in a laboratory. Always think and work safely. (Inland Steel)

CHAPTER **25**

MAINTAINING SAFETY

After studying this chapter, you will be able to:
- ☐ Give reasons why safety on the job is important to yourself and the company.
- ☐ List and discuss the four major phases of a safety program.
- ☐ List four steps in proper job safety training.

Both the company and the employees suffer when accidents happen. Injured employees suffer physical pain. They may lose income. Their insurance benefits may not cover all their expenses.

Through accidents, companies can lose the services of valuable employees. They cannot use the employees' special skills and knowledge for a period of time. The company will also lose money.

Insurance rates are based on accident history. The more accidents a company has the higher their rates will be.

THE SAFETY PROGRAM

Modern companies have well-designed safety programs. These programs start with the new worker. They continue throughout the employee's working life, Fig. 25-1.

These safety programs contain five major phases. The phases are shown in Fig. 25-2.

Safety Engineering

Some jobs are safer than others. The person with a desk job is relatively safe. A person operating a forging press is more likely to get hurt, Fig. 25-3.

Safety engineering designs processes and machines to be safer. Equipment can be engineered to be safely operated, Fig. 25-4. *Hazards* (sources of danger) can be designed out of a process. Guards can be placed over cutter heads and saw blades. Controls can be placed in convenient locations. Emergency stop switches can be located within easy reach.

Tooling can also be designed to be safe, Fig. 25-5. Small parts may be held by clamps. Parts may be

Fig. 25-1. The safety program continues through the work-life of the employee.

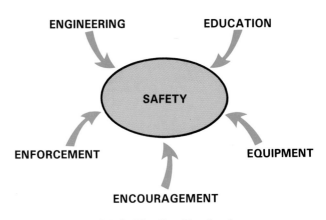

Fig. 25-2. The five Es of safety.

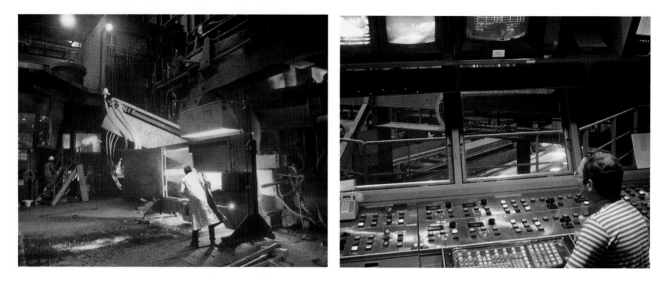

Fig. 25-3. Look at these two photos. Which job is most dangerous? Why?
(American Iron and Steel Institute)

guided safely into cutters. The worker's hands are kept away from tools and dies.

Workers may be removed from very dangerous operations. Mechanical devices may be engineered to do the job instead. Robots, Fig. 25-6, do many dangerous jobs. They are often used to load punch presses, do welding, and apply finishes.

Safety Education

Workers must be educated about safety. They must be taught its importance. Companies hold periodic meetings to discuss these concepts.

A worker must receive careful safety instruction for his or her assigned job. This instruction includes four steps. Look at Fig. 25-7.

The trainer never assumes a person knows how to do the job safely. Each worker should receive complete instructions on safe practices.

Safety Equipment

During training, the worker should be taught about required *safety equipment*. The need for personal protection is important. Each job has its own equipment requirements. Special protection

Fig. 25-4. These high speed metal stamping presses are designed with safety in mind. Note the doors in front of the ram. Also, the controls are on the stand to the right. The operator is a safe distance away from the actual press operation. (American Metal Stamping Assn.)

devices may be provided. Safety equipment protects the worker's sight, hearing, lungs, and skin.

Look at Fig. 25-8. Note that the worker is wearing:
- Dark goggles to protect the eyes.
- Hearing protectors.
- A face shield.
- Leather gloves.
- Long sleeves.
- A hard hat.

Encouragement

Working safely is a habit. It is developed over time. Therefore, workers must be encouraged to work safely.

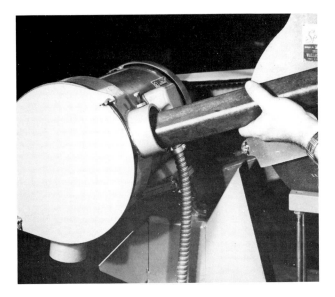

Fig. 25-5. This grinding jig guides the work and protects the worker. (Wallace Supplies Mfg. Co.)

Fig. 25-6. Robots such as this one are capable of doing very dangerous operations. When robots are used humans do not have to be exposed to dangerous environments. (Cincinnati Milacron)

Most large companies have an ongoing safety program. Posters remind workers to work safely. Company newsletters will have articles on safety. Signs will announce the number of days worked without an accident. Safe workers may win special recognition. Often, safety awards, Fig. 25-9, will be given to individuals or departments.

Employees should also be encouraged to report unsafe conditions. Alert workers can always see

Fig. 25-7. The steps in educating workers in job safety.

Fig. 25-8. This worker is wearing appropriate safety protection. (ESB Corp.)

ways to improve operations. They should be encouraged to share their ideas.

Enforcement

Everyone tends to become careless over time. We start to take chances. We drive too fast or run yellow lights. The Police will remind us that this is wrong. They give us a traffic ticket.

The same is true about safety. Workers often have jobs where they must do the same task over and over again. The job becomes routine. Boredom can creep in. With boredom comes carelessness.

Enforcement is making sure that workers follow safety rules. An alert supervisor will remind workers of careless acts. All workers must be required to work safely. Unsafe workers are a hazard (danger). They can hurt themselves and others.

The unsafe worker, like the unsafe driver, may need to be disciplined. She or he must be made to understand that unsafe practices will not be allowed.

SUMMARY

Safety is everybody's job. Employees must be provided a safe work environment. The operations must be engineered to be safe. Proper safety education and equipment must be provided. All workers must be encouraged to work safely. Finally, safety rules must be constantly enforced.

KEY WORDS

All of the following words have been used in this chapter. Do you know their meaning?

Enforcement
Hazard
Safety engineering
Safety equipment

Fig. 25-9. This employee is receiving a special safety award. (National Safety Council)

TEST YOUR KNOWLEDGE

Please do not write in this text. Place your answers on a separate sheet of paper.

1. List and discuss the four major phases of a safety program.
2. What are the four steps in proper job safety training?

ACTIVITIES

1. Design a safety poster that warns of a safety hazard in the home, school, or shop.
2. Make a videotape of bicycle safety.
3. Design a safety device for a machine in your laboratory.
4. Use the Internet to discover the types of workplace hazards regulated by the Occupational Safety and Health Act (OSHA).
5. Write instructions for the safe handling of a tool, equipment, or substance.

Using proper safety equipment is very important. This worker is wearing safety glasses, a respirator, and a lab coat. The tool he is using also collects any dust generated by cutting. (Nilfisk of America)

Unions hold national conventions periodically, such as this one of the United Steelworkers of America. (Dave Rentz, USWA)

CHAPTER 26

WORKING WITH LABOR UNIONS

After studying this chapter, you will be able to:

☐ Explain the purpose of a labor union and tell why workers would want to belong to one.

☐ List the legal steps in forming a union.

☐ List the officers of a union and describe their duties.

☐ Explain the procedures for negotiation of a new contract between a union and a company.

☐ Define a contract and outline the elements in a typical contract.

Workers often feel they have no way to assert their rights and to express their ideas to their bosses. Individual employees feel alone and powerless in dealing with management.

These feelings are the reason workers join together in labor unions. Workers want to get together to promote their rights. They form a union to be officially heard, Fig. 26-1. The *union* is a legal (has rights by law) organization that represents the workers' interests.

The National Labor Relations Act of 1935 (also called the Wagner Act) provided workers a way to be heard. It guaranteed the rights of employees:

• To organize and join a union of their choice.

• To bargain collectively (as one voice) with their employer.

ORGANIZING A UNION

Organizing a union takes several steps. The actual activities will vary from union to union. They will also be different from company to company. The six most common organizing activities, Fig. 26-2, are:

• Forming a plant committee, Fig. 26-3. The union organizers meet with workers who want a union. The organizers work for a national union. They

cannot come into the plant to organize the union. However, workers can promote it during non-working time. The plant committee is a group of workers who want to form the union. They coordinate (bring order to) the organizing effort within the plant.

• Developing a program to promote the union. Not all workers are aware of the union activities. Some do not understand the issues. Others may not want a union. Much like political candidates looking for votes, union organizers try to convince workers that they will be better off if they vote for and join the union.

Fig. 26-1. Union organizers help workers establish a union. (United Steelworkers of America)

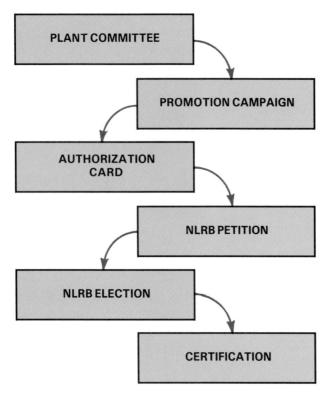

PLANT COMMITTEE

PROMOTION CAMPAIGN

AUTHORIZATION CARD

NLRB PETITION

NLRB ELECTION

CERTIFICATION

Fig. 26-2. These are the most common steps in forming a union.

Promoting the union is done in a number of ways.
- Holding meetings to explain how they work.
- Passing out literature after work, Fig. 26-4.
- Setting up large group meetings and rallies.

- Getting *authorization cards* signed. The plant committee wants a card from each worker, Fig. 26-5. This card lets the union represent the employee. It gives your bargaining rights to the union. The National Labor Relations Act requires authorization cards from 30 percent of the workers. If these are obtained, the union asks management to accept the union. Generally, management will not recognize a union at this point.
- Submitting an *NLRB* (**N**ational **L**abor **R**elations **B**oard) petition. This is a request for an election. The board makes certain that the union has met all legal requirements. If it has, a date for elections is set.
- Holding an NLRB supervised election, Fig. 26-6. All workers who will be eligible to join the union can vote. However, they are not required to do so. If most workers choose the union, it wins.
- Making the union the official bargaining agent for the workers. This is called *certification*. Management must now recognize the union. The two must meet and set pay rates, hours, and working conditions.

ORGANIZING A LOCAL

Most national unions are made up of a number of "locals." These are local chapters (groups) of the

Fig. 26-3. Union organizers select a plant committee to coordinate the organizing activities.
(United Steelworkers of America)

Fig. 26-4. Union organizers pass out leaflets promoting the union.

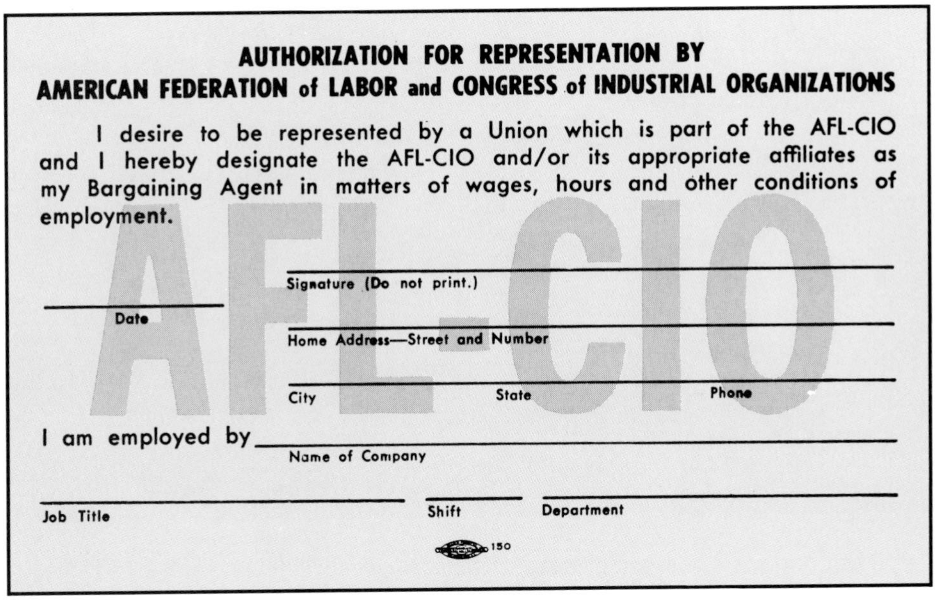

**AUTHORIZATION FOR REPRESENTATION BY
AMERICAN FEDERATION of LABOR and CONGRESS of INDUSTRIAL ORGANIZATIONS**

I desire to be represented by a Union which is part of the AFL-CIO and I hereby designate the AFL-CIO and/or its appropriate affiliates as my Bargaining Agent in matters of wages, hours and other conditions of employment.

_____
Signature (Do not print.)

_____
Date

Home Address—Street and Number

City   State   Phone

I am employed by _____
Name of Company

_____   Shift ____   Department ____
Job Title

⬥ 150

Fig. 26-5. A sample authorization card. If enough workers sign cards, the union may ask the company to recognize it as an "agent" for workers.

national union. The method of organizing locals is set by the national union's constitution and bylaws.

Generally, three major officers run the local. These officers are elected by the membership. The officers and their duties are:

- President.
  - Conducts all meetings of the local union.
  - Appoints committees.
  - Calls special elections as needed.

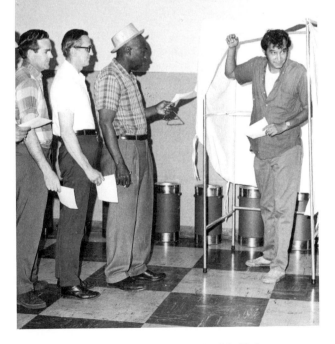

Fig. 26-6. The workers vote to decide if they want a union. (United Steelworkers of America)

- Vice-president.
  - Assists the president.
  - Becomes president if the elected president leaves office.
- Secretary-treasurer.
  - Keeps minutes of all meetings.
  - Receives dues.
  - Keeps financial records.
  - Pays union bills.

Other important union officers are the *shop stewards*. Each steward represents a group of workers. The members elect the shop stewards. Often, one steward is elected from each major department in the plant. The shop stewards are the union officials closest to the workers. They represent the employees in contract discussions.

NEGOTIATING A CONTRACT

The biggest job of the union is to get the workers a fair labor agreement. This is a legal document. It spells out what work must be done for what pay. Union officers and management work out the agreement together. Several meetings may be necessary. These meetings are called *collective bargaining*, Fig. 26-7. Each side makes *proposals* (tells what they want in the agreement). These are followed by each side making counterproposals. This is called bargaining. Each side is trying to change the proposal of the other side.

Next, the union and management will begin to work out their differences. It is a time of give and

Fig. 26-7. The contract is being negotiated. The union team is on one side of a table. Management representatives are on the other.

take. Each side will give up something but tries to get the other side to give up something, too. This is called *negotiation*. Finally, they reach an agreement. This is how pay rates, hours, and working conditions are set.

A contract agreement is signed by both sides, Fig. 26-8. It is then submitted to the workers for approval. This is done at a meeting. The union bargaining team first explains the contract to its members, Fig. 26-9. Then the workers vote. A majority must support it before the contract is adopted.

Fig. 26-9. The labor agreement is submitted to the union (rank and file) members. They must approve it before it goes into force. (United Steelworkers of America)

CONTENTS OF A CONTRACT

A *contract* contains the rules that the workers and the managers must obey. It is generally in force for three years. Then a new contract must be made.

A typical contract will outline:
- The rights of management.
- What employees are to be covered by the contract. (For example, all hourly production workers.)
- Wage rates for various jobs.
- Hours of work for a normal day and overtime.
- Vacation and holidays.
- Policies for hiring and firing workers.

Fig. 26-8. The contract is signed by both management and union officials. (United Steelworkers of America)

- Work rules that describe the employees who can do each type of job.
- Working conditions, including lighting, ventilation, and safety measures.
- Grievance procedure (way to handle complaints from the workers).
- Expiration date (when the contract ends).

GRIEVANCES

The contract is like a rule book. Different people may see its meaning differently. There may be arguments over the use of the contract. If employees feel that management acted against the contract, they can file a complaint. This complaint is called a *grievance*. There are generally four steps in a grievance. It can be settled at any step. These steps, shown in Fig. 26-10, are:

- The employee and the shop steward discuss the complaint with the supervisor.
- If the matter is not settled, the committee of stewards reviews the grievance. If it has merit (deserves to be heard), they present it to the plant manager or personnel director.

- If still unsettled, a representative from the national union studies the grievance. It can be presented to top management.
- If not resolved at this point, the grievance is submitted to *arbitration.* An outside person (arbitrator) hears both sides. He or she gives a ruling. This judgment is binding on both sides. They must live by it.

The grievance procedure is an orderly way to settle disputes. Both sides have to face the problem. It keeps small problems from piling up into a big problem.

SUMMARY

Through unions, workers can express their views as a group. They are organized through a legal procedure. First, plant committees are formed to promote the union. Authorization cards are signed. The union asks for the right to represent workers. A NLRB petition seeks an election. The workers vote for or against the union. If successful, the union is certified. It becomes the bargaining agent for the employees.

STEPS IN THE GRIEVANCE PROCEDURE

1 Steward and worker talk with supervisor.

2 Union committee and plant superintendent or personnel director take up the grievance.

3 A representative of the international union is called in to aid the union. Top company officials represent management.

4 Arbitration

Fig. 26-10. Steps in the grievance procedure. (AFL-CIO)

A local chapter of the union is organized. Officers are elected by the members.

Once organized, the union through its officers, negotiates with the company for a fair labor contract. Union officers and labor union officials work out the agreement (contract) that is then presented to the membership for approval.

The contract sets down conditions under which the workers will work. It sets pay rates, hours, and working conditions. It also contains a procedure to settle disputes. This system is called the grievance procedure.

KEY WORDS

All of the following words have been used in this chapter. Do you know their meaning?

Arbitration
Authorization cards
Certification
Collective bargaining
Contract
Grievance
Negotiation
NLRB
Proposals
Shop steward
Union

TEST YOUR KNOWLEDGE

Please do not write in this text. Place your answers on a separate sheet of paper.

1. Following are the steps for organizing a union. Place the steps in the proper order.
   A. Develop a program to promote the union.
   B. Get workers to sign authorization cards.
   C. Form a plant committee.
   D. Hold an NLRB supervised election.
   E. Petition the NLRB for an election.
   F. Make the union the official bargaining agent for the workers.
2. A smaller union that is part of a large, national union is called a _____ _____.
3. A union will usually have three main officials: a president, a vice-president, and a secretary-treasurer. True or false?
4. A _____ contains the rules that the workers and managers must obey.
5. Working conditions are (never, usually) a part of the contract.
6. List the major steps in settling a grievance.

ACTIVITIES

1. Invite an officer from a union local to discuss organizing and operating a union.
2. Invite a union officer or labor relations director from a company to discuss negotiating a contract.
3. In class, debate the reasons for and against joining a union.
4. Role-play the four steps in the grievance process, from an initial complaint through arbitration and resolution.

Unions sometimes organize demonstrations to inform the public of an issue.
(United Steelworkers of America)

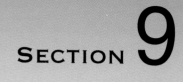

MARKETING THE PRODUCT

CHAPTER 27

DEVELOPING MARKETING PLANS

After studying this chapter, you will be able to:
- ☐ Define the term, marketing.
- ☐ List five major elements in a marketing plan.
- ☐ Define market research and list the data that is collected.
- ☐ Explain the difference between trade names and trademarks.
- ☐ Explain the method used in arriving at a factory price for a product.

Products do not sell themselves; they must be marketed, Fig. 27-1. *Marketing* brings together those who make products with those who buy them. This two-way exchange is shown in Fig. 27-2.

ELEMENTS OF A MARKETING PLAN

A complete marketing plan has five major elements:
- Product. A company must have the right product. It must meet the consumers' wants.
- Price. Customers must see value in the product. The price must be right.
- Promotion. The customer must be made aware of the product and its good features must be explained.
- *Distribution*. When a customer decides to buy, the product must be available. There must be a method of moving the product to its users.
- Service. Products may break down or fail. The company must have a way to repair or replace what it makes.

BEGINNING A MARKETING PLAN

Marketing is based on market research. This area was introduced in Chapter 17. *Market research* gathers data about:
- Who will buy the product.
- Typical customer's background (age, gender, education, income, etc.).

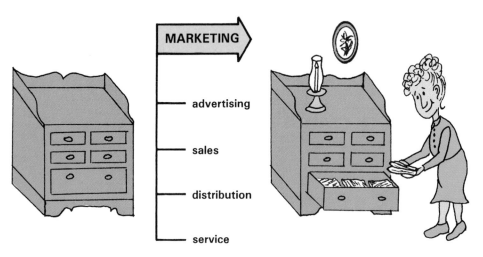

Fig. 27-1. Marketing promotes, sells, distributes, and services products.

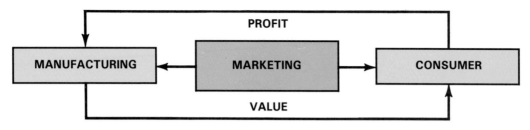

Fig. 27-2. The marketing process brings manufacturers and their products together with users. The user receives value; the manufacturer receives a profit.

- Where the customers live.
- How they would use this product.
- How much people would expect to pay for the product.
- Where the customer would expect to buy the product (discount store, specialty store, hardware store, supermarket, etc.).
- The type of product service expected.

The results of this market research are used to plan other marketing activities such as:

- Developing a trade name and trademark.
- Selecting a marketing theme.
- Pricing the product.

Finally the advertising, sales, distribution, and servicing activities are planned. These areas will be discussed in later chapters.

DEVELOPING A TRADE NAME AND TRADEMARK

Companies identify their products in two ways. They use trade names and trademarks.

Trade Names

A *trade name* is the official name under which a company may do business. Through it the customer comes to recognize the manufacturer. The trade name may be registered and protected by law. No one else can use a company's registered trade name. See Fig. 27-3.

Picking a trade name takes careful thought. The company must live with it for a long time. Generally, it is not wise to use the product name in the trade name. The company's product line may change. It may enlarge or be completely different.

A trade name using the product name may become out-of-date. Changing it can be expensive. Packages, signs, stationery, and thousands of other items must be changed. In the early 1970s the Standard Oil Co. of New Jersey changed its trade name and trademarks. ESSO was changed to EXXON. That change cost over $125 million.

Another example of a trade name change is that of RCA. The company was known as Radio Corporation of America. Then, it stopped making radios. RCA owned a television network and a number of radio and television stations. It also manufactured records, tapes, television sets, and other electronic devices. It also owned a car rental company and manufactured computers. The name no longer described its business. The name was changed to RCA Corporation.

The trade name should identify the company. It should provide an image of the enterprise.

Trademarks

A *trademark* identifies a product. It is the registered property of a company. Like the registered trade name, no one else can use a registered trademark. A trademark, by definition:

- Is a word, name, or symbol, Fig. 27-4.
- Is used by a single company.
- Identifies goods made or sold by the company.
- Separates products made by one company from those made by others.

Fig. 27-3. Some sample trade names on products. (Sonoco Products Co.)

WORDS

SYMBOLS

WORDS AND SYMBOLS

Fig. 27-4. Trademarks are words, symbols, or a combination of the two.

Trademarks are designed to stick in your mind. How many trademarks can you think of? Can you "see" several trademarks in your mind's eye?

Trademarks are carefully designed and selected. They should meet some basic rules. A trademark should be:

- Easy to see and recognize.
- Timely (modern, up to date, in keeping with the times, Fig. 27-5).
- Easily used on advertisements and packages.
- In good taste (not offensive, obscene, or negative to most people).

Look back at Fig. 27-4. Do you feel these trademarks follow the rules?

SELECTING A MARKETING THEME

Trademarks are one important part of a marketing plan. A second part is a theme. The company develops a slogan. It describes their activities or products. Trademarks are fairly stable. They change slowly. The new Sears trademark in Fig. 27-5 is only the fourth one used in over 100 years. On the other hand, marketing themes change fairly often.

Ford Motor Company used the theme, "A better idea," at one time. The theme suggested that engineering was most important. It reflected the emphasis of the company. But times changed. Consumers wanted better cars. They wanted quality and Ford responded. They started improving the quality of their cars. Their theme also changed. It became, "At Ford, quality is Job 1."

Fig. 27-5. Sears, Roebuck and Co. changed its trademark to show a more modern image. The new trademark shows action and movement. It shows that the stores are progressive.

Many companies have themes, Fig. 27-6. They convey an image. They encourage people to think a certain way. They want people to believe:

- General Motors cars and trucks are the "The Mark of Excellence."
- You "Care Enough to Send the Very Best" with Hallmark Cards.
- "You're in Good Hands" if you buy Allstate insurance.
- If you want something to drink, "Coke Is The Real Thing!"

The thoughts people have affect their actions. Good themes will cause people to have positive thoughts. Consumers will believe in the company and its products.

PRICING PRODUCTS

The process of setting product prices is not simple. Pricing must consider three factors. These, shown in Fig. 27-7, are:
- Cost of making and selling the product.
- Competition.
- Customers.

Product Costs

The basic costs, Fig. 27-8, that are considered in pricing a product are:
- *Factory cost*–the actual cost of producing the product.

Fig. 27-7. Factors affecting selling price.

- Labor costs–wages and salaries earned by people producing the product.
- Material cost–cost of material used in making the product.
  - *Overhead*–cost of equipment, utilities, and insurance.
- Administration cost–cost of developing products and managing support functions.
- *Selling cost*–cost of promoting, selling, and distributing.

These costs, plus some profit, set the minimum manufacturer's price. This is the price the manufacturer must charge for the product. Any price below this would produce a poor profit. The product would soon be discontinued.

However, you and I must pay a much higher price. The manufacturer seldom sells products directly to us. They sell to wholesalers and retailers. They, also, expect to make a profit. Their expenses and profit margins are added to the price of the product.

The final selling price is the sum of many levels of expense and profit. Manufacturers, transporters, distributors, and retailers all add on some costs.

Competition

Manufacturer's products will have to compete. Customers compare competing products on several points. One is quality. Generally, higher quality products will sell for a higher price. Product function (how well it works) is also considered. Customers buy what best serves their needs. We are willing to pay more for a product that fits our needs.

The company's reputation is also a major factor in choosing a product. The image that we have of the company is important. We often prefer to buy products from a manufacturer we know. Finally, we react to price. If everything else is equal, the cheaper product sells best.

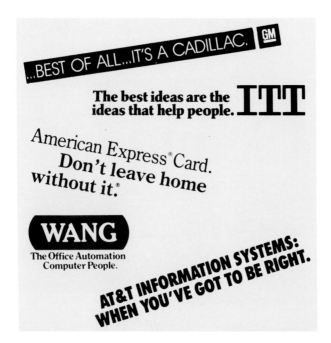

Fig. 27-6. These are some typical company and product themes.

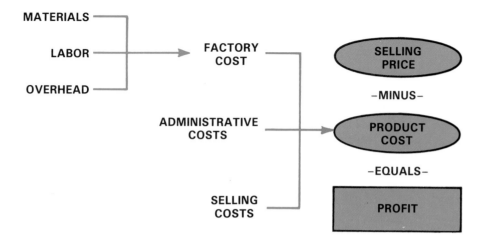

Fig. 27-8. Elements in product cost.

The company will have to decide the way it will face competition. Will it be on quality? Will function be most important? Will the company stress service and guarantees? Will price be the deciding factor?

This decision will affect selling price. In all cases, the customer must see the price as fair. The product must earn the selling price. It must deliver quality, function, or service, or it must compete on price.

Customers and price

A company must "know" its customers. Their tastes, values, and income are important. A product must appeal to customers. It must be attractive to them.

SUMMARY

All products are marketed. Early in the process an image is built. Company trade names and trademarks are selected. The product takes on an image and an identity.

A general marketing theme is then developed. The slogan ties all marketing efforts together. Advertising, selling systems, and packaging are designed to use the theme.

Finally, the product is priced. Costs are considered. Profit margins are added. The customer will decide if the price is fair. If so, the product will sell.

KEY WORDS

All of the following words have been used in this chapter. Do you know their meaning?

Distribution
Factory cost
Market research
Marketing
Overhead
Selling cost
Trade name
Trademark

TEST YOUR KNOWLEDGE

Please do not write in this text. Place your answers on a separate sheet of paper.

1. Advertising, selling, distributing, and servicing a product come under a company activity known as _____.

Matching questions: Match the definition on the left with the correct term on the right.

2. _____ Making customers aware of products.
3. _____ Method of moving product to customers.
4. _____ Arrangement a company makes to have products repaired or replaced.
5. _____ Gathers data about customers' wants and expectations about new products.
6. _____ The official name of a company.
7. _____ Identifies goods made or sold by a company.
8. _____ A slogan describing company activities or products.

A. Market research.
B. Trademarks.
C. Trade name.
D. Promotion.
E. Marketing theme.
F. Distribution.
G. Service.

9. _____ _____ is the actual cost of producing a product. It includes labor costs, material costs, and _____.
10. How does a manufacturing firm set the minimum price that it charges its customers for its products?

ACTIVITIES

1. Develop a trademark and advertising slogan for one of your school's athletic teams or service clubs.

2. Inform others in your school about marketing. Collect ten examples of company trade names, trademarks, and advertising themes and arrange them in a hallway display case. Include written information about the type of data gathered by market research.

3. Research the marketing of American products in other countries. Discuss these questions: What types of products are being sold? Do the people of these countries like the presence of American marketing or are they opposed to it? What would be the positive and negative effects of American products on other cultures?

The design of products, packages, and promotional materials contribute to success in the marketplace. (SAFT America)

CHAPTER 28

PROMOTING PRODUCTS

After studying this chapter, you will be able to:
- ☐ List and describe the two different types of advertisements.
- ☐ List and explain the functions of an advertisement that is effective.
- ☐ Give the three basic steps needed to create an advertisement.
- ☐ List the functions of a good package.
- ☐ Give the basic steps in designing a package.
- ☐ List and describe four types of plastic packages.
- ☐ Name five main considerations in selecting a package.
- ☐ Discuss the three important design considerations in package graphics.

All purchases require making a choice. This is where product promotion enters the scene. It is designed to encourage sales. Promotion influences the customer to select one product over another. See the advertisement in Fig. 28-1.

Product promotion can be done in many ways. Two very important methods are advertising and packaging. Both attract our attention.

ADVERTISING

Advertising is getting the attention of the public using messages. The message is given by print or electronic means. You read, view, or listen to the message. The customers can decide to receive the message or not. The customers are in control of the communication.

Types of Advertising

There are basically two types of advertisements, Fig. 28-2. Most ads are designed to promote either:
- The company or an idea.
- A product.

Fig. 28-1. Consumers must constantly make product choices. (Richard Barella)

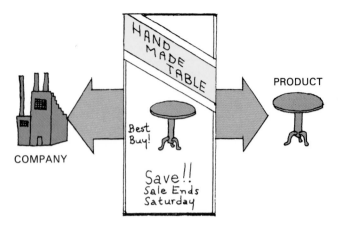

Fig. 28-2. Advertising promotes either the product or the company.

Company and idea advertising

Some advertisements try to get people to think a certain way. These advertisements promote the company image or an idea.

Many *public service advertisements* stress ideas. They want the public to act a certain way. Such advertisements are designed to protect the environment, improve health standards, or increase donations to a cause, Fig. 28-3. Typical idea ads promote forest fire prevention, use of seat belts, and giving to charity.

Other ads promote companies. They do not ask us to buy a specific product. They promote an image of the company. "Get a Piece of the Rock" (Prudential Insurance) and "Quality Goes in Before the Name Goes On" (Zenith) are two examples. Both want you to respect the company.

Product advertising

Most advertising promotes specific products. Television and radio promote products on every program. Newspapers and magazines are full of product advertisements. Billboards describe all kinds of products. You cannot go through a day without seeing or hearing a product advertisement.

Functions of Advertisements

Advertisements call us to act. They are saying, "buy this product," or "believe in this company."

These advertisements are fulfilling a function. To make us act, they take us through four steps. These, shown in Fig. 28-4, are:
- The advertisement must attract our attention. We must want to read, see, or hear the message.
- It must inform us. We learn of the product's availability. We are told of its features and advantages.

- It must persuade us. We must want to use the product or support the idea.
- It must cause action. We must seek the product or behave differently.

Creating Advertising

Advertising is created by people with special training, Fig. 28-5. Often special companies are hired to do the job. These enterprises are called *advertising agencies*. Some companies have their own staff to develop their ads. They are called *in-house advertising departments*.

In either case, creating advertisements follows three basic steps. These, shown in Fig. 28-6, are:
1. The message is developed.
2. The presentation is designed.
3. The advertisement is produced.

One tree can make 3,000,000 matches.

One match can burn 3,000,000 trees.

A Public Service of This Magazine & The Advertising Council

Fig. 28-3. A public service ad draws us to some action for the common good. (The Advertising Council)

Fig. 28-4. An advertisement should attract attention, provide information, persuade customers, and cause action.

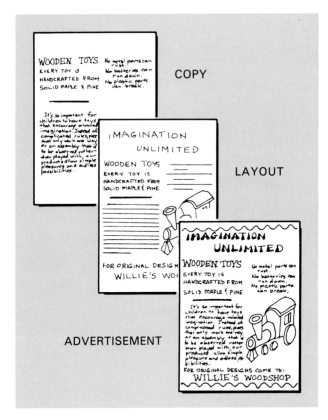

Fig. 28-6. Steps in developing an advertisement.

Developing the message

Advertisements must have a message. The message is developed from the theme. Developing a theme was discussed in Chapter 27. This theme provides the focus for the advertising campaign.

The message is then developed from the theme. Facts and ideas are chosen. The product or idea is described in words.

Messages can take two forms. Those meant to be used on radio or television are called *scripts.*

Fig. 28-5. An artist is preparing an advertising layout. (Ohio Art Co.)

Those used in print media (newspapers, magazines) are called *copy.*

Designing the presentation

A message is not enough. The ad must attract and hold attention. It must be presented well. The method used to do this is called the presentation. It is important to the success of an ad.

For print advertising, the presentation is called a *layout.* It is the way of arranging the information and pictures. Layouts are produced using (Fig. 28-7):
- Rough layouts, (these drawings are also called "thumbnail sketches".)
- Refined layouts.
- Comprehensive (almost complete) layouts.

Several rough layouts are prepared. They show different ways to arrange the advertisement. The better "roughs" are refined. More detail is provided. The best refined idea is given still more attention. It is developed into a near complete (*comprehensive*) state. The comprehensive is approved for use.

Television advertising uses a storyboard to show its presentation. The *storyboard* contains a sketch of each scene. It is used to guide the director. It shows the position of the actors. The background to be included is also shown.

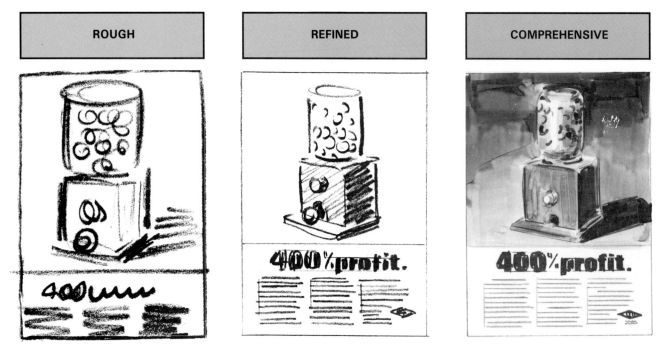

| ROUGH | REFINED | COMPREHENSIVE |

Fig. 28-7. Preparing a layout includes making rough, refined, and comprehensive layouts. (Manufacturing Forum)

Producing the advertising

The creative ideas must be reproduced so customers get the message. Print and electronic media are often used. (Media means all the ways of communicating–newspapers, radio, and TV).

If the message will be in print, type will be set. An artist or photographer will provide illustrations. A layout artist brings together the type and illlustrations to make a printed advertisement, Fig. 20-8. Then, the ad is printed.

| LAYOUT | ADVERTISEMENT |

Fig. 28-8. The art and copy are changed into a finished advertisement. Left. Comprehensive layout shows how ad will look. Right. The ad is printed.

If the media is radio or television, the advertising department may need actors. The art director or an advertising agency will arrange for a stage or location to produce the commercial (name for a radio or TV ad). The ad, Fig. 28-9, comes into our homes.

PACKAGING

A second way to promote a product is with its package, Fig. 28-10. You probably have been attracted by a product's container. It gave you information you thought useful. Perhaps you acted on the information and bought the product.

Functions of a Package

A *package* can serve three main functions. It can, as shown in Fig. 28-11:
• Protect and contain the product.
• Promote the product.
• Provide information to the customer.

Some products can be damaged during shipment. Others are small and easily lost. A package can protect and contain the product. It can keep it from being broken, or damaged by moisture. Products like toothpaste, corn flakes, and orange juice

Fig. 28-10. Packages are a good way to promote a product. (James River Corp.)

Fig. 28-11. Packages attract attention. They also protect and promote the product and provide information. (Reynolds Metals Co.)

Fig. 28-9. The script for a television commercial can be recorded and become a radio advertisement. (Richard Barella)

need to be contained and protected. In fact, most products need some protection as they travel from the factory to you.

Designing Packages

Package design follows three steps:
1. Package type is selected.
2. Package graphics (printing) are designed.
3. Package is printed.

Types of packages

Designers can choose from a large number of package types. Bottles, tubes, cans, cartons, bags, and trays are just a few of those available.

Bottles, cans, and tubes are often used. They can hold liquids, pastes, and granules (grains). These are popular for both consumer and industrial goods.

Two important materials for packaging are:
- Paperboard.
- Plastic.

Paperboard packages

Paperboard (cardboard) can be formed into trays and boxes. The material is cut and scored (creased). Then it is bent into shape. Often, a window is cut into the box. The opening, often covered with plastic film, lets the customer sees the product.

Paperboard packages take many different shapes. Fig. 28-12 shows four. Also shown is the layout for these packages.

Plastic packages

Plastic bottles, tubes, and jars make good containers, too. A number of other packages are made from plastic sheet and film. These, shown in Fig. 28-13, include:
- Blister pack. A plastic blister (formed bubble) is shaped by thermoforming. (See Chapter 10 for a description of the thermoforming process.) The product is placed in the blister. The blister is then glued to a card. The card contains the package graphics (printing). Blister packs are used for hardware, toys, batteries, and other small products. Often the packages are displayed on a rack.
- Skin pack. The product is placed on a special paperboard sheet. Heated plastic film is drawn tightly around the product. (This process also uses thermoforming machines.) The film sticks to the coating of the paperboard. The paperboard sheet contains the package graphics. Skin

pack is used for the same type of products as blisters.
- Bags. Plastic bags are used to hold a variety of products. The bags are usually made from long tubing. The tubing is unrolled to the right length. One end is sealed and cut. The product is then placed into the tube. The second end is sealed, forming the bag.
- Shrink packaging. Shrink packaging usually puts a plastic film over another package. The package is placed between two layers of special film. The sides are sealed. This produces a plastic envelope around the product. The film is then heated. The heat causes the film to shrink. Shrink packaging is used around products like cassette tapes, games, and computer discs. It provides a clear moisture- and dust-resistant cover. Usually, it keeps customers from opening boxes and packages in the store.

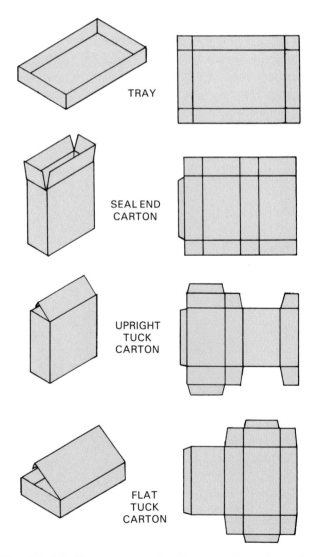

TRAY

SEAL END CARTON

UPRIGHT TUCK CARTON

FLAT TUCK CARTON

Fig. 28-12. These are typical layouts for selected paperboard packages.

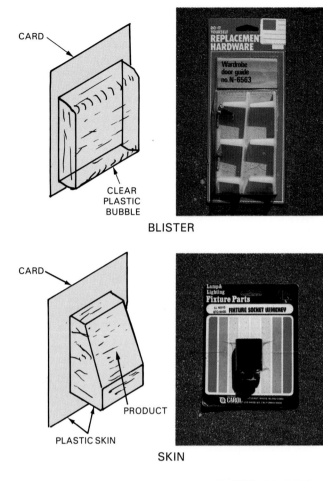

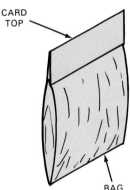

Fig. 28-13. Some common plastic packages.

Selecting a Package

A package must be right for the product. Five major factors are considered. A package is selected to meet the:
- Product requirements.
  - Shape.
  - Form–gas, liquid, or solid.
  - Characteristics–fragile, sharp corners, poison, etc.
  - Number to be sold as a unit.
- Protection requirements.
  - Keep out moisture, dirt, grease, etc.
  - Prevent breakage.
  - Discourage theft.
- Legal requirements.
  - Information required by law.
  - Need for safety.
  - Weight and measurement requirements.
- Market requirements.
  - Sizes and shapes preferred by customers and retailers.
  - Quantities bought at one time.
  - Method of display (shelf, rack, etc.).
  - Ease of handling.
- Cost considerations.
  - Material cost.
  - Cost to manufacture the package and fill it.

Preparing Package Graphics

Packages must be attractive. They also must provide information. Many of the advertising principles discussed earlier apply to packages. Three important design considerations are:
- Product identity.
  - Are the trademark and brand names properly shown?
  - Is the product description clearly presented?
- Package graphics.
  - Do the package colors match the product, Fig. 28-14?
  - Are the graphics pleasing?
  - Is all required information included?
- Customer acceptance.
  - Is the package pleasing both close-up and at a distance?
  - Does the package meet customer's needs?

Producing Packages

Packages are a manufactured product. The actual cutting, forming, and assembling use manufacturing processes. These were presented in

COLOR	IMPRESSION	ASSOCIATED WITH
Black	Solemn	Death, mourning, darkness, emptiness
White	Purity	Cleanliness, winter, Mother's day
Red	Offical, close to the heart	Christmas, Valentine's day, Fourth of July, danger, fire, warmth
Blue	Prize winning, cool and refreshing	Water, sky, cleanliness, clearness
Yellow	Cheerfulness, brightness	Sunlight, caution, daytime
Green	Comfort, natural	St. Patrick's day, mature, growing things
Purple	Dignified, exclusive	Easter, reality, evening
Orange	Happy, glowing, friendly	Halloween, Thanksgiving, fall

Fig. 28-14. Colors are important in packaging. They should support the product's image.

Chapters 10, 11, and 13. Graphics are printed using several methods. These include silkscreen and offset lithography. Typical printing processes are taught in communication classes.

SUMMARY

Products must be promoted. Often advertisements and packages are used for this task. Both are carefully designed. The package, as well as the advertising, should attract customers' attention. Beyond that, they should provide information, persuade customers, and cause action.

Advertising should encourage customers to buy the product. The package should present the product attractively. Also, it should contain and protect the product.

Good advertisements and packages can improve sales. People can be encouraged to buy the product.

KEY WORDS

All of the following words have been used in this chapter. Do you know their meaning?

Advertising
Advertising agencies
Comprehensive
Copy
Layout
Package
Public service advertisements
Script
Storyboard

TEST YOUR KNOWLEDGE

Please do not write in this text. Place your answers on a separate sheet of paper.

1. Indicate which of the following are the two main types of advertisement:
   A. Promotes company or an idea.
   B. Promotes a product.
   C. Promotes a person in the company.
   D. Promotes a process.
2. List and explain the four functions of advertisements.
3. The three steps of creating advertising are: developing the _____, _____ the presentation, and _____ the advertisement.
4. The _____ provides the focus for the advertising campaign.
5. A _____ contains a sketch of each scene in a television commercial.
6. Name the three basic steps needed to design a package.
7. There are four types of plastic packaging. They are:
   A. _____.
   B. _____.
   C. _____.
   D. _____.
8. What are the five main considerations in selecting packages?

ACTIVITIES

1. Find an advertisement that you feel is good and one you feel is bad. Analyze them based on how the person(s) depicted in the ad might feel.
2. Design a package for a baseball, pair of socks, or ten cookies.
3. Develop a point-of-purchase display for ballpoint pens.
4. With a partner, design a poster to promote the sale of a product to help someone with a physical disability.

CHAPTER **29**

SELLING AND DISTRIBUTING PRODUCTS

After studying this chapter, you will be able to:

☐ List and describe the three major channels of distribution used for consumer goods.

☐ Explain the two major types of sales.

☐ Describe the role of the sales manager in a company.

☐ List the steps in making a sale.

Products must move from the manufacturer to the consumer. They may follow any of several paths. These paths are called *channels of distribution*. Consumer goods follow one of three main routes. These are shown in Fig. 29-1.

Fig. 29-1. These are typical channels of distribution for consumer goods.

CHANNELS OF DISTRIBUTION

The simplest path is called direct selling. Manufacturers sell products directly to the customer. You buy the product from the producer. Many encyclopedias, cosmetics, and vacuum cleaners follow this channel. Mail order and catalog sales are also considered direct selling.

Some manufacturers sell directly to retailers. These stores then sell the product to the customers. An *"authorized" dealer* or "franchised" dealer is this type of retailer. Such dealers are the only ones allowed to sell the product. Most new automobiles are sold this way.

Most consumer products follow a third route. They are first sold to wholesalers. The wholesalers resell the products to retail stores. The retail stores make the final sale to the consumer.

SALES

Each step in the channel of distribution involves sales. During a sale the ownership of goods changes hands. Products move from warehouses to stores. From the stores they move to customers, Fig. 29-2.

Types of Sales

There are two major types of sales. These, shown in Fig. 29-3, are industrial sales and retail sales.

Industrial sales

Industrial sales involve several types of action. Raw materials may be sold to primary processors. Industrial materials are sold to secondary manufacturing companies. Finished products move to wholesalers and retailers. These are all examples of industrial sales.

| WAREHOUSE | STORE | CUSTOMER |

Fig. 29-2. Sales move products from warehouses to stores to the customer. (Jack Klasey, Ohio Art Co.)

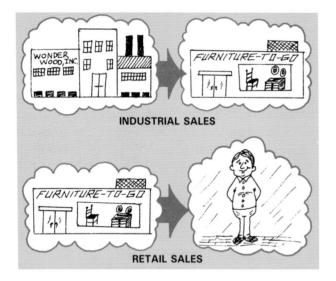

Fig. 29-3. Sales are classified as industrial and retail.

Retail sales

Retail sales means selling to the final consumer. The customer pays for the products. He or she receives them immediately.

THE SALES FORCE

Manufacturers may hire a special sales force. This includes *salespeople*, the people who do the selling to the customer. Sales managers are also hired. They manage the sales effort. The sales effort takes three major steps. These are shown in Fig. 29-4.

Developing a Sales Force

A sales force is developed in the same way as other workforces. The people are first recruited. Recruiters look for qualified people to fill the sales jobs. Human resource people place ads in newspapers. Recruiters visit schools. Some people approach the company looking for sales jobs.

Applicants are screened. They complete applications. Employment officers interview them. Previous sales experience is checked. The best applicants are hired.

Those hired receive special training. They learn the art of selling. The pay plan is also carefully outlined. Many sales people work on salary plus commission. They receive a base salary. The *commission* is a reward for sales completed. They may get a percentage of their total sales.

Directing Salespeople

At least in large companies, regional or district sales managers direct the work of the sales force. They supervise and motivate. They assign sales people to areas called territories. A *territory* may cover a city, several counties, an entire state, or several states.

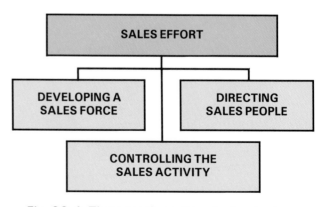

Fig. 29-4. There are three steps in developing a good sales program.

To supervise means to give salespeople direction in their work. A manager must explain company policy, correct poor performance, and reward good performance.

Another part of supervision is to get people to do their best. This is called motivation. We all let down once in a while. It is why coaches take time during the game to give their teams a "pep talk." Sales managers also must find ways to encourage better sales effort from salespeople. They hold sales meetings to urge their people to work harder. They give out sales awards to those who sell more than their quota. (A *quota* is the amount each salesperson is expected to sell.) As new goals are discussed, the sales people are "fired up" to "get out and sell."

Controlling the Sales Effort

All managed activities need to be controlled. By now, you can see that selling is certainly a managed activity. Of the various goals, an important one is the *sales forecast.* This is the sales budget. The company estimates overall expected sales for each reporting period. A period may cover a week, month, or quarter (three months).

Sales forecasts are broken down by region. Regional forecasts are further divided. Each salesperson works toward a sales quota so the sales forecast is met. Various territories are expected to produce scheduled sales. Look at Fig. 29-5.

Failure to reach quotas will call for action. New motivation techniques may be required. Some salespeople might be replaced. Better training may be provided. All action is designed to increase sales.

THE ART OF SELLING

Selling is an art. It takes talent. People can develop their skill in this art. Good salespeople are skilled in, Fig. 29-6:
- Approaching the customer.
- Presenting the product.
- Closing the sale.

Each sales call follows these steps. Each step must be successful. Otherwise, there will be no sale.

Approaching the Customer

The approach to a customer is critical. The salesperson must attract the buyer's attention. Then an interest in the product must be developed.

The approach is based on two key principles. First, an appointment is usually arranged. The

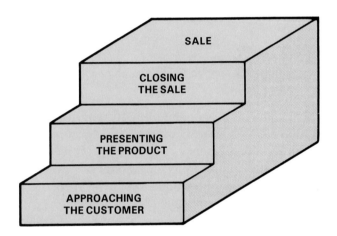

Fig. 29-6. Steps in completing a sale. A good salesperson will try to improve his or her skills in selling.

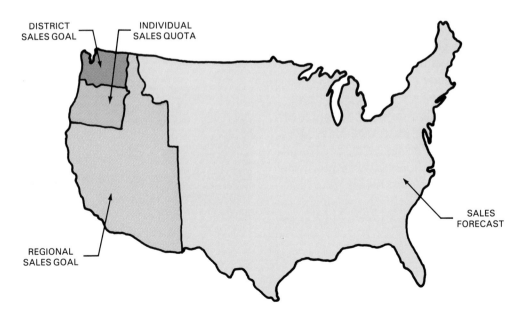

Fig. 29-5. Types of sales goals.

Order Form

Ball

Consumer Products Division
1509 South Macedonia Avenue, Muncie, Indiana 47302

Warehouse No.		Date of Shipment		Delivery Order No.		Ball Customer No.	
P. O. No.		Ppd/Col	Name of Carrier			Type Sale	B/L No.
Date to Ship/Arrive	Date Ordered		Order Placed By:			Routing:	
Special Instructions							

SHIP TO:

C/O

Street

City   State

SOLD TO:

Street

City   State   Zip

Terms

Cases	Wt. Per cs.	Product Code	Description	Cs.per Pallet	No. of Pallets	Cases	Wt. Per cs.	Product Code	Description		Cs. per Pallet	No. of Pallets
	6	60000	½ PT. CAN OR FRZ JAR	170					**BAGS**			
	8	61000	PT. REG. MASON JAR	208			4	51600	PINT	30 COUNT		
	12	62000	QT. REG. MASON JAR	121			4	52400	I-½ PINT			
	20	64000	½ GAL. REG. MASON JAR	56			4	53200	QUART	20 COUNT		
	9	66000	PT. W/M CAN OR FRZ JAR	154			4	56400	2 QUART			
	12	12400	1-½ PT. W/M CAN OR FRZ JAR	121			4	57800	GALLON			
	13	67000	QUART WIDE MOUTH JAR	121			4	58600	2 GALLON			
	21	68000	½ GAL. WIDE MOUTH JAR	56			5	71600	PINT	50 COUNT		
	29	80800	REG. JELLY GLASS 6/12's	42			5	73200	QUART	40 COUNT		
	28	81000	DLX Q C JELLY GLASS 6/12's	49								
	34	81200	DLX Q C JELLY JAR 6/12's	45					**BOXES**			

(REGULAR PAK / ECONOMY PAK markings in right section)

Fig. 29-7. An order form such as this may be used by a manufacturer's sales force. (Ball Corp.)

salesperson must be on time. Salespeople often wait for a customer. The customer should never have to wait for a salesperson.

Secondly, the salesperson should not waste a customer's time. The product should be introduced in a few words. The first words will set the tone for the meeting. Most customers like a business-like approach.

Presenting the Product

The product presentation should:
- Clearly explain the product.
- Describe its features and benefits.
- Answer all the customer's questions.
- Prepare the client for a "yes" buying decision.

The product explanation must be designed for the customer. One type of customer may buy a product to resell it. Another may be buying for his or her own use. Their reasons for wanting it are different. The presentation must take this into consideration. Retailers want profit. The user wants to know how it will make a job easier or life more comfortable.

Closing the Sale

If the presentation is successful, the sale can be closed. When you buy a product in a store the close

is simple. You just pay for it. Usually the clerk gives you the product. An industrial sale does not work this way. The salesperson takes the order. The order is recorded on an order form. The order form, such as the one shown in Fig. 29-7, will list:
- Item.
- Quantity ordered.
- Cost.

Fig. 29-8. Many sales orders are handled by computer.

Fig. 29-9. Most consumer products, like these automobile parts, are sold from inventory. The manufacturer keeps products in a warehouse. (AC Rochester)

- Shipping instructions.
- Billing instructions.
- Other important information (shipping dates, discounts for early payment, etc.).

The order information goes to the factory. An operator usually enters the information on a computer, Fig. 29-8. Often, the order is filled from inventory, Fig. 29-9. The items are shipped to the customer. Some products are not built until they are ordered. Aircraft companies do not keep airliners in inventory. These and other products are designed and built for the customer, Fig. 29-10.

An industrial sale requires time to complete. The product may have to be built after the order is placed. When the customer receives the order the salesperson is long gone. He or she is calling on other customers. Additional sales are being made. Many times, salespeople never see the products they sell. They sell from catalogs or samples.

SUMMARY

Products move from manufacturers to customers. They follow channels of distribution. At each step in the channel a sale is made. Products are bought and sold.

Salespeople create these sales. The sales force is developed, directed, and controlled. They are motivated to approach customers, present products, and close sales.

The success of a company is related to the success of the sales force. Products can be built. They also have to be sold.

Fig. 29-10. This airliner was built to fill an order. (Alaska Airlines)

KEY WORDS

All of the following words have been used in this chapter. Do you know their meaning?
Authorized dealer
Channels of distribution
Commission
Industrial sales
Quota
Retail sales
Sales forecast
Salespeople
Territory

TEST YOUR KNOWLEDGE

Please do not write in this text. Place your answers on a separate sheet of paper.
1. The simplest type of distribution is called _____ selling.
2. List two other types of distribution or selling.
3. If you are selling airplanes to an airline company you are engaged in (retail, industrial) sales.

Matching questions: Match the definition on the left with the correct term on the right.

4. _____ Selling products to a wholesaler.

5. _____ Area to which a salesperson is assigned.

6. _____ An estimate of the future sales volume.

7. _____ Getting customer's attention.

8. _____ Explaining product and features.

9. _____ Getting customer to buy.

10. _____ Place to record an order.

A. Order form.
B. Closing the sale.
C. Territory.
D. Product presentation.
E. Sales approach.
F. Sales forecast.
G. Industrial sales.

ACTIVITIES

1. Develop a list of products that are sold through (a) direct, (b) retailer, and (c) wholesaler-retailer distribution channels.

2. Develop a sales presentation for decorative candles that will be sold to support a trip to EPCOT Center.

3. Arrange to visit a company in your area. Talk to the person who heads the sales department. Ask him or her how they approach sales.

4. Design a sales receipt that could be used by a company that sells a wide range of school supplies.

CHAPTER 30

MAINTAINING AND SERVICING PRODUCTS

After studying this chapter, you will be able to:

☐ Tell the difference between durable and nondurable goods.

☐ Explain the difference between repair and maintenance of products.

☐ List and describe the steps in a product use cycle.

☐ List and explain the steps used to repair products.

☐ Explain the economics of replacement versus repair.

When a customer buys a product its life cycle (time it will be used) starts. The manufacturer's work is not done, however. The customer must know how to properly operate the product. The manufacturer provides directions for use and maintenance. Service information or facilities are also made available.

You will recall that earlier we divided products into two groups. These, Fig. 30-1, were:

• Nondurable or soft goods.

• Durable or hard goods.

Nondurable goods last less than three years. Clothing and food are nondurable goods. Pencils, paper, light bulbs, and motor oil are nondurable.

Durable goods last over three years. Automobiles, bicycles, and refrigerators are durable goods.

Both types of goods require maintenance and service. Clothing must be washed. This is called *maintenance*. Buttons have to be replaced. In this case, the clothing is being serviced.

Cars, trucks, and busses also need maintenance. Engine oil must be changed. Air and oil filters are replaced. Tires are rotated. Many automobiles

Fig. 30-1. Two types of goods. Left. The food and the packages are nondurable goods. (James River Corp.) Right. The wood lathe is a durable product. (Delta International Machinery Co.)

need service, too. Worn parts are replaced. A leaking radiator is repaired.

Most servicing and maintenance is done on durable goods. They are usually more expensive. Therefore, we want them to last longer. It is usually cheaper to repair than to replace durable goods.

PRODUCT USE CYCLE

Products usually follow a common life cycle, Fig. 30-2. First the product is installed. When a product is installed it is set up where it will be used. From time to time it is *maintained* to keep it in working order. After a time, the product is *repaired*: worn and broken parts are replaced. Finally, the product is taken out of service when it is not possible or economical to repair. It is *replaced*.

Installing Products

Some products are not ready to use when they leave the factory. They must be *installed*, Fig. 30-3. The product must be set in place. It is often permanently located. This means the product is fastened down or it is so large that it cannot be moved.

Many products connect to utilities. Installers must run water lines, electrical wiring, or natural gas lines. They attach drains to sewers. Machines are leveled. These activities are all part of installing products.

Product testing is performed after installation, Fig. 30-4. For example, a dishwasher is run through its cycle. A furnace is operated for a period of time. The installed product is then turned over to the customer.

Fig. 30-3. This engine test equipment is being installed. After the components (parts) of the system are in place, they must be connected and tested. (Daimler Benz)

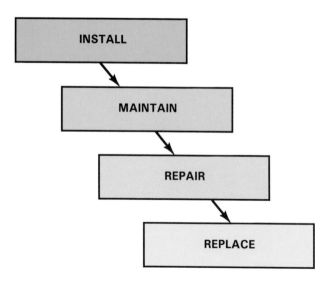

INSTALL

MAINTAIN

REPAIR

REPLACE

Fig. 30-2. Steps in a product's life cycle. Most durable good follow this cycle.

Fig. 30-4. A technician is testing a newly installed CNC machining center. (Kearney & Trecker)

Schedule 2

I : Inspect and if necessary correct, clean, or replace
R : Replace or change   A: Adjust

MAINTENANCE INTERVALS		Number of months or miles (kilometers), whichever comes first											
	Months	5	10	15	20	25	30	35	40	45	50	55	60
	Miles × 1000	5	10	15	20	25	30	35	40	45	50	55	60
MAINTENANCE ITEM	(km × 1000)	(8)	(16)	(24)	(32)	(40)	(48)	(56)	(64)	(72)	(80)	(88)	(96)
Drive belts							I						I
Engine oil		R	R	R	R	R	R	R	R	R	R	R	R
Engine oil filter		R	R	R	R	R	R	R	R	R	R	R	R
Engine timing belt *1		Replace every 60,000 miles (96,000 km)											
Air cleaner element				I*3			R			I*3			R
Spark plugs							R						R
Cooling system							I						I
Engine coolant							R						R
Fuel filter													R
Fuel lines							I*2						I
Idle speed							A*3						A

*1 Replacement of the engine timing belt is required at every 60,000 miles (96,000 km). Failure to replace this belt may result in damage to the engine.

*2 This maintenance is recommended by Mazda. However, it is not necessary for emission warranty coverage or manufacturer recall liability.

*3 This maintenance is required in all states except California. However, we recommend that it also be performed on California vehicles.

Fig. 30-5. This chart is a service schedule for an automobile. These services help keep the car in excellent working order. (Mazda Motors of America)

Maintaining Products

Often, products require attention to keep them working. Durable products require the most maintenance. Automobiles have maintenance schedules, Fig. 30-5, as do many industrial machines. The product must be lubricated and the controls must be adjusted.

Nondurable products are also maintained. Dishes and clothing are washed. Hiking boots are coated with silicone. Shoes are polished. Rugs are vacuumed.

All maintenance is designed to make the product last longer. Wear and breakage are reduced.

Repairing Products

Products will not work forever, however. Parts go out of adjustment. Sometimes they break. Surfaces wear thin or rust through. Bearings wear out. The product stops working. It needs repair.

Repair puts the product back into working order. It is made as much like a new product as possible. There are three major steps in repairing a product. These are shown in Fig. 30-6.

Diagnosing

You cannot fix something unless you know what is wrong. Finding the defect is called *diagnosing*.

The cause for the breakdown is found. Refer to Fig. 30-7.

The owner or repairer studies the defect. The cost of repair is estimated. The owner must then make a decision. Is the product worth fixing? If it is, the defect is repaired.

Correcting defects

Most defects can be corrected. We can hire repair people to work on the product. Sometimes we can repair it ourselves.

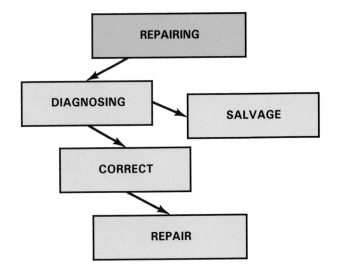

Fig. 30-6. These are the basic steps in repairing.

Fig. 30-7. These technicians are diagnosing a problem in a communication system. (AT&T)

Repair people often receive factory training, Fig. 30-8. They are shown the correct way to repair the product. They learn to use special tools.

The repair people, then, put the product into working order. They order replacement parts for the product, Fig. 30-9. They install and adjust parts. Sometimes, entire subassemblies are replaced. See Fig. 30-10.

Testing

All repair work needs to tested. The repaired product should meet operating standards. Testing serves as the "quality control" step for repair. Proper testing is important to make sure the product works.

Replacing products

Sometimes it costs too much to repair the product. Usually, the repair costs are higher than the product's value. Customers may decide they do not need the product that much. The cost of repair is greater than their need.

Other times a new product is cheaper than repairing the old one. The original manufacturing system may have been highly automatic. Labor costs were, therefore, cheaper. Parts were purchased in large quantities. The product was efficiently manufactured. Its selling cost was reasonable.

Repair seldom enjoys these benefits. The products are repaired one at a time. Replacement parts are ordered as they are needed. Often, a single worker repairs the devices. These individual actions make repairs expensive.

Products not repaired must be recycled. Sometimes they are used for parts. The product is taken apart. Good parts are saved.

Other products are thrown away. They are put into landfills. Still other products are *recycled*. They are ground up, shredded, or melted down. They become raw materials for primary processing. Many steel, aluminum, glass, and paper plants use scrap.

Fig. 30-8. A service person is receiving training on automotive suspension systems. (Arvin Industries)

Fig. 30-9. This employee is filling orders for repair parts. (Goodyear Tire & Rubber Co.)

Fig. 30-10. These trained technicians are repairing a communication switching system. (Northern Telecom)

SUMMARY

Many products need service and maintenance. Maintenance includes all the actions that keep products working. Servicing is repairing broken products.

Servicing involves determining the fault. The defect is diagnosed. Corrective action is often taken. Parts and systems are replaced. Proper operating adjustments are made. The repaired product is tested.

Eventually all products wear out. They are discarded. They can be disassembled for parts. They can be placed in a dump. Finally, they can be recycled to make new products.

KEY WORDS

All of the following words have been used in this chapter. Do you know their meaning?
Diagnosing
Durable goods
Installed
Maintained
Maintenance
Nondurable goods
Recycled
Repaired
Replaced

TEST YOUR KNOWLEDGE

Please do not write in this text. Place your answers on a separate sheet of paper.

1. Goods that last less than a year are called _____ goods.
2. Automobiles and other items that last longer than _____ years are examples of what we call _____ goods.
3. Explain the difference between repair and maintenance.
4. Which of the following are steps in the repairing of products?
   A. See if it is working.
   B. Find the cause for the breakdown.
   C. Fix or replace the part.
   D. Check the product for proper working order.
   E. Determine the cost of the repair.
5. Explain why it is sometimes cheaper to replace than repair products.
6. When a product is worn out and returned to the scrap pile for reuse it is being _____.

ACTIVITIES

1. In a small group, write an owner's manual for a simple product such as a pencil sharpener.
2. Visit a repair service center (automobile, appliance, computer). Ask the manager to demonstrate the steps in servicing the products.
3. Tour a local recycling center or scrap yard to find out how certain products can become the raw materials for primary processing of other products.

PERFORMING FINANCIAL ACTIVITIES

CHAPTER **31**

MAINTAINING FINANCIAL RECORDS

After studying this chapter, you will be able to:

☐ Name three major types of financial records kept by manufacturing companies.

☐ Tell why companies should keep financial records.

☐ List and describe the major types of budgets.

☐ Tell the difference between a company's assets and liabilities.

All companies must manage the use of their money. To do this, they must monitor (review) their financial results. This activity requires financial records. Keeping financial records is often called **accounting**.

Many companies keep three types of financial records. These are:

• Budgets.

• General accounts.

• Cost accounts.

These records are designed to control the use of money. They help managers measure the financial health of the company.

BUDGETS

Budgets were briefly introduced in Chapter 16. You may recall that they are plans written in terms of money. **Budgets** are plans that forecast income and expenses.

Money managers depend upon budgets. The company's financial performance is compared to them. They are the base for measuring financial success.

Sales and Production Forecasts

Manufacturing companies use several types of budgets. These are based on two major types of information:

• Sales forecast–Anticipated sales for a period of time. Sales of each product and model are included.

• Production schedule–A record of products that are to be built in a given period. The schedules consider the sales forecast and the number of products in inventory.

The relationship between these two documents is shown in Fig. 31-1. The sales forecast lists the total

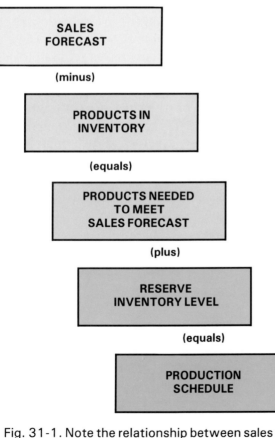

Fig. 31-1. Note the relationship between sales forecasts and production schedules.

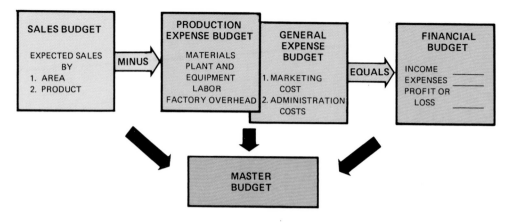

Fig. 31-2. These are major types of budgets.

need for products. Usually, some products are already in the warehouse. These are in finished goods inventory. These products are subtracted from the forecast. The new total is the minimum production level. This many products would exactly meet the sales forecast. However, companies want some reserve inventory. A number of their products should be on hand. These can cover production delays or extra sales. This reserve inventory is added to the minimum production level. The result is a production schedule. The schedule will meet the sales forecast. It also will maintain a reserve inventory.

Types of Budgets

It costs money to produce and market products. These costs are predicted on some basic budgets. These budgets, as shown in Fig. 31-2, are:

- Sales budget–A projection of income from sales, Fig. 31-3. It estimates sales by product and region.
- Production expense budget–An estimate of production costs. This budget is based on the production schedule, Fig. 31-4. The production budget is often divided into four sub-budgets. These are:
  - Labor budget–Estimated cost of human resources needed to meet the production schedule.
  - Materials budget–Estimated cost of materials needed to build scheduled products.
  - Equipment budget–Estimated cost of new equipment needed.
  - Factory overhead budget–Estimated cost of utilities, maintenance, and supervision salaries.
- General expense budget–An estimate of the cost of activities that support production. These activities include administration (corporate management) and marketing (advertising and sales).
- Financial budget–An estimate of income and expenses. It can be presented on a daily, weekly, or monthly basis. This budget tells a manager if income will meet expenses at each point in time. The need to borrow money at some point is

CDE INCORPORATED SALES BUDGET						
	TOTALS		SCHOOL SALES		HOME SALES	
	UNITS	DOLLARS	UNITS	DOLLARS	UNITS	DOLLARS
PRODUCT A @ $2.00						
WEEK 1	15	$ 30.00	9	$ 18.00	6	$ 12.00
2	30	60.00	20	40.00	10	20.00
3	23	46.00	14	28.00	9	18.00
4	22	44.00	13	26.00	9	18.00
TOTAL	90	$180.00	56	$112.00	34	$ 68.00
PRODUCT B @ $1.50						
WEEK 1	20	$ 30.00	9	$ 13.50	11	$ 16.50
2	24	36.00	11	16.50	13	19.50
3	22	33.00	9	13.50	13	19.50
4	18	27.00	8	12.00	10	15.00
TOTAL	84	$126.00	37	$ 55.50	47	$ 70.50

Fig. 31-3. A sample sales budget. It estimates sales of a company by the week.

CDE INCORPORATED PRODUCTION SCHEDULE (BUDGET)			
PRODUCT A			
Week	Sales (1) Forecast	Scheduled (2) Inventory	Production (3) Required
I (April 1-5)	15	20	35
II (April 8-12)	30	20	30
III (April 15-19)	23	10	13
IV (April 22-26)	22	00	12
PRODUCT B			
I (April 1-5)	20	20	40
II (April 8-12)	24	20	24
III (April 15-19)	22	10	12
IV (April 22-26)	18	00	08

Fig. 31-4. A typical production schedule. It estimates levels of production to meet predicted sales.

shown on this budget. It also shows when money will be available to pay debts.
• Master budget–A summary of all budgets. It provides an overview of financial activity.

GENERAL ACCOUNTING

Budgets are a prediction of financial activity. General accounting records this activity. It involves two major tasks:
• Recording financial transactions (dealings).
• Summarizing financial activities.

Recording Transactions

Most accounting systems are based on a ledger or journal, Fig. 31-5. Various financial actions are recorded, Fig. 31-6. Each action is described and dated. The amount of the transaction is entered. Money going out is entered in the debit column. These are expenses. Income is entered in the credit column. Credits should exceed debits. Only then is a profit being made.

Summarizing Financial Activities

Ledgers help accountants record financial actions. Other managers want a more general report such as balance sheets and income statements.

Fig. 31-6. These employees are entering financial data into a computer system. (Union Pacific)

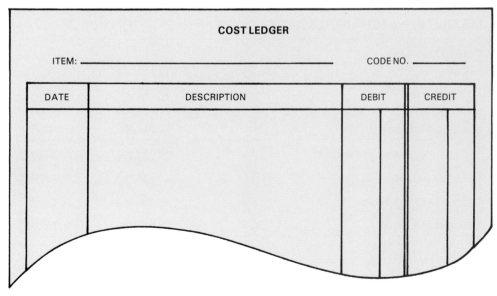

Fig. 31-5. A general ledger form. It keeps track of only one kind of expense or income.

Balance sheets

A balance sheet "balances" assets with liabilities. It lists all the things the company owns, for example materials, equipment, and knowledge. These items are called *assets*. They include:
- Current assets.
  - Cash and securities (stocks and bonds).
  - Accounts receivable (money owed by others to the company).
  - Inventories (materials and goods in plants and warehouses).
  - Other assets.
- Property, plant, and equipment.
  - Land, buildings, and equipment owned by the company.

Balance sheets also list what the company owes. These are called *liabilities*. They include:
- Current liabilities.
  - Accounts payable (money owed to other companies).
  - Salaries and fringe benefits for employees.
  - Long term debts due.
  - Interest and taxes due.
- Long term debt (loan and bonds outstanding).
- Deferred taxes (taxes due at a later date).

The assets should exceed liabilities. A company should own more than it owes. The excess is shown as *shareholders' equity*. This is the actual value of the shareholders' ownership (equity). A recent balance sheet is shown in Fig. 31-7.

CONSOLIDATED BALANCE SHEET
December 31, 19XX and 19YY

ASSETS	19XX	19YY
Current Assets:		
Cash and marketable securities	$ 209,030,000	$ 203,350,000
Receivables	201,610,000	163,380,000
Inventories	248,230,000	243,620,000
Prepaid expenses	10,210,000	11,410,000
Total current assets	669,080,000	621,760,000
Investments in Partially Owned Companies	45,550,000	41,600,000
Receivables and Investments, Related-Party	39,050,000	36,880,000
Other Assets	168,790,000	171,440,000
Property and Equipment	348,940,000	350,480,000
	$1,271,410,000	$1,222,160,000

LIABILITIES and SHAREHOLDERS' EQUITY	19XX	19YY
Current Liabilities:		
Notes payable	$ 13,530,000	$ 123,890,000
Accounts payable	43,740,000	34,170,000
Income taxes	22,060,000	28,610,000
Accrued liabilities	50,040,000	48,540,000
Total current liabilities	129,370,000	235,210,000
Long-Term Debt	367,640,000	372,540,000
Deferred Income Taxes	45,600,000	25,020,000
Shareholders' Equity	728,800,000	589,390,000
	$1,271,410,000	$1,222,160,000

The accompanying notes are an integral part of the consolidated financial statements.

Fig. 31-7. A balance sheet from a large company.

Income statement

The second report is an income statement, Fig. 31-8. This report is also called a profit and loss statement. It shows the financial success for the year. It lists net (total) sales. The cost of the products sold is then subtracted. The result is *gross profit*. Next the general expenses are subtracted. The remainder is called *operating profit*. Finally, other income and expenses are entered. The resulting figure is *"profit before taxes"*. Taxes are subtracted giving the *net income*. This is the actual profit. It is used for:

- Enlarging the company (retained earnings).
- Paying shareholders a dividend.

COST ACCOUNTING

The third financial record system is called cost accounting. It charges each transaction to a product line or plant. Each product or plant is called profit center.

The income for each product or plant is recorded. Also, each expense item is charged to them.

The corporate office's expenses are divided among the profit centers.

Cost accounting is a valuable tool. It pinpoints plants and products that are doing well. Others that need attention are identified.

Cost accounting helps managers to decide which products to discontinue (stop making). Plants that need improvement or closing are also identified.

SUMMARY

Managers must control the company's money. It must be budgeted. Income and expenses are predicted. Each transaction is recorded. Income and expenses are entered into ledgers. These are usually kept on computers.

Each product and plant must make money. Cost accounting keeps track of their progress. Income and expenses for each profit center are recorded. The records are a decision-making tool.

Good financial management helps a company make a profit. This is, after all, the key to staying in business.

CONSOLIDATED STATEMENT OF INCOME
for the years ended December 31, 19XX, 19YY and 19ZZ

	19XX	19YY	19ZZ
Net sales	$1,059,450,000	$855,740,000	$876,530,000
Cost of sales	687,850,000	557,110,000	571,400,000
Gross profit	371,600,000	298,630,000	305,130,000
Selling, general and administrative expenses	183,810,000	150,440,000	139,910,000
Operating profit	187,790,000	148,190,000	165,220,000
Other expense (income), net:			
Interest expense	40,840,000	40,210,000	39,870,000
Other income, net	(29,370,000)	(27,070,000)	(25,390,000)
	11,470,000	13,140,000	14,480,000
Income before income taxes and extraordinary income	176,320,000	135,050,000	150,740,000
Income taxes	69,760,000	57,410,000	62,420,000
Income before extraordinary income ($1.50 per share in 1982)	106,560,000	77,640,000	88,320,000
Extraordinary income from retirement of debentures	–	14,510,000	–
Net income	$ 106,560,000	$ 92,150,000	$ 88,320,000
Earnings per share	$1.93	$1.78	$1.73

The accompanying notes are an integral part of the consolidated financial statements.

Fig. 31-8. A typical income statement.

KEY WORDS

All of the following words have been used in this chapter. Do you know their meaning?

Accounting
Assets
Budgets
Liabilities
Shareholders' equity

TEST YOUR KNOWLEDGE

Please do not write in this text. Place your answers on a separate sheet of paper.

1. What are three major types of financial records kept by manufacturing companies?

2. List and describe the major types of budgets.

3. All the things a company has are called _____; what the company owes is called _____.

4. List the uses for profits.

ACTIVITIES

1. Keep a general account of how much you spend (debits) and how much you earn (credits) for one month. Think about whether you are managing your finances well. Create a monthly personal budget based on this analysis.

2. List your assets and liabilities. Using the figures you have, calculate your net worth (assets minus liabilities).

3. Obtain the annual report of a company from someone you know who works for the company or from the library. Identify the company's earnings and expenditures for a given year.

CHAPTER 32

CLOSING THE ENTERPRISE

After studying this chapter, you will be able to:
□ Describe the process of dissolving a company.
□ Name the two types of bankruptcy and explain how they differ.
□ List the steps a company must follow in going through dissolution.

The process of closing all company activities is called *dissolution*. The company that was built is dissolved. It is taken apart. People that were hired leave. Plant, equipment, materials, and finished goods are sold. Patents and product plans are sold. The company was once a sum of its parts. It is now broken into pieces.

There are two types of dissolution. These, as shown in Fig. 32-1, are:
• Voluntary dissolution.
• Involuntary dissolution.

VOLUNTARY DISSOLUTION

The owners may close the company because they want to do so. They may enter into *voluntary dissolution*. They file a form to dissolve the corporation. It is called a "Certificate of Dissolution" or "Articles of Dissolution."

Voluntary dissolution may be caused by unprofitability. The company may be losing money. The owners close the company before it fails. Dissatisfaction with the company is another reason. The owners may feel they have better uses for their money. They can close the business and sell the assets. This money can be invested elsewhere.

INVOLUNTARY DISSOLUTION

Some companies are forced to dissolve. A court order may close them down. The assets are sold to raise money. Three main reasons may cause *involuntary dissolution*. These are:
• Inability to pay debts (called *bankruptcy*).
• Dishonest financial activity (fraud and other criminal acts).
• Loss of a charter (state refuses to renew the charter, usually because of illegal activity).

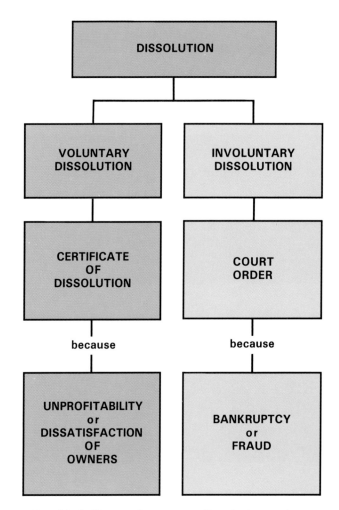

Fig. 32-1. Types of company dissolution actions.

Fig. 32-2. A busy plant becomes an empty place during dissolution.

STEPS IN DISSOLUTION

Dissolving a company is an orderly activity. Four major tasks must be completed. These are:
1. Filing the proper legal documents.
2. Closing operations.
3. Selling the corporate assets.
4. Distributing the company's money.

Filing Legal Documents

Two legal documents can start dissolution. The company officers can file a Certificate of Dissolution. This document must be approved by the stockholders. It tells everyone that the owners are closing the company. The corporation is starting voluntary dissolution.

The company may receive a court order to close the company. This action is usually started by a lawsuit. *Creditors* (people who are owed money) demand payment. The company may not be able to meet this demand. The corporation files for bankruptcy. This action starts involuntary dissolution. The courts oversee the dissolution activity.

Another type of bankruptcy does not dissolve the company. It allows the company to *reorganize*.

Fig. 32-3. When a company dissolves it sells its assets. Common types of assets are shown. A–Plant and equipment. B–Materials and work-in-process. C–Finished products. D–Information.

Debt is restructured (changed). Operations are improved. The company is reborn. This is called Chapter 11 Bankruptcy.

Closing Operations

During dissolution the company closes its operations. All sales activities stop. Deliveries of products cease. Employees are laid off. They lose their jobs. The busy corporation becomes an empty shell, Fig. 32-2. All activity stops.

Selling Assets

The company still owns property. This property is called assets. Most companies have four types of assets. These, as shown in Fig. 32-3, are:
- Plant and equipment.
- Material and work-in-process.
- Finished goods.
- Knowledge (this includes product plans, process information, etc.).

These assets must be sold. They are converted (changed) into cash. Some items may be sold in private sales. Another company may buy the equipment. The real estate (buildings and land) may be sold separately. Materials may be sold back to the suppliers.

Often, assets are sold at a public sale. An auction sale may be held. Advertisements, such as those shown in Fig. 32-4, are placed in newspapers. Buyers come to bid on the assets, Fig. 32-5.

Distributing Cash

The final step in dissolution is paying debts. Often there is not enough cash to meet all debts. The debts are then paid in a specific order, Fig. 32-6. This order is set by law. Taxes are paid first. If money is left, then legal costs are paid. The employees come next. They must receive their wages and salaries. Any remaining money must pay creditors. People holding loans and bonds receive their

Fig. 32-4. These advertisements for auctions of the assets of companies were placed in newspapers.

Fig. 32-5. The assets of a company may be sold at a public sale. They are often auctioned off.

payment. This payment may cover all or part of the debt. Finally, the owners (stockholders) receive any money that is left. In involuntary dissolution, the owners seldom receive any money.

SUMMARY

The stockholders are the greatest risk takers. They bought into the company to make money.

They can also lose their investment (money). This is the basic element of capitalism–our form of business ownership. People invest their money. They provide the capital needed to buy the plant and equipment. They also pay early development costs for the product. The investors are "betting on a winner." If they are right, they make money. They receive dividends. Also, the stock becomes more valuable.

Fig. 32-6. When a company closes and there is not enough money to pay everyone, the debts are paid off in a certain order.

Likewise, they can lose money. A wrong decision can lead to bankruptcy. The company is dissolved. The assets are sold to raise cash. As many bills as possible are paid. The company dies.

KEY WORDS

All of the following words have been used in this chapter. Do you know their meaning?

Bankruptcy
Creditor
Dissolution
Involuntary dissolution
Voluntary dissolution

TEST YOUR KNOWLEDGE

Please do not write in this text. Place your answers on a separate sheet of paper.

1. What are the two types of dissolutions?
2. Give the causes for each type of dissolution.
3. List the steps in dissolving a company.
4. One of the legal documents that starts dissolution is called a _____ of Dissolution.

5. Companies going into bankruptcy have four types of assets that are sold. Indicate which of the following are assets.
   A. Good will.
   B. Orders from customers.
   C. Work force.
   D. Plant and equipment.
   E. Material and work-in-process.
   F. Finished goods.
   G. Knowledge.
   H. All of the above.
   I. None of the above.

ACTIVITIES

1. Obtain an announcement for an auction sale related to closing a business. Determine who caused the closing and if it was voluntary or involuntary. (Note: most ads of this type will tell who ordered the sale to be held.)
2. Go to the local library and look for music cassettes or CDs whose theme is the dissolution or dividing of businesses (farms, factories, corporations) and the effect on the people who used to work there. Listen to the music and write about what you heard.
3. Invite a stockbroker to speak to your class about investments and risk taking. Prepare questions for the speaker beforehand.

CHAPTER 33

DEVELOPMENT OF MANUFACTURE

After studying this chapter, you will be able to:
☐ List and describe the four major periods in the development of every society.
☐ Describe the scientific management used in the factory system of manufacture.
☐ Discuss the changes beginning to appear in modern manufacture.
☐ Define general terms related to the development of manufacture.

Humans have always produced goods to meet their needs. The system used has changed over time. This change can be seen in four major periods:
• Hunting and fishing period.
• Agricultural period.
• Handicraft period.
• Industrial period.

HUNTING AND FISHING PERIOD

During the *hunting and fishing period*, the early humans lived off the land. They hunted animals and harvested wild berries, fruits, herbs, and roots. They fished the lakes and streams. These people were at the mercy of nature.

Very little manufacturing took place during this period, Fig. 33-1. Crude weapons and clothing were produced. Tree limbs were formed into clubs. Sharp stones became spearheads and knives. Hides were sewn into clothing.

Life was hard and primitive. The family was the basic unit. The family made products to meet its needs.

AGRICULTURAL PERIOD

As the human population of the earth grew, people could no longer depend on nature for food.

Droughts led to famine. People starved to death. The survivors moved to the river valleys to farm. This was the beginning of the *agricultural period.*

To water their crops, they built irrigation systems. The crops gave them a dependable source of food. Large numbers of people could be supported on small amounts of land.

The agricultural period was the start of most early civilizations. People were farmers ruled by kings. These civilizations developed along Tigris and Euphrates rivers in Iraq (about 3500 B.C.), and along the Nile in Egypt. They were good examples of agricultural economies.

HANDICRAFT PERIOD

Gradually, people became better at growing food. They produced more than they needed. This allowed some people to do different work. This is

Fig. 33-1. Early hunters and fishers used crude tools to make simple products. This hunter is using a bow drill for drilling a hole.

Fig. 33-2. These young people are practicing skills from the handicraft era.

called *division of labor.* Not all people were needed as farmers and rulers. Some could develop a *handicraft* (skill at making one type of product). The skilled trades were born as people practiced their handicraft. Some became carpenters; others, cobblers (shoemakers) or blacksmiths, Fig. 33-2. Other crafts were born. Each person did the work she or he could do best.

People traded the products of their labor for things they needed or wanted. The carpenter traded construction work for food. The cobbler exchanged shoes for fish. A local economy (trade) developed. The various members of a town or community produced all the goods for their area.

This system grew and developed. Certain areas became known for a special handicraft. One community became known for its fine furniture making. Another was famous for clock manufacture.

Trade expanded as communities began to exchange goods. A wholesale trade started. Traders would buy goods in one area. They would haul them to other communities. There the goods would be traded.

Money was introduced to help in this trade. The trader did not have to exchange one kind of goods for another. Products were bought and sold for money.

INDUSTRIAL PERIOD

The output of the handicraft system was limited. Work was done in a small shop by skilled workers,

Fig. 33-3. Their output was controlled by their physical skills and speed.

However, populations were growing. People needed more and better products. This demand led to the factory system.

Manufacturing became centralized. It was moved from small shops into a central location. Specialized tools and machines were developed.

Fig. 33-3. This worker practices a skill common to the handicraft period. (Lenox China Co.)

Water and steam power was used. Later, electric power replaced these early sources.

Work was separated into jobs. Labor was divided. Less skill was required to do each job, Fig. 33-4. Fixed hours and wages were set.

Special people, called managers, were employed to run the factory. This new system was called industry. It soon became the major employer of people. In the United States, industrial employment passed agriculture employment by 1890.

The process of moving from an agricultural to an industrial economy is called *industrialization*. It generally requires:

- Products designed with interchangeable parts (used by Eli Whitney as early as 1798).
- Continuous processing of materials (used by Oliver Evans).
- Material handling systems to move products from operation to operation (used by Henry Ford–the movable conveyor), Fig. 33-5.
- Division of labor so that each worker builds only one part of the whole product (this system is used in most factories).

Out of the factory system there also came the corporate form of ownership. The investors were protected from company debts. This allowed companies to raise the large sums of money needed to develop factories.

Scientific Management

The factory system also gave birth to professional managers, Fig. 33-6. Often the owners did

Fig. 33-4. This worker completes only part of the total job of making a microchip. Each person is doing part of the total job.

Fig. 33-5. These dishwashers are moved (conveyed) between manufacturing operations.

Fig. 33-6. Most companies employ trained professional managers.

not mange their companies. Special managers were hired for the job.

These managers worked at developing efficient operations. Frederick Taylor and others studied worker actions. Their work provided the basis for modern motion study. Jobs were studied to develop the most efficient techniques. Wasted or unnecessary actions were removed.

MANUFACTURING TODAY

Manufacturing is continuing to change. It still uses division of labor, continuous process, material movement, and interchangeable parts. However, machines are being used for more things, Fig. 33-7.

Fig. 33-7. Machines are replacing workers in many factory jobs. These robots can pick up parts and move them from one place to another on the factory floor. (Kearney and Trecker)

Computers are making decisions that people used to make. Sensors, small devices that can "feel" or "see" shapes and surfaces, are making quality checks. Robots are replacing people in routine factory jobs. Machining centers (complex machines controlled by computers) are doing complex jobs with little human supervision.

People are taking on a new role in manufacturing. Early factories used people to do the heavy work. They moved parts, ran machines, and loaded shipments. People are still doing these tasks but to a lesser extent. The modern manufacturer uses more labor-saving devices. Many employees are becoming *communicators* (information handlers). They program machines and computers. They complete reports on production, sales, quality, etc. They plan for company activities. Less and less are people the direct producers of products. More and more they design and plan products and systems.

SUMMARY

We are part of a slowly changing society. Industry is moving through a whole series of changes. Manufacturing started with people producing products for personal use.

Then the population divided according to skill and interests. People become farmers, skilled craftspersons, and rulers (government leaders).

More developed civilizations industrialize. They move their manufacture into factories. Work is done in central locations. Workers are given specific tasks to do.

Later, countries move into a post-industrialization (after industrialization) period. This era will be discussed in the next chapter.

Not all countries or peoples are at the same stage of development. Some peoples are still in the hunting and fishing stage. Others are in their agriculture period. Still others are in the handicraft stage. Most developed countries are well into or through their industrialization. However, all groups will go through the four stages.

KEY WORDS

All of the following words have been used in this chapter. Do you know their meaning?

Agricultural period
Communicators
Division of labor
Handicraft
Hunting and fishing period
Industrialization

TEST YOUR KNOWLEDGE

Please do not write in this text. Place your answers on a separate sheet of paper.

1. Every society goes through four major stages. From the following list select the stages and place them in the order they occur.
    A. Nomadic period.
    B. Hunting and fishing period.
    C. Communication period.
    D. Prehistoric period.
    E. Agricultural period.
    F. Manufacturing period.
    G. Industrial period.
    H. Handicraft period.
2. Give the four basic requirements needed for industrialization.
3. Today, in manufacturing, more workers are _____, which means they are information handlers.
4. Telling a computer what to do by punching in information is known as _____.

ACTIVITIES

1. Select one of the periods of society growth. Prepare a report describing the manufacturing activity in that period. Check your school's library or media center for information.
2. Invite an historian to class to discuss the development of manufacturing through history.

CHAPTER 34

MANUFACTURING AND THE FUTURE

After studying this chapter, you will be able to:
- ☐ Discuss the change from an industrial society to an information society.
- ☐ Define the term high technology.
- ☐ Explain high technology's effect upon our society.
- ☐ List the four areas where high technology is used in manufacturing.
- ☐ Discuss how high technology is used in the four manufacturing areas.

As you learned in Chapter 33, the industrial world is rapidly changing. We are moving from an industrial society to an information society.

During the agriculture period people worked with nature. They tried to control and improve on the natural world. Better types of grains were developed. Irrigation was introduced. Sprays were used to control pests.

The industrial period matched people with a human-built world. People worked with machines. These machines were used to build products and structures, Fig. 34-1.

The information period causes people to interact with people. People share information with other people. We are able to receive new information almost immediately. The telephone lets us talk directly to one another over long distances. Computers, too, send information across long distances. Fiber optic lines and communications satellites interconnect every part of the world. We are becoming a world dependent on information.

INFORMATION AND MANUFACTURING

The movement to a communication society does not mean manufacturing is becoming less import-

ant. It is going to be different, however. The number of people actually producing products is becoming smaller. Reports say that 10 to 15 percent of the work force is doing the manufacturing operations.

Many other people are managing operations. They are *professional workers*, such as engineers, accountants, designers, and sales managers. Because professional workers use information so many times they are called *information workers*. See Fig. 34-2. They use information to manage others, to develop production systems, and to control outputs.

A second group working in manufacturing is the *production workers*. They use information, too. But their main skill is working with machines and materials, Fig. 34-3.

Fig. 34-1. The industrial period emphasized using machines to produce materials. (Bethlehem Steel Co.)

Fig. 34-2. Professional workers are basically information workers. Some use mathematics and science information; others use sales and research information. (AC Rochester)

MANUFACTURING AND TECHNOLOGY

Managers and production workers have always used technology. They have used tools and systems to improve their work. Today, the use of new breakthroughs have made improvements come faster. The useful application of recent discoveries in science and other fields is called *high technology*. New information is incorporated into products quickly. The pace of improvement has quickened. New developments in computers have resulted in machines that need less hand control. This means that machines can do more work alone. High tech is being used in many areas of manufacturing. Four important areas, shown in Fig. 34-4, are:

1. Design and engineering.
2. Planning and scheduling.
3. Material processing.
4. Quality control.

Design and Engineering

Some of the earliest uses of high tech were in design and engineering. These activities are closely related to mathematics. They, therefore, could be adapted to computer processing. Lines could be described as starting at point A and ending at point B. The computer could deal with this data.

The result was *Computer-Aided Design*, or CAD for short. Early CAD programs could only draw in two dimensions. They could show only width and length. More advanced programs let the designer show objects in three dimensions, Fig. 34-5.

A recent study tried to find out when CAD will be widely used. The researchers estimated in the near future more than:

- One-fourth of all machined parts will be designed by CAD.
- One-fourth of all tooling will be designed by CAD.
- One-half of all mechanical drawings for prototype development will be done on CAD systems.

Some people predict that 80 percent of drawings in industry will be done on CAD systems within eight years.

Planning and Scheduling

Scheduling is another use for computer technology. The result is more efficient use of human, material, and equipment resources. Also, efficient inventory control is important.

Fig. 34-3. Production workers use machines to process materials. (Goodyear Tire & Rubber Co.)

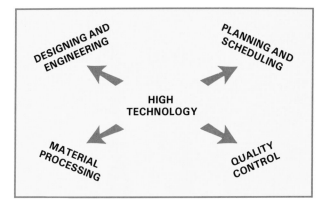

Fig. 34-4. High technology is used in many areas of manufacturing.

A new inventory technique where the computer is useful is called "just in time." As you recall from an earlier chapter, this means materials should arrive in the plant "just in time" for processing. Purchased parts should arrive "just in time" for assembling. Final products should be completed "just in time" to meet orders. All these actions reduce costs. Money is not used to buy extra materials or parts. Finished products are not held in warehouses waiting for orders.

In a like manner, computers are scheduling the use of equipment and people. They schedule machines for maximum use. They provide carefully maintained work schedules for people. Proper scheduling increases productivity without making people work harder.

The computer is essential for this type of scheduling, Fig. 34-6. It is the only inexpensive way to maintain the necessary records.

Material Processing

Much is being done to improve material processing. Primary processing activities are using computer *process control*. This technique uses computers to control the operation of the manufacturing process. The system:
- Improves product quality.
- Saves raw material, reduces waste.
- Reduces energy use.
- Increases productivity.

The system uses *sensors*, such as electronic eyes and heat probes, to gather information. The data is fed into computers. The computers analyze the information and adjust the process.

Process control improves the utilization (get more lumber out) of logs in sawmills. Also, steel is rolled to a more even thickness. Paper is produced to more exact standards, Fig. 34-7.

Secondary processing has also been improved by high technology. Computer controlled equipment is used to machine materials, spray finishes, and weld metals. An example is the computer controlled press shown in Fig. 34-8.

More complex machines have been designed. They will complete a number of machining operations without an operator. The machine positions the work. It then performs the required operations. Also, the machine can change tools between each operation. These machines, shown in Fig. 34-9, are called *machining centers*.

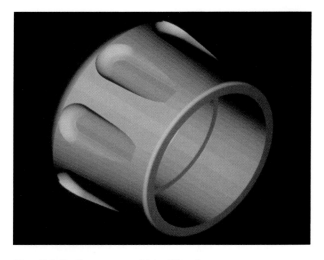

Fig. 34-5. Computer-Aided Design systems can show parts in three dimensions. (Schlumberger CAD/CAM)

Fig. 34-6. This employee is learning how to use a computer inventory system. (AC Rochester)

Manufacturing and the Future 277

Fig. 34-7. Left. A process control system controls the trim saws in this saw mill. Right. This steel is produced using a process control system. (Inland Steel Co.)

Several machining centers can be connected to make up a complete system. Robots can move parts from one center to the next. A complete part or

Fig. 34-8. The computer on the right of this machine controls the operation of this stamping press. (Cincinnati, Inc.)

product can be produced under computer control. These systems are often called the factory of the future. However, they are here today. Fig. 34-10 shows such a factory. The blurred objects at the lower left are moving robot vehicles called Automated Guided Vehicles (AGVs). AGVs move parts from storage areas to manufacturing lines as they are needed.

Some robots are being equipped with machine vision systems. Machine vision systems use computers to analyze a video image of a product. These systems can be used to control a process, position a robot, or for inspection of parts.

Quality Control

High technology has also found great use in the area of quality control. Various automatic devices measure product features. This information is used to adjust machines. Also, defective products are removed from production.

Quality control is extremely important in industry today. New methods of inspection, designing quality problems out of the product, and better tooling help to make better products. Quality starts when the designer picks up a pencil to sketch ideas. Quality must come first as the product is manufactured. When the product is used by the customer, the care taken in its making must show. The quality must shine through.

Fig. 34-9. A flexible machining system employing two CNC machining centers with automatic pallet (work holder) loading and storage. (Mazak Corp.)

Fig. 34-10. An automated factory uses computers to control machine processes.
(Westech Automation Systems)

SUMMARY

Manufacturing is very important to many societies. Each society must produce products to meet its needs. However, nothing remains the same for long. For example, in 1900 one-third of all working Americans were farmers. Today only about three percent of the labor force is needed to grow our crops. In fact, more people work full-time in universities than on farms. This does not mean farming is less important. It is more efficient. The farmers in North America are among the most productive in the world.

Likewise, manufacturing is changing. We are becoming more productive. Automatic machines are taking over the manufacture of products. Fewer workers are needed to meet our need for goods.

Manufacturing jobs are becoming "information based." Employees use information to guide machines and people. The manufacturing jobs of the future will be different. They will require fewer hand skills. Skills of the mind will be needed. Each of us needs to be ready for this change.

KEY WORDS

All of the following words have been used in this chapter. Do you know their meaning?

Computer-Aided Design (CAD)
High technology
Information workers
Machining centers
Process control
Sensors

TEST YOUR KNOWLEDGE

Please do not write in this text. Place your answers on a separate sheet of paper.

1. Indicate which of the following statements best describes an information society.
   A. In an information society, people are looking for more information.
   B. It is easy to get information in an information society.
   C. In an information society, people interact with people, using computers, telephones, and other means of communicating.
2. High technology is a term that means the use of _____ _____ in manufacturing.
3. List and describe four important uses of high technology in manufacturing.
4. List the four advantages of computer process control.

ACTIVITIES

1. Visit a "living" museum or fair where people practice handicrafts from another era such as weaving, blacksmithing, or pottery making. Think about the modern processes that have replaced these skills in most places.
2. Create a poster with pictures depicting various countries of the world in the four stages of development.
3. Ours has been called an information society. A negative aspect of such a society is overexposure to information, termed "information overload." As a class, list sources of information overload. Then, discuss issues of waste, invasion of privacy, and roadsides cluttered with billboards and signs.
4. Write and design a newsletter of interest to manufacturing students using a microcomputer and a software package. Print it on an output device and distribute it.
5. Visit a computer-aided design (CAD) workstation at a school or place of business for a demonstration of the software's capabilities.
6. Write a futuristic story that includes descriptions of jobs people will be performing.

CHAPTER 35

CAREERS IN MANUFACTURING

After studying this chapter, you will be able to:
- ☐ List types of information needed to select a job.
- ☐ List types of personal information helpful in choosing a job.
- ☐ Describe how to match personal goals with job requirements.
- ☐ List the resources you will have to work with on the job.

Millions of Americans go to work each day. These people chose to work. At some point they decided which job they wanted, Fig. 35-1.

Some people made the choice after careful thought. Others took the first job available. Many people enjoy their work but others do not. The level of job satisfaction is related to the decision process. People who carefully choose their jobs are usually happier.

In order to select a job, you will require three types of information.
- Personal information.
- Job requirements.
- Job future.

PERSONAL INFORMATION

Each person has personal goals and abilities. These should enter into your career decision.

In selecting a career ask yourself two basic questions:
- What do I want out of life (personal goals)?
- What abilities and interests do I have?

Personal Goals

Not everyone wants the same thing out of life. Some want security and safety. Others want adventure and challenges. Some people like to be home every night. Others enjoy traveling. Some people want to be close to their parents and childhood friends. Others enjoy making new friends.

Each job puts demands on people. These demands affect the individual's life. The first step in choosing a career path is defining a lifestyle (way of life). You must decide what you want out of life, your *personal goals*. You might develop a list of your personal goals.

For example, from this list you can answer questions about yourself. You might decide that you:
- Want to live in a small communtiy close to your hometown.
- Want to know when and how long you are expected to work each day.
- Like to have jobs planned for you.
- Like to work with machines and materials.
- Want the security of set pay rates.

Fig. 35-1. Many people work for a living. At some point they had to choose and apply for a job. (Miller Electric Co.)

You would probably not like to be a salesperson or a plant manager. You would more likely enjoy a production job.

Job Requirements

Your personal goals can be matched with job requirements. Each job has its own specific demands, called *job requirements*. These demands may be arranged under three headings.
- Type of responsibility.
- Resources used.
- Skills required.

Responsibility

One measure of job requirements is responsibility. Some jobs require the employee to take little responsibility, Fig. 35-2. The job is set up by others. The task is totally planned. The worker must only do the job. Many production jobs and clerical tasks fall into this group.

Other jobs require the employee to decide how to do the job, Fig. 35-3. The worker must know how to organize and complete an entire task. Skilled production (tool and die, repair, etc.), accounting, and sales positions are examples of this type of job.

Both of these job groups require people to be responsible for their own work. Other jobs require people to be responsible for other people's work. These jobs are management positions, Fig. 35-4.

Fig. 35-3. This machinist must set up and complete the entire task. (U.S. Army)

Managers get work done by directing other people's efforts.

Resources

Jobs also require working with resources. Basically jobs require people to work with:
- Information.
- Machines.
- People.

Fig. 35-2. The workers in this machinery repair shop complete work planned by other people. (Inland Steel Co.)

Fig. 35-4. Managers are required to get work done by guiding other people. (Goodyear Tire & Rubber Co.)

The balance between these three resources varies with each job. Accountants work primarily with information. They use machines (computers) to aid in their work. The information they process is used by people. But the most important resource is information.

Many other jobs involve operating machines, Fig. 35-5. Information helps the employee use the machines correctly. Contact with people is limited. Skill in using machines to process materials is the most important part of these jobs. In choosing a career path, you must consider the resources with which you work best.

Skills required

All jobs require some kind of skill. The workers must know certain information. They also must be able to do certain things. For example, product designers must know the elements of a good design. They must also be able to sketch, build models, and communicate.

JOB FUTURE

Finally, you should consider the job's future. Some job areas are growing. Others are rapidly disappearing.

Jobs requiring little or no training are disappearing. Self-service gasoline stations require fewer employees than older stations. Fast food restaurants also use fewer workers. Automation is rapidly replacing the typical production worker.

Jobs requiring special abilities show promise. People with computer skills are in demand. Good managers are always needed. Sales people with "people" skills can easily find jobs.

Another thing to look for in job future is advancement. Some jobs are dead ends. The person has little opportunity to learn advanced skills in these jobs. Movement to better jobs is difficult. Many unskilled and semiskilled (some skill) jobs fall into this category. Manual (hand skill) laborers, machine operators, and warehouse workers often have little chance for advancement. Their work does not lead into more skilled jobs.

It is wise to choose a job that has a *career ladder*. Many jobs are the first step to a series of other jobs, Fig. 35-6. A successful salesperson can become district sales manager. An accountant can become the manager of cost accounting. A production supervisor can become a department head. The first steps

Fig. 35-5. This mold maker must be highly skilled. (Goodyear Tire & Rubber Co.)

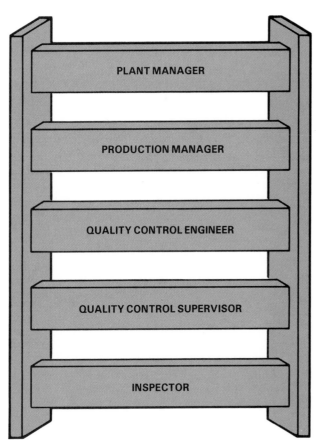

Fig. 35-6. Many jobs have a career ladder you can climb. You can move up to better jobs if you have ability and work hard.

can lead to additional promotions (new jobs with greater responsibility). Some individuals climb the ladder to top management. They become vice-presidents and presidents.

Job applicants (seekers) should consider the job ladder. The highest paying job may not be the best one. It may be a dead end job. Often a lower paying job with advancement opportunities is a better choice.

SUMMARY

You are approaching the age requiring career decision. This is one of the most important decisions each of us makes. You should carefully decide what you want out of life. Then, match this decision with various jobs. Consider their requirements and future. Careful planning will help insure a happy, secure work life.

KEY WORDS

All of the following words have been used in this chapter. Do you know their meaning?
Career ladder
Job requirements
Personal goals

TEST YOUR KNOWLEDGE

Please do not write in this text. Place your answers on a separate sheet of paper.
1. Indicate which three of the following types of information are most important in selecting a job.
   A. Beginning pay.
   B. Amount of vacation.
   C. Personal information about own interests, goals, and abilities.
   D. Tasks and abilities required by the job.
   E. Future that can be expected of the job.
2. How would you respond to the statement: "Everyone wants the same things out of life"?
3. Basically, jobs will require people to work with three type of resources: _____, _____, and people.
4. What does the term "career ladder" mean and why is it important to a job search?

ACTIVITIES

1. Write a series of statements that describe what you want out of life and what you want from your job. Look in the Help Wanted section of a newspaper for jobs you think would fit your personal goals.
2. Use the *Occupational Outlook Handbook* in the library to learn about the future of a job that interests you. Write a short report on your findings.
3. Devise a game that teaches young people about careers in math, science, and technology.

GLOSSARY

Accounting: the practice and process of keeping financial records.

Acoustical properties: how a material absorbs, transmits, or reflects sound waves.

Adaptation: changing a product by improving it. For example, the electric typewriter is an adaptation of the manual typewriter.

Advertising agencies: special companies that are hired to create advertisements and marketing messages.

Advertising: getting the attention of the public using messages.

Agricultural period: the period in human history when primitive people began to grow crops for food instead of hunting and gathering food from the wild.

Air drying: reducing wood moisture by allowing air to move around the lumber and carry away excess moisture.

Alloy: a mixture of pure metals that yields certain qualities. For example, brass is an alloy of copper and zinc.

Annealing: a heat-treating process that relieves internal stresses in a part and softens any work hardening.

Anodizing: a process that oxidizes the surface of a part, giving a layer of oxide that will resist corrosion. Anodizing is often used on aluminum and magnesium parts.

Apprenticeship: training that combines on-the-job and classroom instruction. The on-the-job portion is provided by a skilled worker. A special teacher provides the classroom portion.

Arbitration: the process where an outside person hears both sides of a dispute and issues a ruling that both sides must live with.

Area: the measure of a surface in which the length is multiplied by the width. Area is used to measure materials and the floor space of buildings.

Articles of Incorporation: the legal documents filed with a state government to legally establish a company.

Assembling: the process of putting a product together out of separate parts.

Assembly: a group of parts that make up one product. For example, a pencil is an assembly of wood, graphite, metal, rubber, glue, and paint.

Assembly drawing: a drawing that shows how the parts of a product fit together.

Assets: the things that a company owns, such as cash, property, and equipment.

Atomic closeness: occurs when the molecules of two parts are as close together as are atoms inside each part; created by bonding processes.

Authorization cards: cards that are signed by union members giving a union the authority to negotiate for employees.

Authorized dealer: a retailer who buys directly from the manufacturer and is the only person allowed to sell a product in a certain area.

Automation: giving simple, repetitive jobs to machines, computers, and robots.

Bankruptcy: a state in which a company cannot pay its debts; the company is dissolved or reorganized.

Basic oxygen process: a steelmaking process that reduces the carbon content of iron by injecting pure oxygen into molten iron.

Batch processing: the intermittent manufacture of raw materials in groups called batches.

Bench rule: a ruler for measuring small parts, marked in 1/8 inch increments.

Bending: one of the forming forces used to form material; produced by presses.

Bill of materials: a list of the materials that are needed to make one product.

Blow molding: a forming process that uses molten plastic or glass. A tube of molten material is placed in the mold. The mold closes and air is blown into the center of the tube forcing the material into the shape of the mold.

Board of Directors: a group of people elected by the stockholders to represent their interests. The board sets company policy.

Bonding agent: a substance used to fasten parts together.

Bonding: permanently fastening parts together using heat, pressure, and/or a bonding agent.

Brazing: a bonding process that uses copper, silver, and aluminum alloys as the bonding agent. A close-fitting clean joint is prepared. The molten alloy is applied to the joint area. There it hardens and bonds the parts together.

Budget: an estimate of income and expenses.

Budgets: plans that a business uses to forecast income and expenses.

Bylaws: detailed information that outlines how a company will be run. The stockholders have the power to develop and change the bylaws.

C

Calipers: a tool that is used to measure two parallel surfaces. The distance between the caliper legs is measured with a rule. There are inside and outside calipers.

Cant: the square center of a log that is cut into lumber on a gang saw in a sawmill.

Capital: the plant and equipment used to produce products, the permanent physical resources of a company.

Career ladder: this is the concept that if you start at an entry level job you can advance to other jobs after you gain experience.

Case hardening: a hardening process that produces a layer of hard metal on a soft core. Heated parts are placed in a carbon-rich substance. The parts absorb the carbon into a thin layer. The interior of the parts is not changed.

Casting: a process in which an industrial material is first made into a liquid. The liquid material is poured or forced into a prepared mold. The material is allowed to solidify. The solid material is then removed from the mold.

Cavity: the void in a casting or forming mold where the part will take shape.

Ceramics: a range of materials that have a crystalline structure, are inorganic (never living), and can be either metallic or nonmetallic. Ceramic materials are generally stable and are not greatly affected by heat, weather, or chemicals. They have high melting points and are stiff, brittle, and rigid.

Certification: making the union the official bargaining agent for the workers. Management must now recognize the union, and the two must meet and set pay rates, hours, and working conditions.

Channels of distribution: the paths that products follow from the manufacturer to the consumer. A product may follow any of several paths: retailer, direct, and wholesaler-retailer.

Chemical cleaning: using liquids or vapors to remove dirt and grease. Chemical cleaning is a basic part of many finishing processes.

Chemical conditioning: the changing of materials using chemicals. For example, when a chemical called a hardener is added to liquid polyesters the liquid becomes solid.

Chemical processes: methods of processing raw materials that use chemical reactions. For example, plastics are formed by chemical reactions.

Chemical properties: the ability of a material to resist chemicals.

Chuck: a spinning mold used to shape metal in metal spinning. Also, the part of a lathe that holds and spins the workpiece.

Clear-cutting: a method for harvesting trees that cuts down all trees regardless of age or species.

Coke: a clean-burning high-carbon fuel made from coal. Coke is coal with the impurities burnt out of it.

Cold forming: forming of metals that occurs below the point of recrystallization.

Collective bargaining: negotiations between an employer and a labor union.

Combination set: a set of measuring tools that has a 45 and 90 degree head, a protractor head, and a center-finding head. All the heads will fit on a single rule but are used separately. See Fig. 8-15 on page 71 to see what one looks like.

Commission: a fee paid to the member of a sales force for the sales he or she completes.

Communication: transforming information into messages that can be transmitted (moved) from the source to a receiver.

Communicators: employees that are becoming information handlers. They do more planning than actual production work.

Company: a group of people who work together to produce a product or service for a profit.

Competitive analysis: companies carefully study the products of their competitors. From this study a company can determine the need to improve its own products.

Competitive price: a price at which a product can be produced cheaply enough to sell at a price similar to like products on the market.

Composites: materials that are made of two or more substances that are bonded together by adhesion. A composite has two parts, a filler and a matrix. The filler usually provides the bulk while the matrix holds the filler together. Composites can be either natural or synthetic.

Comprehensive: an advertisement that has been developed to an almost complete state.

Compression: a forming force that squeezes the material into the desired shape.

Compression strength: the squeezing force a sample of material can withstand.

Computer-Aided Design (CAD): using computers to create and store drawings for products.

Conditioning: changing the properties of a material by mechanical, thermal, or chemical means.

Construction: using manufactured goods and industrial materials to build structures on a site.

Consumer products: manufactured goods that are ready to use; no further processing is needed to use the product. Consumer products are bought from retail stores, dealers, or catalogs.

Continuous manufacturing: a type of manufacturing that produces products in a steady flow. Materials go in and finished products come out at a steady rate.

Contract: contains the rules that the workers and the managers must obey.

Controlling: comparing or verifying the results of the employees' work with the company plan.

Converted finishes: changing the surface of a material by chemical action. Converted finishes add no material as a coating. The surface molecules are changed to make a protective skin or layer. Chemicals in the air and water will not damage the material.

Cope: the top half of a mold.

Copy: the message to be given in a print advertisement.

Corporate charter: a document issued by the state that legally authorizes the company to do business in the state.

Corporation: a legally created business unit. It is an "artificial being" in the eyes of the law.

Curtain coating: a finishing process where the surface of the material is flooded with finishing material. The excess runs off and is collected. Curtain coating is often used to coat flat parts or sheet stock.

Custom manufacturing: used to make small numbers of products. The company produces them to a customer's specifications. Custom manufacture is the most expensive type of manufacturing; often used to make large products.

Cutting motion: the movement between the workpiece and the tool that creates a chip and removes material.

D

Debt financing: a type of financing in which a company borrows money. Someone will provide money for a period of time. This money is called a loan. The company must repay the money plus interest.

Density: a measure of the weight of a certain volume of material. The volume of the sample objects must be constant. Density is given as pounds per cubic inch (lb/in^3), pounds per cubic foot (lb/ft^3), or grams per liter (g/L).

Department head: a person who runs one department in a plant, such as accounting or assembly.

Depth gage: a tool used to measure the depth of a hole, groove, or other feature.

Depth of cut: the difference between the original surface and the newly machined surface.

Deskilling: a method used to control labor costs by making a job simpler.

Detail drawing: a drawing that gives the exact size of a part as well as the size and location of all features. These features may include holes, notches, curves, and tapers.

Diagnosing: determining what is wrong with a product that needs repair.

Diameter: the length of a line that passes through the center of a circle.

Die casting: a type of casting used with nonferrous metals. The metal is melted and then forced into the mold. The mold is water-cooled and ejects the solidified part.

Die sets: a pair of dies that have shapes machined or engraved on their faces. The shape on one half of the die fits the shape on the other half.

Dies: a shaping device used in forming processes. Dies are flat pieces of hard materials. They must be harder than the material they are forming. Dies generally have a shape built into them. There are three types of dies: open dies, die sets, and shaped dies. Dies can also have blades designed to cut special shapes such as curves, circles, or whole outlines.

Dimensions: the size measurements for a part.

Directing: assigning employees to jobs and encouraging them to complete their work efficiently.

Directional drilling: a technique that allows wells to be drilled at an angle or along a curve to reach oil or gas.

Dispatching: directing employees to complete their scheduled tasks efficiently.

Dissolution: the process of closing all of a company's activities.

Distribution: the task of getting the product to the customer.

Dividends: payments made to the owners of a company. It rewards them for investing their money in the company.

Dividers: a tool used to measure the distance between two points. The points of the divider are placed on the two points to be measured. The divider is placed next to a rule and the distance is read off.

Division of labor: the task of making a product is divided into small jobs. Workers are trained to do one job. Also, the development of people who could practice a handicraft instead of growing food in early societies.

Draft: the sloped sides of a pattern. If a pattern has no draft, it cannot be removed from the sand without causing damage to the mold.

Drag: the bottom half of a mold.

Draw bench: a forming machine with a shaped one-piece die and a drive mechanism. Draw benches are used to stretch a bar or sheet over a die, and to pull a wire or bar through a hole in a die.

Drawing: a shaped die process. One die pulls sheet metal into the other die. Drawing is used to make automotive body parts and baking pans.

Drift mining: a method used to reach a mineral vein that comes to the surface at some point. A tunnel is dug into the vein, which is serviced by rail cars that move along the drift shaft.

Drilling: a method used to reach underground liquid resources such as oil and water. A small round hole is drilled using a derrick and a drill bit that grinds up the rock as it drills.

Drop forging: a forming process where a die is dropped onto the material. Many wrenches, sockets, and pliers are drop forged.

Drop hammers: a forging machine that raises the upper die and then allows it to fall on the material to shape it. Gravity pulls the upper die onto the lower die.

Drying: a process that removes moisture from a material. Drying can happen naturally or can be aided by applying heat.

Durable goods: products made to last more than three years. Automobiles, bicycles, and refrigerators are durable goods.

E

Edge: the second largest surface of a part.

Ejected: this occurs when a solidified part is pushed out of a mold.

Elastic stage: during this stage a material under stress will stretch. When the stress is removed the material will return to its original size and shape. No deformation has occurred.

Elastomer: an adhesive, often called contact cement, that has low strength. It is useful for attaching plastic laminates to panels.

Electrical and magnetic properties: the measure of a material's reaction to electrical current and external electromagnetic forces. The principal measures of these properties are electrical conductivity, electrical resistivity, and magnetic permeability.

Electrical discharge machining (EDM): a process that uses electric sparks to remove material. The sparks break away small particles of the workpiece that are carried away by a solution.

Electrocoating: a finishing process that uses unlike charges to attract finishing materials to the parts.

Electroplating: deposits a layer of metal on a base material. Often, layers of different metals are applied to obtain the desired results. The electroplating process uses electricity to deposit the plating metal.

Electrostatic spraying: a finishing process that uses electrically charged paint and parts to reduce overspray and ensure good coverage.

Employment: placing qualified people in jobs.

Enamel: a coating that forms a protective and decorative coating by polymerization.

End: the smallest surface of a part.

Energy: resource powers machines, lights work areas, heats and cools factories, moves materials, and performs many other tasks. The energy may be electrical, chemical, mechanical, thermal (heat), or nuclear.

Enforcement: making sure that workers follow safety rules.

Engineering materials: solid materials that have a rigid structure and hold their size and shape under normal conditions.

Enterprise: a single business unit, that is also called a company.

Equipment: the machines that process materials. They are used to produce industrial, military, and consumer products.

Equity financing: a method of raising money where ownership rights to the company are sold. People are sold stock and become part owners of the company.

Exhaustible resource: a resource whose supply is finite; it can be used up and no more of the resource will be available.

Expediting: following up to make sure work stays on schedule.

Expendable mold: a mold that is destroyed after one use.

Expenses: the costs incurred by a company in producing a product.

Extrusion process: a material is forced through a shaped hole in a one-piece die. The material flows through the die taking on the shape of the opening. Extrusion can produce shapes in metals, plastics, and ceramics.

F

Face: the largest surface of a part.

Factory cost: a company's actual cost of producing a product.

Feed motion: a motion that brings new material into contact with the tool.

Fiberboard: a synthetic composite made from wood fibers. The fibers are held in place by the natural glue in the fibers called lignin.

Filler: the substance that provides the bulk for a composite material. The filler can be fibers, flakes, sheets, or particles that are the base for a composite.

Finances: the money used to purchase the resources needed to develop and engineer new products, buy material, pay for labor, and purchase machines.

Finishing: a surface treatment that protects or decorates a material. Finishing involves three steps: selecting a finishing material, preparing the surface to accept the finish, and applying the finish.

Firing: a thermal conditioning process used on ceramics. Firing melts the glassy part of the ceramic. Upon cooling, the product will be particles held together by the glassy material.

Fixed path: devices that move product or materials from one fixed point to another in a plant.

Flame cutting: a separating process that uses burning gases to separate the excess material from the workpiece.

Flask: the container that encloses the sand in an expendable mold.

Flow bonding: a bonding process that heats, but does not melt, the base metal. The heated metal is bonded by melting a different material into the joint to serve as a bonding agent.

Flow process chart: a chart that shows the step-by-step arrangement of tasks to complete a part.

Forecast: management's estimates of the demand for products.

Forest products: all products that are made from wood.

Forming: processes that change the size and shape, but not the volume of the material. The material will weigh the same before and after a forming process.

Fracture point: the point at which a material under stress breaks into two or more parts.

Function: the ability of a product to do a job.

Fusion bonding: a bonding process that uses the same material as the base metal to create the weld. Thick parts require the use of a filler rod. This rod is made of the same material as the base metal. It provides more metal to produce a strong weld. The heat is provided by burning gases or by electric sparks.

G

Galvanizing: the process of coating steel with zinc so that it resists corrosion.

Gating: the path into the cavity that the liquid material follows.

Goals: the end to which effort is directed by a system, company, or individual.

Gravity mold: a mold that is filled by pouring the liquid material into the top. No additional pressure is used.

Green sand casting: a casting process that uses moist sand packed around a pattern.

Grievance: a complaint that is made by employees who feel that management has broken the rules of a labor contract.

H

Handicraft: a skill at making one type of product. Some people in early societies became carpenters, cobblers, and blacksmiths instead of having to grow food.

Hardening: increasing the hardness of a material using conditioning processes.

Harvesting: a method that collects a growing resource.

Hazard: sources of danger in a manufacturing plant.

Heat treating: the thermal conditioning of metals using a process of heating and cooling solid metal to produce certain mechanical properties. Heat treating includes the three major groups: hardening, tempering, and annealing.

High technology: the useful application of recent discoveries in science and other fields into new products.

High-energy rate (HER) process: a forming process that uses high energy sources to provide forming force. These include: explosive materials and rapidly changing electromagnetic fields. These processes are used in special applications.

Hot forming: all forming processes that are done above the point of recrystallization.

Hunting and fishing period: a period in history when humans lived off the land. They hunted animals and fish, and harvested wild berries, fruits, herbs, and roots.

I

Ideation: a process designers use to move from ideas in their mind to ideas on paper.

Imitation: a common product development technique. A company will produce a product much like those of other companies, letting someone else identify and build the market.

Impulse sealing: a bonding process used to seal plastic films that employs heat generated by a pulse of electricity through a wire.

Industrial products: materials and equipment used by companies to produce products. Industrial materials need further processing before becoming useful products.

Industrial sales: the sales of goods to anyone but the final customer.

Industrialization: the process of moving from an agricultural to an industrial economy.

Industry: this term can be described as: all economic activity; or as the productive activities– communication, transportation, manufacturing, and construction; or as a group of companies that compete against one another, such as the publishing industry.

Information workers: professional workers that use great amounts of information.

Injection molding: a method used to mold plastics. Plastic is heated to a liquid state and then forced into a mold. When the part has solidified, the mold opens and the part is ejected.

Innovation: a product development technique where a totally new product is developed. The videocassette recorder, CD player, and the microchip are examples of innovations.

Inorganic coatings: coatings made up of metals or ceramic materials.

Inputs: the resources needed to make a product. These inputs may be grouped into seven main classes: natural resources, human resources, capital, knowledge, finances, time, and energy.

Inspection: a process that ensures only quality products leave the plant. Inspection includes checking: materials entering the plant, purchased parts, work-in-progress, and finished products.

Installed: when a product is installed it is set up in the place where it will be used. It is unpacked, hooked up to utilities, adjusted, and tested.

Intermittent manufacturing: a type of manufacturing that produces the number of parts that are needed, then stops.

Inventory control: controlling the amount of material on hand.

Involuntary dissolution: this occurs when a company is forced to dissolve. The assets are sold to raise money. Three reasons may cause involuntary dissolution: bankruptcy, dishonest financial activity, loss of state charter.

J

Job requirements: what each job demands of the employee.

Job-lot manufacture: intermittent manufacture that produces finished products.

Joint: the point where parts come together. There are five basic types of joints: butt, T-joint, corner, lap, and skarf.

K

Kiln dried: lumber with a moisture content of 6 to 12 percent. Green lumber is placed in a large oven called a kiln. Air circulation, heat, and humidity are carefully controlled as the lumber is dried.

L

Lacquer: a material containing a polymer coating and a solvent. A lacquer dries as the solvent evaporates.

Laminations: heavy timbers produced from layers of veneer or lumber. The timber is held together with synthetic adhesives.

Laser: a device that generates an intense light beam that can be used for cutting. The word laser stands for *l*ight *a*mplification by *s*timulated *e*mission of *r*adiation. A laser amplifies light. This intense light beam produces heat when it strikes a surface. This heat will cut a workpiece.

Layout: the arrangement of a print advertisement that has been prepared for printing.

Lay out: the process of measuring and marking a part so that it can be made. The markings show where every feature should be on the part.

Lead time: the time needed to manufacture a product or part.

Length: the largest dimension of a part.

Levels of authority: responsibility and decision- making paths within a company.

Liabilities: the money that the company owes to other companies and to individuals.

Linear measure: the length of a material in units. Used to determine the size of a product or how much is being sold (such as pipe or rope).

Loan: an amount of money that is lent to a company for a period of time. The loan must be paid back with interest.

Lumber: pieces of wood (a natural composite) that have been made to a certain size for construction and other uses.

M

Machine screw: threaded fasteners that are used to assemble metal parts. They have round, flat, or oval heads and a shank of uniform diameter and threads along its full length.

Machine tools: machines that are used to build other machines.

Machining centers: a type of separating machine that uses computer control and can perform many different operations.

Machining: changing size and shape of a part by removing excess material.

Machinist's rule: a ruler that has scales (markings) that will measure down to 1/64 in.

Maintained: when service has been performed on a product to keep it in good working order.

Maintenance: the tasks that are performed on a product to keep it in good working order.

Management: brings together the inputs of people, machines, materials, finances, and people to produce and sell products.

Management structure: the way a company is organized, how responsibility flows and how decision making is divided.

Manufacturing engineer: a professional person who organizes manufacturing operations.

Manufacturing: the activity that changes materials to make them more useful.

Marketing: the activity that brings together those who make products with the people who buy them.

Market research: the process that gathers data about: who buys the product, the customer's background, where they live, how they use the product, how much should it cost, where to buy it, and the type of service expected. The results of this market research are used to plan other marketing activities. It is used to study customer's thinking about products. The information gathered is used either product development and product improvement.

Material handling: the methods used to move material around a manufacturing plant.

Material processing: changing the size, shape, and looks of materials to fit human needs. Changing the form of materials takes three steps: obtaining natural resources, producing industrial materials, and making finished products.

Matrix: the agent that holds the filler together in a composite. It acts as the bonding agent for the filler.

Measurement: the process of describing a part's size using a standard for comparison. This allows the part to be duplicated from the measurements only.

Mechanical cleaning: cleaning processes that use abrasives, wire brushes, or metal shot to remove dirt and roughness.

Mechanical conditioning: using physical force to modify the internal structure of a material.

Mechanical fastening: permanently or temporarily holding parts together using mechanical devices (like screws) or mechanical force.

Mechanical processes: methods that use mechanical force to change the resource, such as cutting or crushing.

Mechanical properties: the ability of a material to withstand mechanical forces. These forces are compression, tension, shear, and torsion.

Metal spinning: a forming process that uses one-piece molds. A thin disc of metal is spun and then forced over a spinning mold. Large lighting reflectors, satellite antennae, and tank ends are formed using the metal spinning process.

Metals: an engineering material with a crystalline, inorganic structure. Usually processed using heat or using forming techniques.

Micrometer: a very precise measurement tool used for linear dimensions.

Military products: the materials and machines used for the defense of a country. These goods are special products made for the use of a country's military forces.

Mining: the process of digging resources out of the earth.

Mock-up: an appearance model. It shows what the product will look like.

Models: a three-dimensional representation of a product. There are two major types of models: mock-ups and prototypes.

Mold: a container to hold a liquid material until it solidifies. A correctly shaped cavity is built into the mold. There are two types of molds: expendable and permanent.

Molding: a process that heats plastic to a liquid or softened state, forces the plastic into a cavity of the desired shape, and then allows the plastic to cool and set into its new shape.

N

Negotiation: discussions held to work out a labor contract between an employer and the workers.

NLRB: the National Labor Relations Board, a federal agency that oversees labor relations between workers and employers.

Nondurable goods: products that are made to last less than three years. Clothing, food, pencils, paper, light bulbs, and motor oil are nondurable goods.

Nontraditional machining: machining processes that do not use a "tool" as we use the word. They use heat, light, chemical action, or electrical sparks to produce a cut.

O

One-piece die: a type of die used to give shape to a material. Used in thermoforming and metal spinning processes. Also called molds.

Open die: the simplest type of die. An open die is two flat, hard plates. One half of the die does not move. The other half moves to hit (hammer) or put pressure (squeeze) on the material between the dies.

Open-pit mining: a type of mining used when the resource is close to the surface.

Operations: the processes that shape and assemble a product.

Operation sheet: a form used to record the sequence of operations needed to produce a product.

Optical properties: characteristics that describe how a material reacts to light waves. The two main optical properties are opacity and color.

Organic coatings: coatings made of natural or synthetic polymers. Organic finishes are classified into four groups: paint, varnish, enamel, and lacquer.

Organizing: dividing tasks into jobs and establishing lines of authority (who gives orders to whom).

Orthographic projection: a method of presenting a product in drawings by showing the top, front, and right side views.

Outputs: the things that come out of a manufacturing system. Outputs can be desirable (products) and unwanted (pollution, noise, waste, etc.).

Overhead: the cost of equipment, utilities, and insurance needed to produce the product.

Overspray: finishing material from a spray gun that misses the product or does not adhere to the surface. It is wasted and pollutes the air.

P

Package: a device that protects, contains, promotes, and provides information to the customer about the product.

Paint: a class of finishing materials that contains a liquid that forms a coating by polymerization. (This is a linking of molecules into strong chains.) Many paints have a coloring agent added.

Parison: a heated tube of plastic or glass material that is placed in a mold for blow molding.

Particleboard: a synthetic wood composite made from chips, shavings, or flakes held together with a synthetic glue. The most common types are: standard particleboard, waferboard, flakeboard, and oriented strand board.

Parting compound: a powder that makes removing the pattern from an expendable mold easier.

Partnership: an association of two or more people to run a business.

Pattern: a pattern is a device that is the exact shape of the finished part. Patterns are used to make expendable molds.

Permanent molds: molds that can be used over and over again. They will produce many parts before they wear out. Permanent molds are more expensive than expendable molds. There are two types of permanent molds: gravity and pressure.

Personal goals: what each person wants out of life.

Physical properties: characteristics that describe the size, density, or surface texture of a product.

Pilot run: a test run of a production system. The system is tried out to see if it works. The pilot run is designed to "debug" (correct) the system.

Planning: setting goals and the course of action that is to be followed.

Plant manager: an individual is in charge of an entire production facility. This person manages all activities at a single plant.

Plasma spraying: a finishing process that uses a gun to vaporize metal or ceramic materials. Hot gases carry the particles to the workpiece. This process deposits a thin, even coating on metal, plastic, and ceramic parts.

Plastic stage: during this stage a material starts to yield to stress that is applied. The material will be permanently deformed into a new shape.

Plywood: a synthetic wood composite made of sheets of veneer. The grain of the core and the face veneers run in the same direction. Except in thin plywood, the crossbands are at right angles to the face veneers. Other plywood has cores made of particleboard or solid lumber.

Point of recrystallization: the lowest temperature that a material can be formed without causing internal stresses. At this point, the material will form easily.

Polymers: natural and synthetic compounds made of molecules that contain carbon. A single molecule is called a mer or monomer (meaning single mer). Polymers are made by combining monomers into a chain-like structure.

Porosity: this is the relationship of open space to solid space in a material. A porous material will be lighter than a nonporous material. Porous materials contain air within themselves and make good heat insulators.

Precision measurement: a very accurate type of measurement. Readings are given to greater than .001″ accuracy.

President: a full-time manager hired by the board of directors. The president is the top manager in a company.

Press fit: a type of fit where parts are forced together. The friction between the two pieces keeps them assembled. A shaft may be pressed into a hole.

Press forging: a forming process that uses squeezing action. It is used to shape many automotive and aircraft parts such as camshafts, piston rods, and crankshafts.

Pressure mold: a type of mold that has the liquid material forced into it. This type of mold must be built to withstand the force of a clamping system and the pressure from the material as it is forced into the mold.

Primary processes: processes that change raw materials into a usable form for further manufacture. Changing logs into lumber is an example.

Primary processing: the first step in manufacturing where raw materials are processed into industrial materials.

Process control: using computers to control the operation of manufacturing processes.

Processes: the actions that are performed to raw materials to turn them into usable products.

Process layout: a type of plant layout where machines are grouped by the process they perform.

Product engineering: the process of preparing a design for production. The design is specified and tested for operation and safety.

Product layout: places machines in a plant according to the sequence of operations. It is used in most continuous manufacturing plants.

Product: the output of any manufacturing system. Products can be made for consumers, industry, or for military purposes.

Production planners: people who schedule and organize the manufacturing system to make sure that products are produced on time and at the lowest cost.

Productivity: a measure of the output per unit of labor.

Profit: any income that is left over after the expenses, taxes, and manufacturing costs are paid. Profits allow the company to reward its owners for investing in the company, become more productive, and develop new products and technology. Without profits, companies soon run out of money and disappear.

Profit-centered: companies that are formed to make money for the owners.

Properties: the qualities of a material such as hardness, opacity, strength, and so forth. Properties tell the designer how the material will perform or behave during use.

Proposals: a statement that tells the other side in a negotiation what one side wants in an agreement.

Proprietorship: a business enterprise owned by one person.

Prototype: a working model. Prototypes are used to check the operation of the final product.

Protractor: a tool used to check angles other than 90 degrees or 45 degrees.

Public service advertisements: advertisements that are designed to get the public to act a certain way, such as to protect the environment, improve health standards, or increase donations to a certain cause.

Purchasing: the practice of buying the materials needed to manufacture products; it brings the suppliers and users together.

Q

Quality circle: groups of workers that meet to discuss ways to improve the company and its operations.

Quality control: activities that ensure products meet standards. This function of a company has two tasks: motivating workers to produce quality products, and inspecting products to remove substandard items.

Quota: the amount of product that a salesperson is expected to sell.

R

Rake: the slope of the tool face away from the workpiece. Rake causes the chip to curl away from the cut.

Raw materials: natural resources found on or in the earth or seas. Manufacturing starts with raw materials.

Recruitment: a company's search for qualified workers to fill jobs.

Recycled: when a product cannot be repaired, the materials in that product are reprocessed for other use.

Refined sketch: a sketch that shows shape and size of a product idea. It gives a fairly accurate view of the designer's ideas.

Relief angle: the clearance behind the cutting parts of the tool. Relief angles also keep most of the tool from rubbing on the workpiece.

Rendering: a colored pictorial sketch used to show the final appearance of a product design.

Renewable resource: biological materials that can be grown to replace the materials we use. Trees and food plants are examples.

Repair: worn and broken parts are replaced to restore the product to proper working order.

Replace: the product is taken out of service when it is not possible or economical to repair it, and a new product is purchased to do the old product's job.

Resistance welding: an assembly process that uses heat and pressure. This process is based on a material's ability to resist the flow of electric current. Resistance welding uses resistance to melt the material. The material is then squeezed and held to form the weld.

Resource control: making sure that resources are being fully utilized, and not sitting idle or being wasted.

Resource flow: the flow of materials and people inside a plant.

Retail sales: selling products to the final consumer, who receives the product immediately.

Retained earnings: profits that are kept by the company to invest in additional productive capital. It pays for such things as new machines and new buildings.

Riddle: the sifting of sand over a pattern when an expendable mold is prepared.

Roll forming: a forming process that uses smooth rolls to give a curve to a straight piece without changing its cross section. For example, roll forming will produce a curved I-beam, but the "I" shape of the beam will not change.

Rolls: a type of forming device. They can be either smooth or formed.

Rough sketch: the first sketch a designer makes. You might think of the rough sketch as a "library of ideas."

Routing: determining the production path for each product going through the plant.

S

Safety engineering: a practice that designs processes and machines to be safer.

Safety equipment: devices that protect a worker's sight, hearing, lungs, and skin.

Sales forecast: a company's estimate of expected sales for a period of time.

Salespeople: people hired by a company to present products to the customer.

Scheduling: deciding when each production activity will take place and when it will be finished.

Scrap: waste material created by a manufacturing process, such as sawdust from a sawmill or steel chips from a machine shop. Every effort should be made to keep scrap to a minimum.

Script: the written message of a radio or television advertisement. It is followed as the advertisement is produced.

Seam weld: a resistance welding process that uses rolling electrodes. The process produces a continuous weld.

Seaming: a fastening technique using mechanical force. It is widely used to fasten sheet metal parts. The parts are bent so they lock together.

Seasoning: the process of reducing the moisture content of lumber through drying in order to make it more stable.

Secondary processes: manufacturing methods that change standard stock into finished products.

Seed tree cutting: all trees in an area, except for four or five large ones, are cut. The large trees reseed the area.

Selective cutting: a harvesting technique in that mature trees are selected and cut. Younger trees are left standing.

Selling cost: the cost of promoting, selling, and distributing a product.

Sensors: devices that change heat, light, sound, or other types of energy into electrical signals that can be used by a computer or other control systems.

Separating: processes that remove excess material to change the size, shape, or surface of a part. There are two groups of separating processes: machining and shearing.

Shaft mining: mining method used for deeply buried mineral deposits. A main shaft and an air shaft are dug down to the level of the deposit. The material is mined by digging horizontal tunnels from the vertical shaft.

Shaped dies: a type of die used to give shape to a material. Used in thermoforming and metal spinning processes. Also called molds.

Shareholders' equity: the actual value of the shareholders' ownership.

Shear strength: the force that is required to cause parts of a material to slide past each other and separate.

Shearing: a separating process that uses opposed edges to fracture (break) the excess material away from the workpiece.

Sheet metal screw: a fastening device with threads that extend the full length of its shank.

Shop steward: a union officer who represents a group of workers.

Shrink fit: a type of fit where heat is used to expand parts so that when they cool and contract a tight fit is created between the parts.

Sinter: heating a material so that it becomes a solid mass without melting the material.

Size: how large or small an object is, described by a measurement standard.

Slip casting: a casting process that uses slip (clay suspended in water). The slip is poured into plaster molds. The molds absorb water. The clay accumulates on the mold walls. When the wall reaches the correct thickness, the excess slip is poured out. The mold is opened, the casting is removed and allowed to dry.

Slope mining: a method used for a shallow mineral deposit. A sloping tunnel is dug down to the deposit. The minerals are often carried to the surface on a moving platform called a conveyor.

Slurry: ground up coal that is mixed with water for pipeline transport.

Soldering: a bonding process that uses tin-lead alloys as the bonding agent. A close-fitting clean joint is prepared. The molten alloy is applied to the joint area. There it hardens and bonds the parts together.

Specifying: to determine the size, material, and quality requirements for a product.

Spot welding: a heat and pressure bonding technique that uses electrical resistance to melt the material. The material is then squeezed and held to form the weld. Spot welding occurs at one "spot," hence the name.

Square: a measuring tool used to check right (90°) angles.

Stamping: drawing operations that combine shearing and drawing.

Standard measurement: a type of measurement where the dimensions are held to the nearest fraction of an inch (1/4, 1/8, etc.).

Standard stock: a material that has been changed so it has certain qualities. It has a certain size, and shape.

Stations: cavities in a single die. Each cavity performs one step of the forming to be done on a part. The material is moved from one station to the next. The part leaves the die completely formed.

Stock: ownership rights to the company, bought by people investing in the company.

Stockholders: are the owners of a corporation. They buy a portion of the company, but they do not run the company.

Storyboard: a set of drawings that contains a sketch of each scene of a television commercial. It is used to guide the production of the commercial.

Stretch forming: a draw bench pulls a material beyond its elastic limit and then pushes a die into the material. Commonly used in the aircraft industry.

Struck: this occurs when the mold is filled with sand. Before the mold can be turned over, the sand is leveled off, or struck.

Supervisors: individuals who assign jobs to and supervise production workers.

Surface coating: a protective layer of material. This material seals the surface against the environment, and in many cases adds color and improves the appearance. Coatings are of two basic types–organic or inorganic.

Surface measure: a method used to measure many materials. Two typical measures are linear measure and area. Pipe is measured in linear units, while land is measured by area (such as square miles or acres).

Surface texture: a term that describes the surface finish of an object, be it smooth, rough, or textured in some way.

Suspension: a liquid where particles of a solid material are mixed with but not dissolved in the liquid. Slip, which is used to cast ceramic products, is a suspension.

Systems drawing: drawings that are used to show electrical, pneumatic (air), and hydraulic (fluid) systems. They show the location of parts in the system and connections.

T

Taconite: a low-grade iron ore. Taconite must be preprocessed at the mine.

Tape rule: a common measuring tool that has markings on a flexible tape of steel, cloth, or plastic.

Technical data sheet: information sheets that describe the characteristics of a product to a designer or engineer.

Technological developments: advancements in science and technology that give designers new product ideas. Companies must never stop gathering information about new developments.

Technology: a way of doing things. It is the knowledge of efficient (timesaving) action.

Tempering: a thermal conditioning process that removes internal stresses in materials.

Tensile strength: the amount of force needed to pull a material apart, expressed in force per unit of area; also, the ability of a material to resist this force.

Territory: an area that is assigned to a salesperson. A territory may cover a city, several counties, an entire state, or several states.

Thermal conditioning: changing the internal properties of a material using controlled heating and cooling.

Thermal processes: processes that use heat to change a material, such as steelmaking changes iron into steel.

Thermal properties: describes a material's response to changes in temperature. **Thermoforming:** a forming process that holds and heats sheet material in a frame. The hot material is lowered over a mold. The air in the mold is drawn out. Atmospheric pressure forces the plastic into the cavity.

Thermoplastic adhesives: adhesives usually resins suspended in water (solvent). They form a bond when the solvent evaporates or is absorbed into the material.

Thermoplastics: a material contains many long polymer chains that are not directly connected to each other except by weak atomic bonds. The bonds will weaken if the material is heated, allowing thermoplastics to be shaped over and over again.

Thermosets: polymers that take on a permanent shape when heat and pressure are applied. Thermosets have long polymer chains that develop cross-links between the chains when heated. These links form a rigid structure by connecting the chains.

Thermosetting adhesives: adhesives in the form of powders or liquids that cure by chemical action. Adding water or a catalyst starts the curing action. Heat will often speed up the curing process.

Thickness: the smallest dimension of a part.

Time: the human and machine time needed to process, produce, and sell products and structures.

Time clock: a device that automatically prints an employee's starting and ending times on a card.

Tool: a device that enhances hand work.

Tooling: devices such as jigs, fixtures, patterns, and templates that help workers make products better and faster. Tooling is designed for three purposes: to increase speed, accuracy, and safety.

Torsional strength: the twisting force needed to cause the material to shear and separate.

Trade name: the official name of a company. A trade name may be registered and protected by law. No one else can use a company's registered trade name.

Trademark: a word, name, or symbol that identifies a product. A trademark is the property of a company.

Training: the process of preparing workers for jobs.

Transportation: converting energy into power to move people and goods from one location to another.

U

Underground mining: a mining method that uses digging tunnels to reach the material. There are three major underground mining methods: shaft mining, drift mining, and slope mining.

Union: a legal organization that represents workers' interests.

Units: single, complete items used for counting purposes. For example, plywood is sold by the sheet.

Unlimited liability: exists when the owner of a business is responsible for all debts of the company (if it is a proprietorship or a partnership). The owner must pay the debts with his or her own money.

V

Varnish: a clear oil-based paint.

Veneer: a thin sheet of wood that is cut from a log. The log is unwound much like paper from a roll.

Vertical drilling: the most common type of drilling; the result is a hole that runs straight up and down.

Vice presidents: people who are in charge of a major part of the company such as sales, marketing, engineering, manufacturing, or personnel.

Volume: the three-dimensional space that a thing or substance occupies. Volume is described in cubic units.

Voluntary dissolution: this occurs when the owners of a business close the company because they want to do so.

W

Wage rates: a type of labor cost, the amount of money the worker is paid.

Warm forming: describes forming heated materials that are not above the point of recrystallization.

Waste: unusable by-products created by many manufacturing processes that are not really wanted.

Weight: how heavy an object or substance is, compared to a standard. Weight is used to measure materials that are hard to break into units, such as sand or clay. It is easier to weigh an amount of clay than to sell a certain volume of clay.

Width: the second largest dimension of a part.

Wood screws: fastening devices that depend on the friction of the threads against the material.

Work hardening: a mechanical conditioning process that changes the internal structure of metals. Pounding or squeezing action changes the grain structure of metals.

Workers: the people who do the actual production.

Y

Yarding: the method used to move fallen trees to a central point for transport to a sawmill.

Yield point: beyond this point, additional stress will permanently deform a material.

INDEX

Designing material handling systems, variable path devices, 189, 190
Designing packages,
  paperboard, 244
  plastic, 244, 245
  types, 244
Designing products, 163-168
  design objectives, 163-165
  design process, 165-167
Designing the presentation, 241, 242
Designing tooling, 186, 187
Designs,
  communicating, 166, 167
  preliminary, 165
  refining, 165, 166
  specifying, 169-173
Deskilling, 204
Detail drawings, 169-171
Determining consumer needs and wants, 158, 159
Determining financial needs, 153, 154
Determining needs, 193
Developing a management structure, 151, 152
  line and functional staff, 152, 153
  line and staff organizations, 152, 153
  line organizations, 152
Developing a sales force, 248, 249
Developing a trade name and trademark, trade names, 234
Developing a trade name and trademark, trademarks, 234, 235
Developing marketing plans,
  beginning, 233, 234
  elements, 233
  pricing products, 236, 237
  selecting a marketing theme, 235, 236
  trade name and trademark, 234, 235
Development of manufacture,
  agricultural period, 271
  handicraft period, 271, 272
  hunting and fishing period, 271
  industrial period, 272, 273
  manufacturing today, 273, 274
Developments, technological, 160-162
Devices,
  clamping, 100, 101
  fixed path, 188-190
  shaping devices, 85-91
  variable path, 189, 190
Diagnosing, 255, 256
Diameter, 65
Diameter measuring tools, 69
Die, 105
Die casting, 80

Die sets, 86, 87
Dies,
  blow molding, 88-90
  die sets, 86, 87
  extrusion, 88-90
  metal spinning, 88
  open, 86
  shaped dies or molds, 87, 88
Dies or molds, shaped, 87, 88
Dimensions, 65
Dipping, 134
Directing, 142
Directing salespeople, 248, 249
Directional drilling, 48
Dispatching, 211
Dissolution,
  involuntary, 265
  steps in, 266-268
  voluntary, 265
Distributing and selling products, 247-251
Distributing cash, 267, 268
Distribution, 233
Distribution, channels, 247
Dividends, 140
Dividers, 68
Division of labor, 179, 272
Draft, 78
Drag, 78
Draw bench, 92, 93
Drawing, 87, 91
Drawings,
  assembly, 170, 171
  detail, 169-171
  engineering, 169-172
  systems, 171, 172
Drift mining, 47
Drilling, 47
Drilling machines, 102, 103
Drop forging, 86
Drop hammers, 92
Drying, 111, 112
Durable goods, 253

▬▬▬▬▬ E ▬▬▬▬▬

Edge, 65
Education, safety, 220, 221
Efficiency, worker, 203, 204
Elastic stage, 85
Elasticity and stiffness, 32
Elastomer, 123
Electrical and magnetic properties, 34, 35
Electrical discharge machining (EDM), 98
Electrocoating, 134
Electroplating, 134, 135
Electrostatic spraying, 133
Elements of a marketing plan, 233
Employees, selecting, 194
Employees, training, 195

Employing workers,
  determining needs, 193
  gathering information, 194
  recruiting applicants, 193, 194
  selecting employees, 194
Employment, 193
Enamel, 130
Encouragement, safety program, 221, 222
End, 65
Energy, 15
Enforcement, safety program, 222
Engineering, and design, 276, 277
Engineering, safety, 219-221
Engineering drawings,
  assembly drawings, 170, 171
  detail drawings, 169-171
  systems drawings, 171, 172
Engineering manufacturing facilities,
  designing material handling systems, 188-190
  designing tooling, 186, 187
  improving manufacturing systems, 190, 191
  preparing plant layout, 187-189
  selecting and sequencing operations, 183-186
Engineering materials, selecting and purchasing, 26-29
Engineering materials, types, 21-29
Engineering products, specifying designs, 169-173
Engineering products, testing products, 173, 174
Enterprise, 11
  closing the, 265-269
  organizing and financing, 147-155
Equipment, 17
Equipment, safety, 220, 222
Equity financing, 154
Essentials of separating, 95-99
Essentials of separating, tool or cutting element, 95, 96
Establishing control systems, 201-209
Establishing control systems, factors to control, 202-208
Establishing product needs,
  consumer approach, 157, 158
  determining consumer needs and wants, 158, 159
  production approach, 157, 158
  sources of product ideas, 159-162
  identifying product ideas, 158
Evaluating performance, 202
Exhaustible resources, 45, 46
Expediting, 211
Expendable molds, 76
Expenses, 139
Extrusion, 88-90
Extrusion process, 88